A FORM OF FRIENDSHIP

THE MUSEUM ON THE SQUARE

MUSEUM OF MODERN ART IN WARSAW 2024

A FORM OF FRIENDSHIP

MICHAŁ MURAWSKI

WITH CONTRIBUTIONS FROM
ZYGMUNT BORAWSKI, MARTA EJSMONT, TOMASZ FUDALA,
TARAS GEMBIK, MARLENA HAPPACH, AGATA JAKUBOWSKA, DOROTA JĘDRUCH,
YULIA KRIVICH, JOANNA MYTKOWSKA, THOMAS PHIFER, DEYAN SUDJIC,
SARAH WILSON, MAJA WIRKUS, AND ARTUR ŻMIJEWSKI

THE MUSEUM ON THE SQUARE

Is it possible (or desirable, or appropriate) to try to distill—perhaps even to concoct—an ideology for a building (and, by extension, for the institution it houses)? This is what this book has ended up trying to do for the new building of the Museum of Modern Art (MSN) in Warsaw. Its initial purpose was to tell a selective, subjective, multivocal story about the creation of the building, whose mighty edifice constitutes the concrete culmination of a two-decades-long process of vision, compromise, public-forming, and institution-building. In the course of putting together the book, however, its narrative has become fixated on several core forms, structures, colors, and ideas. In particular, it has hinged itself to the strange, fraught idea of "Friendship (of the Peoples)"—a notion which was spawned in the Soviet 1930s, and which carries rather traumatic connotations in Warsaw and other places incorporated (usually by force) into the Soviet-dominated state-socialist geopolitical bloc. Yet, the book asks, might the idea of Friendship—with its Stalinist provenance and its associations with Russian/Soviet imperialist domination—be unmoored from this toxic origin? Can it provide some pointers toward new, emergent forms of solidarity, collectivity, care, and artistic and political action? And can the Museum's spectacular new building—the artworks it houses, the aesthetic practices it promotes, the publics and communities it brings together—function as a vessel or a *form* for a new type of (de-Stalinized, decolonized) political friendship (with a small "f") to coalesce?

The story the book tells arises from the *context*, the spatio-temporal and infrastructural nexus within which the building exists. But it does not ignore the *content* of the Museum, gaining inspiration and direction from some of the core items contained in its collection. The artworks at the center of the narrative—by sculptor Alina Szapocznikow and multimedia collagist Zofia Kulik—themselves engage with and relate to the complex and intense spatio-temporal constellation within which the Museum sits. And this constellation is co-constituted by the ensemble of the Palace of Culture and Science (completed in 1955), a 231-meter-high, multifunctional skyscraper "gifted" by Stalin to the people of Warsaw as a gesture of Soviet "Friendship" with Poland (or rather, given the asymmetric nature of this relation, as a gesture of Soviet Friendship *over* Poland), and Parade Square, the enormous and amorphous public space which envelops the Palace and on which the Museum is located.

The book's long introductory essay is subdivided into three sections, titled **FORM**, **FRIENDSHIP**, and **BATTLE**. It provides a broad-sweep overview of the book's remaining sections, tracing the see-saw dialectics—of openness and closedness, whiteness and darkness, expropriation and appropriation, publicness and privateness, amputation and integration, dismemberment and remembering, violence and resistance, provinciality and planetariness, and friendship and solidarity—which co-constitute the Museum's cradle and conjuncture.

The first section, **FORM**, takes as its point of departure Zofia Kulik's understanding of the relationship between what she (following her teacher, architect Oskar Hansen) calls Closed Form and Open Form. **FORM** interrogates the manner in which Kulik's dialectic of form constitutes, to some extent, the animus of her practice—in particular of those works which focus explicitly on the Palace and square. This section refers also to Hansen's understanding of form, and to artist Piotr Uklański's kindred notion of the "empty sign." It tries to make sense of the way in which the binary relationship between closedness and openness is built into the edifice of the Museum itself (its shape, materiality, and color), and into its relationship to the Palace, the square, and its "cousin" building, the TR Warszawa theater, whose construction is scheduled to begin shortly after the opening of the Museum.

The second section, **FRIENDSHIP**, takes its cue from Alina Szapocznikow's *Monument to Polish-Soviet Friendship* (1954), a socialist-realist sculpture which once stood in the entrance hall of the Palace of Culture, and which today—dismembered, having lost its arms and banner during removal from the Palace in 1992—occupies a prominent spot in the new Museum building. **FRIENDSHIP** examines the history of the Soviet-derived notion of "Friendship of the Peoples," which arose in the Stalinist 1930s as a Russocentric faux stand-in for socialist internationalism. It places Szapocznikow's work in the context of several other monuments within and outside the Soviet Bloc, including in Georgia, Russia, Kyrgyzstan, Korea, Senegal, and Ukraine. It provides a brief history of the development of practices, ideologies, and aesthetics of Friendship from the 1930s until the present, and considers some of the ways in which the ideology of Friendship manifests in aesthetic practices and public culture, but also in economic processes and everyday life. Building on an informal research program which I conducted while preparing this book, this section of the essay pinpoints a surprising contradiction. While most scholars and thinkers see Friendship—and the many monuments to it—as an obfuscatory ideological appendage of Russian (or Chinese) imperialism and violence, some also find in it seeds of promise and possibility for a differential, progressive form of political friendship (with a small "f") to emerge.

Leaving this positive trajectory not quite articulated, **BATTLE** takes a step back into the negative to acknowledge some of the forms of violence and dispossession amidst which the Museum's building has taken shape. The titular battle took place in June 2009, during which several hundred petty traders resisting eviction were violently cleared—by riot police, tear gas, and water cannon—from the temporary hangar on Parade Square which served as their workplace, known as KDT (Kupieckie Domy Towarowe—Merchants' Department Store). The Museum stands on part of the former KDT site, and the traders were dispersed, among other reasons, in order to allow its construction to begin. But there are other instances, processes, and specters of violence, both local and global, looming over and crystallizing around the Museum's home on Parade Square, in the shadow of the Palace of Culture: property reprivatization and dispossession, an act of self-immolation, and the mass displacement and multiple crises triggered by Russia's war against Ukraine. **BATTLE** considers some of the ways in which the Museum (-as-institution and -as-building) has been implicated in or marked by these forms and processes of violence. But it also reflects on how the Museum-as-institution has sought (and may continue to seek) to engage, critique, or contest these (and other) violences; and speculates how the Museum-as-building can provide a powerful infrastructure to bolster, broadcast, and reflect processes of contestation and resistance.

In this way, the essay brings together the two main concepts animating the narrative of the book: *form* and *friendship*. It inches toward some possible answers to the question of how the Museum building may come into being as a new form of friendship. Or a structure of (or infrastructure for) solidarity. A critical (or *radical*) institution and building, rooted (the Latin word for root is *radix*) in the struggles, traumas, histories, and futurities pertinent to its particular geopolitical constellation. Cognizant of planetary battles and urgencies, but picking its battles carefully, engaging only where the experience and/or knowledge at its disposal (whether that of Museum employees, or of the broader commons coalescing around the Museum) equips and entitles it to.

So, we return to the positive. To the promise contained in the idea of (lowercase) friendship. Here, the significance of the nodal placing of Szapocznikow's dismembered sculpture in the Museum building becomes clear. For it may be possible to acknowledge (and learn from) the traumatic provenance of Friendship, but at the same time seek to cleave, salvage, and fashion something new from what remains—a different form, one no longer burdened by the toxic encumbrances of that inheritance. To build on the storehouse of shared worlds, wounds, materialities, ruinations, memories, traumas, violences, and solidarities that the state-socialist project engendered (intentionally or otherwise), from Havana to Ho Chi Minh City, via Warsaw and Kyiv, Kharkiv and Kakhovka. And, in the process, for the contours of a different form(ation) of politics and aesthetics to congeal.

The book's remaining chapters constitute a series of conversations and visual interventions, which bring together a variety of voices to hone in on some of the themes, forms, and structures introduced in the opening essay. **CHAPTER 2** provides a visual retelling of the story of the Battle of KDT, through a selection of stills from Artur Żmijewski's film documenting the eviction of the traders and their resistance. **CHAPTER 3**, a conversation featuring art historians Sarah Wilson and Agata Jakubowska, considers the œuvre of Alina Szapocznikow seen through the prism of *Friendship*. Thinking with Szapocznikow's monument, it suggests the idea of "bare friendship," a dismembered and stripped-down state from which future forms of relationality and reconciliation may spring. **CHAPTER 4** interrogates the questions and concepts at the heart of the book in the wake of new conjunctures and uncertainties following Russia's full-scale invasion of Ukraine on February 24, 2022. Construction of the Museum slowed, as many of the Ukrainian nationals working on the site returned home to fight, while at the same time the Museum's offices on Pańska Street saw the birth of an important new institution: the "Sunflower" Solidarity Community Center (known in Polish as a "Dom Kultury," a House of Culture), two of whose co-founders, Yulia Krivich and Taras Gembik, are in conversation here. What new forms, shapes, and styles of solidarity emerge in a museum at the epicenter of a humanitarian catastrophe? What will be the role of *concepts* and *practices* of solidarity and F(f)riendship in the Museum-to-be? **CHAPTER 5** reflects on the centrality of the Museum, focusing on the transformation of a section of Parade Square into the (as-yet-unnamed) Central Square of Warsaw, the site of Phifer's building—whose redevelopment is currently underway in parallel with the Museum's construction. It takes the form of a discussion between then City Architect of Warsaw Marlena Happach, architect and designer of the Central Square project Zygmunt Borawski, and architectural historian Dorota Jędruch. **CHAPTER 6** provides a subjective timeline of the long becoming of the Museum (-as-institution and -as-building), authored by MSN curator—and longest-serving member of the Museum team, in post since 2005—

architectural historian Tomasz Fudala. **CHAPTER 7** is an afterword, reflecting on the long process of the Museum's construction, on the materiality of the finished product, and on the Museum's potential for the creation of publicness. It brings together architect Thomas Phifer, director Joanna Mytkowska, and architecture and design critic, curator, and theorist Deyan Sudjic, who also served on the jury of the 2007 competition for the Museum building. The book closes with a selection of photographs by **MARTA EJSMONT**, who documented the building's construction, zooming in and out on the equipment, debris, and infrastructure which comprise the form and structure of the finished edifice; and photographs by **MAJA WIRKUS** taken in June 2024, once the Museum had acquired its (almost) finished form.

ACKNOWLEDGMENTS

This book has benefited from the labor, wisdom, insight, critique, and friendship of many. I would like to thank in the first instance Joanna Mytkowska, Kasia Szotkowska-Beylin, Maciej Kropiwnicki, Łukasz Mojsak, and Tom Phifer for entrusting me with the rather paralyzing responsibility of trying to put together a story about an edifice which they, and their many colleagues and friends, have spent decades conjuring and eventually creating. Special thanks to Maciej, Kasia, and Łukasz for guiding the project through successive phases of conception and implementation, and for not only wresting copy from me but forcing me, constantly, to think. During the final phases of work, the text benefited from the careful critical attention of English-Polish translator Aleksandra Paszkowska and English-language editor Darren Durham. Thank you to all of you, and to all of your colleagues within and around MSN, for creating and sustaining an institution—even and especially in the hardest and most trying times—which thrives on (self-)criticality and a sincere ethic of political contestation.

The ideas which congeal in this book were enabled by a process of research and dialog, which came to a head during two symposia in Tbilisi and Berlin held in 2022 and 2023. Thanks to the team of the Tbilisi Architecture Biennial—especially Tinatin Gurgenidze—for encouraging these ideas, creating a forum, and providing resources to sustain and develop them, and to other friends in Tbilisi who bolstered and lubricated this discourse, especially David Brodsky and Ana Chorgolashvili. The discussions at the ICKPA (ISKRA) festival in Berlin, funnily enough, were also Saqartvelo-centric. Friendship and hospitality go hand-in-hand. Thank you, Zviad Gelbakhiani and David Chikhladze, for making them happen, and to Daša Anosova for animating them (despite the fact that easyJet scandalously sabotaged her plan to take part).

Throughout the process of cobbling it together, this story and ideology has been enabled and reshaped by the thoughts, actions, experience, and wisdom of Adam Przywara, Lidia Klein, Zofia Kulik, Darya Tsymbalyuk, and further (anonymous) friends. And especially of Shoshana Hedayati, whose wicked, angelic love is like no other form of friendship known on Earth (and probably beyond it).

AFTER THE BATTLE, AN AMPUTATED FORM OF FRIENDSHIP RETURNS

PART I

FORM

CLOSED FORM, OR BYZANTIUM IN OUR HEADS

Since its conception in the distant early 2000s, the building of the Museum of Modern Art (MSN) has always had to do complex dances with the Palace of Culture and Science (PKiN). These dances have taken on a succession of forms. First, there was the desire for an *iconic* sensuous signature building (a Gehry-esque anti-Palace), which, it was hoped, would trigger a Polish version of the then famous "Bilbao effect." Later, a decision was taken that the building should be *aniconic*, that it should ignore the Palace, co-exist with but refuse to engage with it—a postulate met by Christian Kerez's building, which won the international architectural competition in 2007. Finally, we have Thomas Phifer's building, which replicates or mirrors some of the Palace's monumental symmetries while retaining a commitment to simplicity and purity.

This dance around the Palace mimics or enacts the distinction between Open Form and Closed Form theorized by architect and educator Oskar Hansen in the 1950s–1970s and later explored and critiqued by artist Zofia Kulik—part of whose archive is not only housed in the Museum-as-institution, but is displayed as a permanent exhibit in the Museum-as-museum. For Hansen, the Palace is the paradigm of Closed Form, the embodiment of everything regressive about architecture. In his own words, "The Palace—uncontested in its enormity and aggressive in its form, subordinates to itself all the remaining elements of Warsaw's landscape by means of the contrast of form and scale."[1] Questioning the modernist dictates of her former teacher, Kulik's work after 1989 took a turn toward fascination with Closed Form. At this point, the Palace also began to feature with increasing prominence in the artist's complex symmetrical compositions.

The first task of this essay is to make sense of the *formal* character of the relationship between the Museum and the Palace. The binary opposition between Closed Form

1 Jola Gola, ed., *Oskar Hansen. Zobaczyć świat*, exh. cat. (Warsaw: Zachęta—Narodowa Galeria Sztuki, Akademia Sztuk Pięknych w Warszawie, 2005), 102–4.

and Open Form is one possible direction for analysis, but a commensurable category is the opposition between Culture One (avant-garde, horizontal, open, dynamic, future-oriented) and Culture Two (socialist-realist, vertical, closed, static, past-fixated)—the two cultures of Soviet architecture, as identified in the seminal book by theorist of architecture Vladimir Paperny.[2] Alina Szapocznikow's **(SEE CHAPTER 3)** distinction—as articulated in her letters to her husband Ryszard Stanisławski—between "lovely, human, true, heartfelt" and "nice, cultured, polite"—may also serve as a point of juxtaposition.[3]

C1/C2 × OF/CF

If the Palace of Culture is unambiguously Culture Two/Closed Form (C2/CF), is the Museum a clear-cut specimen of Culture One/Open Form (C1/OF)? According to the program brief of the planned Museum headquarters (2014), the very "mission" of the building is to provide a "counterbalance" in the space of the city "to the excessive dominance of the Palace of Culture and Science."[4] The new Museum building, the statement continues, "will counterpose a lack of transparency with transparency, superhuman scale with human scale, excess with simplicity, an anti-social attitude with a social attitude, the past with the future." So far, so C1/OF.

Similar utterances abound. The Museum's official history book, published for its eighteenth birthday in 2023, also describes the Palace—in implicit contrast to the Museum—as "a historicizing, unfunctional, imperial, and anti-modernist building in its expression."[5] A particularly dramatic formulation of a C2/CF vs. C1/OF-esque binary was delivered by Jerzy Blomberg, then head of the Museum's investment department, during a virtual walk around the construction site uploaded onto the MSN website in May 2021.[6] Here, Blomberg characterizes the Palace as a "feudal oppressor," "feudal in form and socialist in content," a "defensive building, with all its crenela-

2 Vladimir Paperny, *Architecture in the Age of Stalin: Culture Two*, trans. John Hill and Roann Barris (New York: Cambridge University Press, 2002).

3 Agata Jakubowska and Katarzyna Szotkowska-Beylin, eds., *Lovely, Human, True, Heartfelt: The Letters of Alina Szapocznikow and Ryszard Stanisławski 1948–1971*, trans. Jennifer Croft (Warsaw: Museum of Modern Art, 2012), 67.

4 "Wytyczne programowe dla wspólnej siedziby Muzeum Sztuki Nowoczesnej w Warszawie i TR Warszawa," April 1, 2014, https://artmuseum.pl/public/upload/files/msn-program-pl-03092013.pdf.

5 Stach Szabłowski, "Ballada o urzeczywistnieniu (pewnej instytucji)," in *Wszystko od razu. Pierwsze 18 lat MSN*, ed. Katarzyna Szotkowska-Beylin (Warsaw: Muzeum Sztuki Nowoczesnej w Warszawie, 2023), 19.

6 "Wirtualny spacer po budowie nowej siedziby Muzeum," Muzeum Sztuki Nowoczesnej w Warszawie, May 15, 2021, https://artmuseum.pl/pl/doc/video-wirtualny-spacer-po-budowie-nowej-siedziby-muzeum.

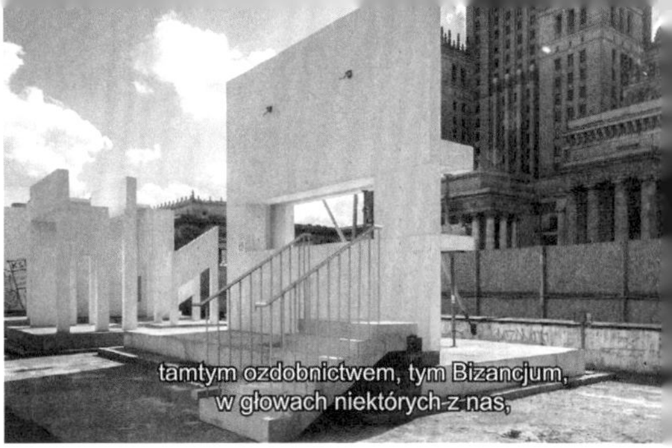

FIG. 1 SCREENSHOT FROM "VIRTUAL GUIDED TOUR OF THE CONSTRUCTION SITE OF THE MUSEUM'S NEW BUILDING," MAY 15, 2021, AVAILABLE ON THE MSN WEBSITE. THE SUBTITLE READS, "THAT DECORATIVENESS, THAT BYZANTIUM IN SOME OF OUR HEADS."

tions and pinnacles."[7] The Museum building, he says, is the "*complete opposite*" of the Palace, in that it will be "entirely open, accessible on multiple levels," "transparent from all four sides." Blomberg contrasts the "Byzantine" decorativeness of PKiN with the "pure form" of the new Museum building. Returning repeatedly to the theme of the *struggle* between Palace and Museum, he goes so far as to claim that we are in the midst of a "civilizational war" between "Byzantium" and its negation. "We live now in a world in which there is a constant struggle between decorativeness, between the Byzantium in some of our heads," and between the "souls and hearts of others, who want a city that is open, simple, honest, accessible, egalitarian." Blomberg's words are underscored by a photograph from the construction site **[FIG. 1]**, which juxtaposes sparkling white fragments of the Museum façade with the monumental, vertical, phallic, over-decorated edifice of the Palace. The photograph—taken in the experimental section of the construction site, at which samples of the poured concrete were tested for durability against the elements, but also for the purpose of obtaining the optimal shade of white for the concrete mix—illustrates this struggle "quite spectacularly," said Blomberg.

The opposition articulated most forcefully by Blomberg, but discernible also in the program brief of the planned Museum building, is seductive for a city such as Warsaw, which is eager to assert its postcommunist (or postcolonial) sovereignty.[8] The starkness of the contrast, which sounded cringingly jarring to me in May 2021, gained in actuality following Russia's full-scale invasion of Ukraine. During the early months of 2022, the Palace reacquired an oppressive affect.

7 Blomberg is alluding here to one of the official definitions of socialist-realist aesthetics, which—in the words of Andrei Zhdanov—was to be "socialist in form and national in content." See Michał Murawski, *The Palace Complex: A Stalinist Skyscraper, Capitalist Warsaw, and a City Transfixed* (Bloomington: Indiana University Press, 2019), 42.

8 The relationship between postcommunist/postsocialist/post-Soviet and postcolonial experiences is of increasing interest to scholars and theorists, but the debate on the equivalence of the two "posts" continues to rage. For influential early interventions, see David Chioni Moore, "Is the Post- in Postcolonial the Post- in Post-Soviet? Toward a Global Postcolonial Critique," *PMLA* 116, no. 1 (2001): 111–28; and Gayatri Chakravorty Spivak, Nancy Condee, Harsha Ram, and Vitaly Chernetsky, "Are We Postcolonial? Post-Soviet Space," *PMLA* 121, no. 3 (2006): 828–36. An ever-growing literature exists with reference to Poland. See, e.g., Clare Cavanagh, "Postcolonial Poland," *Common Knowledge* 10, no. 1 (2004): 82–92; and Adam Kola, *Socjalistyczny postkolonializm. Rekonsolidacja pamięci* (Toruń: Wydawnictwa Naukowe Uniwersytetu Mikołaja Kopernika, 2018).

At the same time, the Museum-under-construction diverted space and resources in its temporary HQ at 3 Pańska Street to the Ukrainian-run "Sunflower" Solidarity Community Center. The Sunflower devoted its work to providing material, symbolic, and ideational support for Ukraine, and to some of the hundreds of thousands of displaced Ukrainians arriving at Warsaw's central railway station, in the immediate vicinity of Pańska Street. The Ukrainians who came to the Museum, some carrying visible signs of trauma, some having lost their homes and livelihoods, were fleeing from a neocolonial Russian army meting out death and oppression. This army, and the state it represented, claimed that it perpetrated this horror in the name of the legacy of the "Russian world (*russkiy mir*)," personified by the Soviet Union and its victory over Nazi Germany in 1945.[9] The Palace, opened in 1955, one decade after this victory and Poland's "liberation" by the Red Army, is the most visible legacy in Poland of the Soviet Union in all its oppressiveness and brutality. The Museum did not merely host, but for a time *became* the Sunflower (in the words of Yulia Krivich, for a moment after the full-scale invasion it spontaneously "took control" of the Museum) **(CHAPTER 4)**. Through this process of the Museum-becoming-Sunflower, then, the Manichean confrontation articulated by Blomberg—between evil Palace and good Museum—acquired a tragic actuality.

Yet, it cannot be that simple. As former City Architect of Warsaw Marlena Happach observes in **CHAPTER 5**, Parade Square, and in particular Świętokrzyski Park, became a favored spot for the coming-together of young Ukrainians who had relocated to Warsaw following the full-scale invasion. In the weeks immediately after February 24, the Palace itself was regularly illuminated in the yellow and blue of the Ukrainian flag. Parade Square hosted concerts and appearances by Ukrainian musicians and cultural figures, such as poet and rock star Serhiy Zhadan. Meanwhile, the Sunflower itself chose as its Polish name the somewhat Soviet-sounding appellation "House of Culture" to characterize its institutional type. Seemingly taking her cue from the Sunflower, MSN Director Joanna Mytkowska describes the entire Museum as a "Solidarity House of Culture" in her contribution to the eighteenth birthday book—thereby attesting to the lasting influence that the emergence of the Sunflower had on the form and ethic of MSN. Finally, *Monument to Polish-Soviet Friendship* (1954) by Polish-Jewish sculptor Alina Szapocznikow,

9 The word *mir* has two meanings in Russian, referring both to "world" and to "peace." It may be more appropriately translated as *Pax Russica*, or the world that has been *pacified* by Russia, by means of war.

one of the largest and most expensive works of art in the Museum, which formerly stood in the entrance hall of the Palace of Culture, will be very prominently placed in the new building, on one of the landings of its monumental staircase, looking back in the direction of the Palace (**CHAPTER 3**). We will come back to the significance of notions such as "solidarity" and "friendship" for the functioning of the Museum toward the end of this chapter. For now, however, we should explore the extent to which the Museum building itself constitutes as clear a negation or opposition to the Palace as its mission statement suggests. Is it really a clear case of C1/OF vs. C2/CF?

A JAR ON A HILL

I sat down for my first conversation with Thomas Phifer on a steaming hot day in July 2021, on the terrace of Bar Studio, the café of the historic Studio Theater, located in the Palace's north-eastern wing. Phifer launched into an invocation of "Anecdote of the Jar," a 1919 short poem by American modernist Wallace Stevens. The poet, said Phifer, "talks about putting a glass jar on a Tennessee hilltop, and about how the landscape and the trees grow up around it and all of a sudden become ordered by this jar." The Museum, "this white building," said Phifer, "will be that jar because it's so startling, so solid, so white, so optimistic, that I think it will begin to order this place." So far, so bold, but also so ambivalent. Purity, whiteness (indisputable), and transparency (arguable) may well belong to C1/OF. But the jar's centrality, its capacity to engineer or "order" its surroundings, fits more comfortably within the authoritarian register of C2/CF. Stevens writes of his jar: "It took dominion everywhere / The jar was gray and bare / It did not give of bird or bush / Like nothing else in Tennessee."[10]

Phifer's allusions and adjectives of choice were very un-modernist. He talked a lot about the Museum's central staircase. This would be a "central space of a really heroic nature. The spaces are grand. There's more space there than is needed." This gratuitous excess of space and volume, in its disregard for use value, fits the classic definition of architectural monumentality.[11] I asked Phifer, who has a reputation as a die-hard modernist, whether the Museum would in fact wind up being a modernist building. "Oh, I have no idea," he replied. The question prompted him to describe the year he spent living

10 Wallace Stevens, "Anecdote of the Jar," 1919, https://www.poetryfoundation.org/poetrymagazine/poems/14575/anecdote-of-the-jar.
11 Archaeologist Bruce Trigger defines monumentality in terms of scale or elaboration beyond use value. See Bruce G. Trigger, "Monumental architecture: A thermodynamic explanation of symbolic behavior," *World Archaeology* 22, no. 2 (1990): 119–32.

in Italy as a twenty-three-year-old architecture student, discovering the Pantheon and the Baths of Caracalla in Rome. Caracalla, he said, was "one hundred times bigger than it needed to be," and the Museum should be "a contemporary Roman building." "I think it will have that kind of Baths of Caracalla presence as a museum." Or rather, something in between the Baths of Caracalla and the most spectacular realizations by the master of modernist monumentality, Louis Kahn—the Parliament of Bangladesh in Dhaka and the library of the Phillips Exeter Academy in New Hampshire. All of Khan's work, said Phifer, "is based on the center with these things around it." Inspired by Kahn and Caracalla, therefore, Phifer said he aimed to create a center that takes the form of a "classical, big, grand, top-lit stair, that's bigger than it ever had to be."

In an interview with architectural historian Lidia Klein, published by the Museum on its website, Phifer speaks of the Museum's centrality in a similar vein, but also builds up a sense of continuity with the Palace of Culture, Stalin's gift to Warsaw. The central space within the Museum, he says, "magnifies the experience, so that you can feel the heroic nature of the building, this central space." In this way, "we elevate the presence of art in the city, so that it becomes the gift to the city."[12]

OBSESSION WITH CLOSED FORM

I asked Phifer whether the presence of such a monumental center is the thing that distinguished his design for the Museum, successfully executed and built, from the failed project which preceded it. It's not that simple, he replied. His most successful buildings, he said, are those which are characterized by collaboration, by the ability to listen to people who are connected to sites or institutions by experience or expertise. In Warsaw, he said, he listened for a long time, changed the design multiple times, and "screwed up a lot." He listened to Museum Director Joanna Mytkowska, to the curatorial team, to historians, but especially to artists.

I did not ask Phifer whether he met Zofia Kulik, but it is her œuvre that Phifer's comments call to my mind. Kulik has a long history of extremely thoughtful engagement with the Palace of Culture, with Parade Square, and with the monumental aesthetics and symmetries they embody. Kulik's

12 "Architekt Thomas Phifer i Lidia Klein rozmawiają o projekcie nowej siedziby Muzeum Sztuki Nowoczesnej w Warszawie," *Facebook* / Museum of Modern Art in Warsaw, August 28, 2021, https://www.facebook.com/MuzeumSztukiNowoczesnej/videos/architekt-thomas-phifer-i-lidia-klein-rozmawiaj%C4%85-o-projekcie-nowej-siedziby-muze/518857939214491/?locale=cs_CZ.

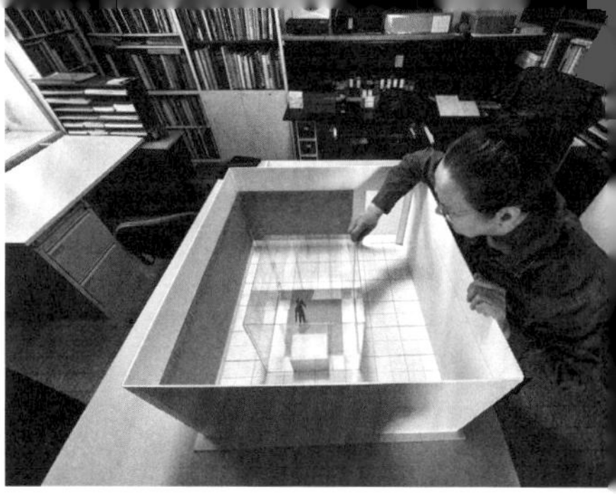

FIG. 2 ZOFIA KULIK IN HER ARCHIVE AND STUDIO IN ŁOMIANKI WITH A MODEL OF THE PURPOSE-BUILT SPACE INSIDE MSN, HOUSING THE ARCHIVE OF THE ARTISTIC DUO KWIEKULIK

œuvre will have a direct museological presence within the building. The archive of the artistic duo she co-comprised with former partner Przemysław Kwiek, KwieKulik, has been relocated from Kulik's home in the Warsaw suburb of Łomianki to the Museum, where it occupies a purpose-built space created by Kulik, in consultation with German architect Johanna Meyer-Grohbruegge **[FIG. 2]**.[13] The folders and dividers constituting the KwieKulik archive are housed in a transparent inner sanctum—accessible only to researchers—within the designated room in the Museum, which Kulik describes as an "archquarium." The KwieKulik room will also display an updated version of *Aggregate*, a monumental timeline of the duo's work from the 1960s until its dissolution, as well as *The Ambassadors of the Past II*, a new version of Kulik's *Made in the GDR, USSR, Czechoslovakia and Poland*, a "travesty" collage of Holbein's *The Ambassadors*. In the 2006 original, the role of Holbein's skull is played by Warsaw's Ujazdowski Castle Centre for Contemporary Art. In the 2024 version, the Museum of Modern Art becomes the skull.

I paid a visit to Zofia Kulik in her home-cum-studio in Łomianki while she finalized preparation of the transfer of part of the archive to the Museum. In her explanation, "the skull is normally viewed as a reference to *vanitas* or *memento mori*," a reminder of the "brittleness" of human (and, in this context, institutional) existence, as well as—in the original version of the work—to the unwillingness of existing institutions in Eastern Europe to collect, house, and "care for" the neo-avant-garde art produced in the region during the late socialist and postsocialist period. "On the other hand," Kulik told me, "the skull is the last part of the human body which remains, while the rest has been eaten by bugs. So there is a double meaning here." The ambivalence concerns, on the one side, the power of the Museum's capacity to choose which art to musealize, but also pertains to the brittleness or permanence of institutions themselves. This is a major concern in Poland and other countries in the region, where art institutions have sometimes found themselves vulnerable to the whims

13 Her personal archive, however, will remain in Łomianki.

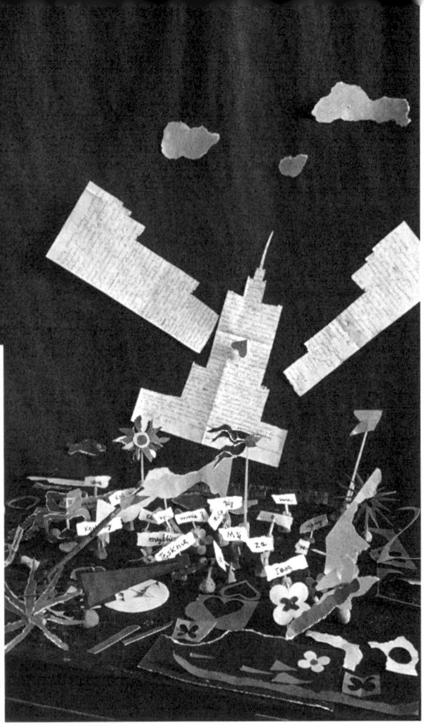

FIG. 3 ZOFIA KULIK, *LETTER FROM MILAN (ACTIVITY ON A SUITCASE)* (DETAIL OF THE SERIES), 1972, 35 MM COLOR SLIDE

and fancies of populist and reactionary governments. And it is a concern that receives architectural expression in the form of the Museum itself, to whose "monumentality" and "permanence," vis-à-vis the hugeness of PKiN, its architect attaches particular importance.

Kulik's engagement with the Palace began in her late 1960s student days, during which time she studied under Oskar Hansen at Warsaw's Academy of Fine Arts (ASP), graduating in 1971. Its most notable early manifestation was her extraordinary 1972 photographic narrative, *Letter from Milan (Activity on a Suitcase)*, built on her correspondence with Kwiek during her four-month residency in Italy [FIG. 3]. In this work, a brown suitcase, laid on its side with a luggage tag marked "Milan" attached to it, plays the part of Parade Square. On the square/suitcase, little clay figurines hold a perverted May Day demonstration. The placards they brandish, as if cut out from Kulik's letters to Kwiek, contain one-word slogans alluding to love. It's a love parade. In the first "act" of the composition, a silhouette of the Palace, cut from a letter by Kwiek to Kulik, presides over the demonstration. Kwiek's letter—a report on artistic undertakings occurring in Warsaw during Kulik's absence—is dry and technical, devoid of pleasantries or emotions.[14] In successive acts, however, the scene becomes increasingly chaotic, apocalyptic. The placards fall onto the floor, the trees and flowers

14 Luiza Nader, "Materializing Conceptual Affects: The Love Discourse of Zofia Kulik's *Letter from Milan* (1972)," in *Conceptualism and Materiality: Matters of Art and Politics*, ed. Christian Berger (Leiden: Brill, 2019), 298–319.

are trampled. The clay figurines lose their anthropomorphic character, and grow into foreboding phallic, abstract, magma-like formations. Eventually, everything is flattened, plastered over with an uneven layer of clay. In the final scene, a ghostly black-and-white photograph of a woman stretching out her arms is laid atop the wasteland. Over the course of the last act, the Palace gradually takes off and flies to the heavens. It acquires wings made out of the two fragments of letter which have been removed from it in order to obtain the Palace's silhouette.

The scene has been brilliantly analyzed by art historian Luiza Nader, who interprets it with reference to psychoanalysis and Kulik's own concept of "actioning" (*czynnościowanie*), or performative enactment. For Nader, *Letter from Milan* is an actioning of Kulik's asymmetrical love-relation with Kwiek. Here, the figure of the Palace—in its embodiment of maleness, patriarchy, authority, and Closed Form—corresponds to the figure of the aloof male partner. In art historian Edit Andras's reading, Kwiek himself is *transformed into* the Palace.[15]

The dispersed, dismembered female body performs an incoherent emotive parade for the distant male lover. It is not really clear whether the lover-Palace flies off indifferently into the sun, rejecting the elaborate, perverted enactment of love, or whether he is actually defeated, repelled, forced to fly away by it. Either way, things don't end well. The disjointed, infantilized female(s) grow(s) and become(s) monstrous, in Nader's interpretation, reaching for the departed Palace in an eschatological iteration of the Freudian-Kleinian *fort!/da!* game. And in the end she/they is/are annihilated, along with everything else. Even the sun disappears.[16]

Letter from Milan prefigures the multiple failed attempts to reconfigure the architectural surroundings of the Palace. The clay figures bring to mind the many attempts to erect high-rise buildings in the Palace's vicinity, thereby counteracting its "dominance" over the cityscape. Since the late 1970s, and especially after 1989, a number of them have been built in Warsaw, within several hundred meters' distance of the Palace. Until the construction of the Museum, however, no buildings were erected on Parade Square itself.

Let us look again at Kwiek's letter, from which the figure of the Palace is cut. Its two side fragments reappear in the composition in act III, and become attached to the Palace as

15 Edit András, "'Yes' for General and Social Issues, 'No' for Anything Private: Matrix P (the Public, the Private, the Personal, and the Political) in Zofia Kulik's Art," in *Zofia Kulik: Methodology, My Love*, ed. Agata Jakubowska (Warsaw: Museum of Modern Art in Warsaw, 2019), 77–98.
16 Nader, "Materializing Conceptual Affects," 313–315.

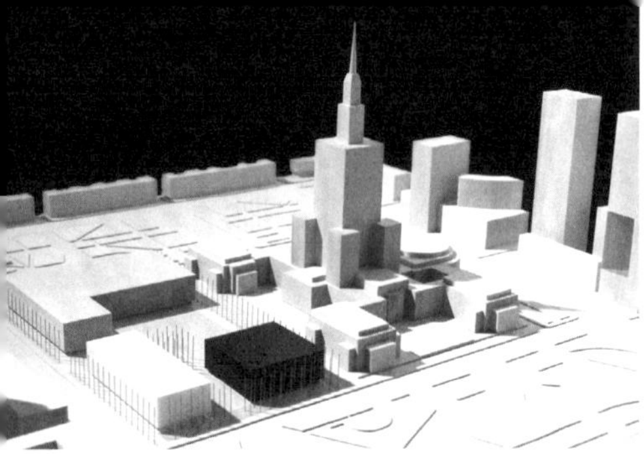

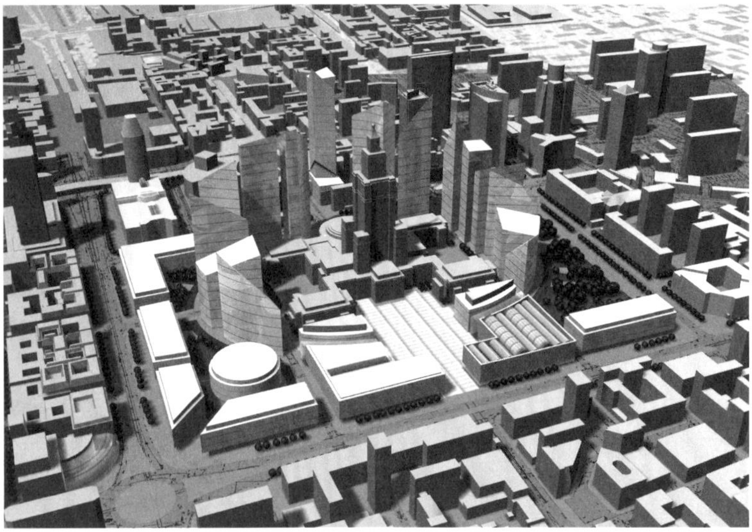

FIG. 4 THOMAS PHIFER AND PARTNERS, MUSEUM OF MODERN ART IN WARSAW AND TR WARSZAWA THEATER SITE DESIGN MODEL, 2015
FIG. 5 CENTRAL WARSAW MASTERPLAN BY BARTŁOMIEJ BIEŁYSZEW, ANDRZEJ SKOPIŃSKI, AND ANDRZEJ FABIERKIEWICZ, PROPOSAL A, 2007, VIEW FROM ROMAN DMOWSKI ROUNDABOUT

wings, allowing it to flutter away from the scene of devastation taking place on the square/suitcase. These fragments have a ziggurat-like shape, loosely resembling the letter L. This shape is determined by their co-constituting the visual negative of the Palace, filling those small sections of the rectangular frame which the Palace does not occupy. There is a remarkable similarity between the shape of the wings and the shape of the cousin white-and-black edifices of the Museum of Modern Art and the TR Warszawa theater, which together create an L shape [FIG. 4]. Kulik's side wings prefigure the shape of the Museum and TR buildings, and the symmetry of its relationship to the Palace of Culture.

The shape of the Museum-theater L was not invented by Thomas Phifer or the Museum. It is a product of the Parade Square masterplan, approved by the city in 2010, but dating back in its first iteration to 2003, according to whose (very restrictive) strictures the Museum is being built. Following the masterplan, the L of the Museum and theater is to be mirrored on the other side of the square by another L, whose function has not yet been determined [FIG. 5]. Initially, it was considered as a permanent home for the KDT traders evicted from their hangar on Parade Square in 2009. This designation, however, was not recommended in the 2010 masterplan, which allows for a mixture of commercial and cultural services on the site. To this date, no one knows what will be in the other L. The shape of each of them directly mirrors the shape of the side wings of the Palace, which protrude into the surrounding cityscape on all four sides. The side wings themselves also mirror the stepped, fortress-like shape of PKiN. If the building was to fall on its side, it would fit like a Tetris block into the space between the two Ls, which is conceived by the creators of the plan and the politicians implementing it as a democratic "agora" for the post-totalitarian city. In other words, ironically or not, this agora has the same shape as the afternoon shadow cast by the Palace itself toward the east. Surely, this is Closed Form.[17]

In *Letter from Milan*, Kulik deployed the Palace—and its two prophetic, L-shaped side wings—as a pure, caricatural embodiment or enactment of Closed Form. The narrative appears to suggest that the eradication or disappearance of the Palace—or at least of its specter or complex, and the patriarchy it edifies and embodies—is a necessary condition for the city (and society) to change, even if this change, judging by the chaos the Palace's departure unleashes on the square/suitcase, does not bring any good in its wake. The ambivalence of the scene forecast by Kulik, then, mirrors the ambivalence of her interpretation of PKiN—its form, politics, and function—which, in Nader's words, "manifests itself as a force with both a positive as well as a negative influence on the world."[18]

Kwiek and Kulik were manifestly not interested in form alone. In their 1970s actions, KwieKulik adapted a student exercise of Oskar Hansen's, "Revealing Complex Form," into a method they called "The Art of Revealing Complex Form." In the words of art historians Łukasz Ronduda and Georg Schölhammer, Kwiek and Kulik "tried to strip the exercise of its purely formal dimension and relate it to the complex sociopolitical-economic situation."[19] Their explorations of form were always political and normative, grounded in a project to alter not just geometries, but also power.[20] Yet these alterations were meant to take place within the ideological strictures of official Marxism-Leninism, and to contribute to the project of improving socialist society. In 1976, Kwiek and Kulik applied to join the

17 Whatever type of form it is, both the post-totalitarian naivete of the agora and the totalitarian delusion of Parade Square are subtly but sympathetically travestied in the design for the new Warsaw Central Square executed by A-A Collective. In the words of architect Zygmunt Borawski, the design was driven by "delight" at the "fabulous posthumous dialectic of bourgeois speculation and Soviet authoritarianism" (**CHAPTER 5**).

18 Nader, "Materializing Conceptual Affects," 314.

19 Łukasz Ronduda and Georg Schöllhammer, eds., *KwieKulik* (Warsaw: Museum of Modern Art; Wrocław: BWA Wrocław; Vienna: ERSTE Foundation, 2012), 466.

20 Izabela Kowalczyk, "The Geometry of Power in Zofia Kulik's Work," *n.paradoxa*, no. 11 (October 1997).

Polish United Workers' Party (PZPR), but their applications were never approved. They withdrew them only after the declaration of martial law by the government of First Secretary of the PZPR General Wojciech Jaruzelski in 1981, the purpose of which was to crush the political momentum activated by the independent trade union "Solidarity."[21]

Then came 1989. Zofia and Przemysław's relationship had broken apart by 1988, and KwieKulik with it. The Polish People's Republic fell. The Palace—and its complex—went nowhere. It did not flutter away. And Kulik's engagement with Closed Form only intensified. In 1990 she wrote:

> I am fascinated by Closed Forms.
> Centricity, symmetry, multiplication, order, figural ornament, imposing upon myself certain preexisting patterns of structures (monuments, medals, mandalas, carpets and gates) that I try to fill with my own madness—these constitute my formal and constructive rules of composition.

These words were part of a self-commentary for the catalog of the first major exhibition of the *Idioms of the Soc-ages* series.[22] They were written, Kulik later recalled, "in an absolute amok. I did not know myself what I was writing. I somehow drew it from my guts, only later my consciousness caught up with it."[23] They signal, explicitly, her *rebellion* and even *revenge* against the binary dictates of Hansen's (and, implicitly, Kwiek's) obsessive quest for Open Form. In order "to spite myself, and to spite KwieKulik, too,"[24] Kulik—first "from the gut," but then consciously, meticulously, painstakingly—cultivates not only an *obsession*, but also an *archive* of Closed Forms.

Her works from the period from 1989 until the early 2000s take the form of large, symmetrical photo-montages (she sometimes calls them "photo-carpets") incorporating a range of images, symbols, and shapes associated with various forms and iterations of totalitarian power [FIGS. 6.1–6.4]. Most often, these are symbols or objects from communist Poland, but there are also fascist, Soviet, Chinese communist, Buddhist, and Catholic artefacts. Many of the works from this period feature the spindly male body of her muse, artist Zbigniew Libera,

21 On strategies of ideological sincerity and overidentification in the work of KwieKulik, see Tomasz Załuski, "How to Live and Work with Two Artistic Biographies: Zofia Kulik's Archival Drive," in Jakubowska, *Methodology, My Love*; and Eliza Rose, "Giving Back the Gift: Predicaments of Patronage and an *Offering* from Włodzimierz Borowski," *Slavic Review* 82, no. 1 (2023): 112–136.

22 *Zofia Kulik: Idiomy socwiecza / Idioms of the Soc-ages*, exh. cat. (Łomianki-Lublin: n.p., 1990).

23 "Bunt neoawangardowej artystki," *Artmix*, no. 9 (March 2005), quoted from the English translation of the interview published on Zofia Kulik's website as "The rebellion of a neo-avant-garde artist: conversation between Zofia Kulik and Joanna Turowicz," http://kulikzofia.pl/en/archiwum/bunt-neoawangardowej-artystki/.

24 Ibid.

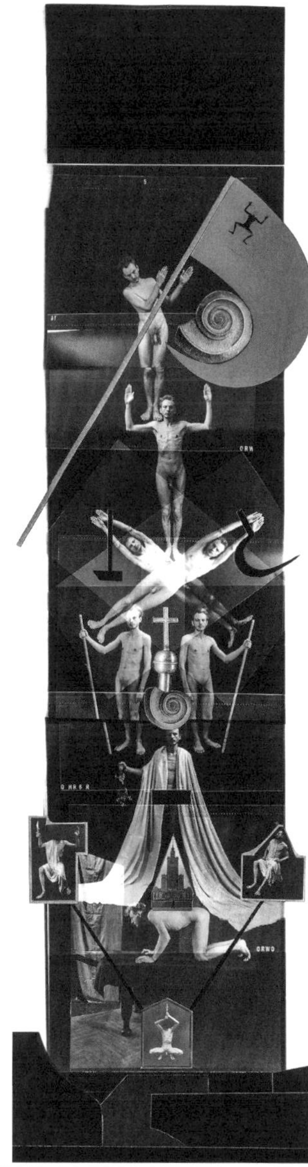

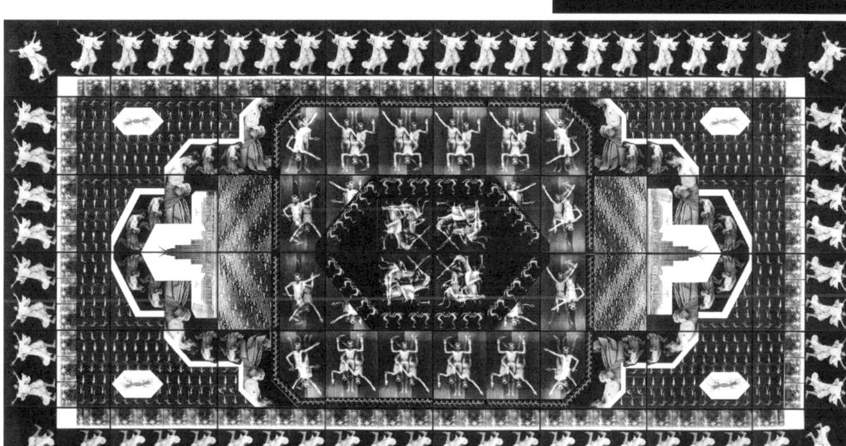

FIG. 6.1 ZOFIA KULIK, *MONUMENT I*, 1989, FROM THE *IDIOMS OF THE SOC-AGES* SERIES, MULTIPLE-EXPOSURE PHOTOGRAPH, 90 × 25 CM
FIG. 6.2 ZOFIA KULIK, HUMAN *MOTIF I*, 1989, FROM *THE IDIOMS OF THE SOC-AGES* SERIES, MULTIPLE-EXPOSURE PHOTOGRAPH, 252 × 480 CM

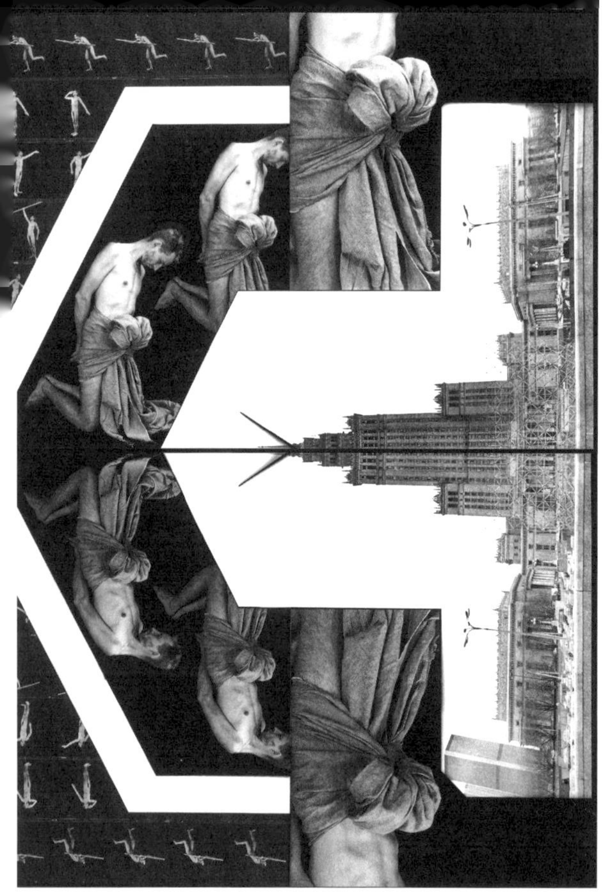

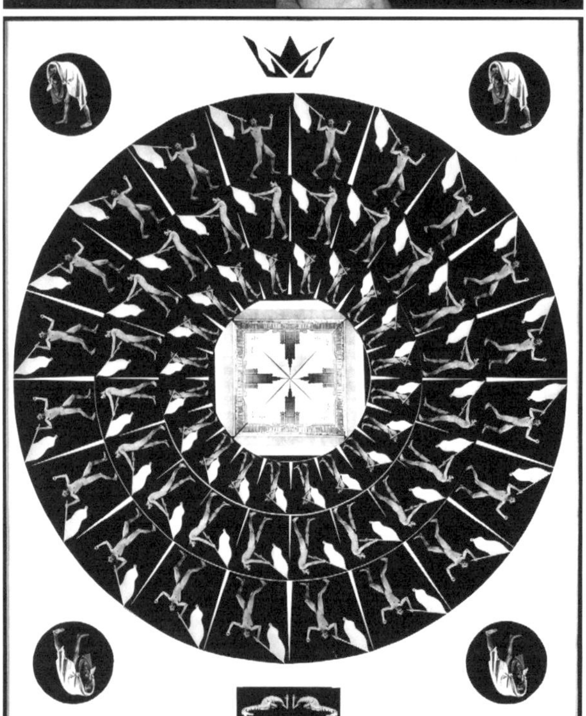

FIG. 6.3 ZOFIA KULIK, *HUMAN MOTIF I*, 1989, DETAIL
FIG. 6.4 ZOFIA KULIK, *MAN WITH A FLAG II*, 1989, FROM THE *MANDALAS* SERIES, MULTIPLE-EXPOSURE PHOTOGRAPH, 60 × 50 CM

performing all sorts of elaborate poses and contortions: holding flags, having his phallus replaced by the spear-like head of a flagpole, gesturing in the manner of Lenin, or even doing a Nazi salute. None of the images are random or accidental. All come from Kulik's enormous archive, some stemming from the KwieKulik years, others collected since that time. One of the most popular motifs, and certainly the most frequently occurring architectural object in these photo-carpets, is the Palace of Culture and Science.

Kulik, then, was fixated on the Palace. In common with many Varsovians, but more so than most of them, she has (or had?) a "Palace complex." Kulik's ongoing engagement with the Palace elaborated Hansen's precept to *reveal the complexity of its form*. It did so not against the Palace, but with it, appropriating what Stalinist ideologue Edmund Goldzamt called its "architectural power" in order to pervert the de-ideologized, re-theologized political climate of postsocialist Poland. In doing so, Kulik diagnosed and deployed the manner in which the Palace would become an object of hatred for the country's reactionary, misogynistic right-wing, and a political tool for those—including Kulik—who opposed them.[25]

Oskar Hansen also had a Palace complex. The Palace came up constantly in his ruminations,[26] and became the anti-hero of his final exhibition, held at the Foksal Gallery Foundation in Warsaw in 2005, the year of his death.[27] And Kulik was neither the first nor the only one of Hansen's students who rebelled or took revenge against Open Form. Writer Filip Springer documents some of these frustrations and rebellions in his biography of Zofia and Oskar Hansen. During the famous action on Morel Hill in Elbląg in 1971—in which Kwiek and Kulik also took part—a seminar room discussion on CF vs. OF became a pitched dialogical battle, with props, held out in the snow. The "black group" represented CF. The "white group," which Hansen also joined, represented OF. The exercise became the stuff of legend, but student participants recalled that they, not Hansen, had initiated the idea of moving it outside. While confined to the seminar room, Hansen stood over everyone, "policing us so that we do not depart from the sources of Open Form," said Wiktor Gutt, "we felt that he was *enclosing* us within [Open Form]"

25 See Zofia Kulik's presentation "Far away from wars. I am deathly afraid," at the 3rd Kyoto University-Inamori Foundation Joint Kyoto Prize Symposium, July 10, 2016, https://ocw.kyoto-u.ac.jp/en/course/154/?video_id=1922.

26 Gola, *Oskar Hansen. Zobaczyć świat*, 102–4.

27 The exhibition was titled *Dream of Warsaw*, see Murawski, *The Palace Complex*, 226–230; Łukasz Stanek, "Oskar and Zofia Hansen: Me, You, Us and the State," in *Team 10 East. Revisionist Architecture in Real Existing Modernism* (Warsaw: Museum of Modern Art, 2014), 240–41.

[emphasis added].[28] Another former student, Emil Cieślar, recalls that during his work as Hansen's assistant at the Warsaw Academy of Fine Arts in the early 1960s, shortly after Hansen had first published his ideas on OF, he "began to notice that this philosophy of Hansen's is in many ways a closed doctrine, something very stiff, formal."[29] Cieślar resigned from Hansen's studio and from the Academy, in reaction to the "aesthetic tightening" of the concept of OF.[30] In Kwiek's own recollections, one newly graduated student cornered his professor at a post-viva party: "Hey, Oskar! You can break your whole Open Form on the sharp edge of your ass!"[31] So, Kulik—whose rebellion did not happen until 1989—stayed loyal to OF much longer than most. No other rebellion, however, was as enduring, constant, and methodical as Kulik's.

What is the color of Open Form? Hansen seemed to think that OF was white and CF was black. A similar contrast between the blackness of CF and the whiteness of OF was suggested by him as a principle animating the design of his theoretical monograph, published posthumously in 2005. The book consists of a long series of comparisons between buildings, urbanistic compositions, even natural formations, accompanied by explanations of which forms are open and which are closed. As it is not always immediately clear which is which, the color-coded design device—black and white bands running across the tops and bottoms of the book's pages—is supposed to aid the reader's navigation through—or rather adherence to—its binary ideology.[32]

WHITE POPE, BLACK POPE

Thomas Phifer puts a lot of emphasis not only on the excessive enormity of the Museum and its central space, but also on the radiant brilliance of its façade, "so solid and so white." However, the white box of the Museum does not exist in splendid isolation. For the design idea to be complete, the black steel box of the TR Warszawa—which, in fact, will be a "very dark shade of purple," in Phifer's qualification—needs to be built alongside. The idea to separate the black theater from the white Museum was Phifer's. As he states, it's all about the "shadow and darkness of the theater and the vitrine of light and white of the museum." The purpose of the "whiteness," says Phifer, "allows for the art to

28 Filip Springer, *Zaczyn. O Zofii i Oskarze Hansenach* (Kraków: Karakter; Warsaw: Muzeum Sztuki Nowoczesnej w Warszawie, 2013), 207.
29 Ibid., 210.
30 Ibid., 211.
31 Ibid., 213; the Polish expression, "o kant dupy potłuc" emphasizes uselessness and obsolescence.
32 Gola, *Oskar Hansen. Zobaczyć świat*, 4.

be elevated in those spaces. The authenticity of that white concrete allows the art to be elevated and displayed." The "authenticity of the black space," meanwhile, performs an equivalent function for the theater: "in the museum, the art is elevated by the light. In TR, the theater is elevated by the darkness, by the shadows."[33] This may make some sense with regard to the functioning of the interiors of the theater and the Museum, even if Phifer seems to be incanting here a hymn to the white cube. It makes less sense with regard to the exteriors of each. Presumably, the intention here is not so much for form to follow function, than to signal functionalism. The white building is the Museum, the black one is the theater: *fonctionnalisme parlant*. Or, as Yulia Krivich, co-founder of the Sunflower, put it, at first glance, the Museum resembles "a white cube squared" **(CHAPTER 4)**.

For Joanna Mytkowska, the whiteness has both an interior and an exterior role. On one level, it realizes Zofia and Oskar Hansen's tenet about making architecture into a "background," not just for art, but also for the coming together of people and the formation of publics.[34] The ground-level transparency of the space, and the unusual level of accessibility of its auditorium, central staircase, and entire lobby level (open spaces and galleries alike) via multiple entrances from the street and the Square, is also predicated, says Mytkowska, on open access for the public, which, she suggests, makes for an effective negation of white-cube dynamics. On another level, the whiteness allows the building to dissolve into the city. "In most weather conditions we see the building under construction from our offices on Pańska Street. But if it's foggy, we can barely see it, as if it's disappeared." **(CHAPTER 7)**. Architecture critic Deyan Sudjic, a member of the first competition jury, points to the paradoxical relationship between the shining material permanence of the pure white concrete façade and its seeming "dematerialization" in the Warsaw fog.

Paradoxes aside, it is noteworthy how closely the—jarringly binary—contrast between white Museum and black theater mirrors the color method employed by Hansen to distinguish between CF and OF—all the more so since MSN as an institution places itself so heavily in Hansen's debt, lineage, and—to use a subversive phrase of Zofia Kulik's—"dowry."[35] But this contrast between blackness and whiteness built into the design of the Museum and theater complex was augured in another artistic con-

33 Thomas Phifer interviewed by Lidia Klein, August 28, 2021.
34 Hansen's theory of background is referred to throughout his work, especially with regard to his idea of "nonmonumentality." See Gola, *Oskar Hansen. Zobaczyć świat*, passim.
35 See András, "'Yes' for General and Social Issues," 90.

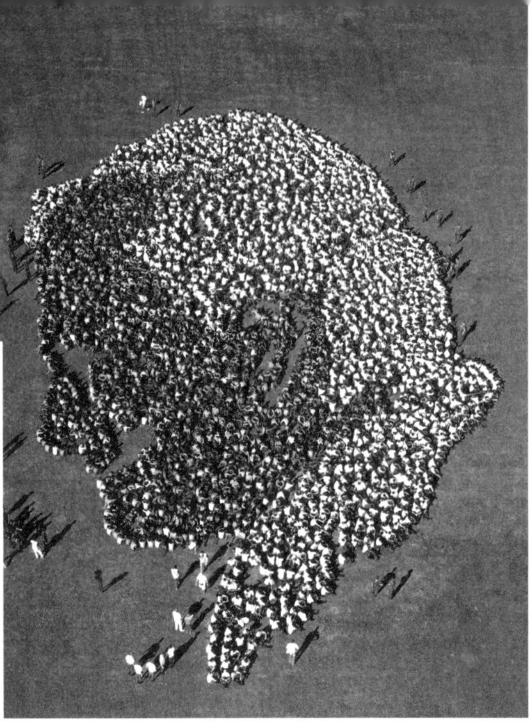

FIG. 7 PIOTR UKLAŃSKI, *UNTITLED (POPE JOHN PAUL II)*, 2004, COLOR PHOTOGRAPH, 200 × 175 CM

catenation. The very first artwork purchased for the collection of the Museum of Modern Art, at its inception in 2005, was Piotr Uklański's aerial photograph *Untitled (Pope John Paul II)*. Realized for the São Paulo Biennale in 2004, this is a monumental, even totalitarian work of choreography **[FIG. 7]**. 3,500 Brazilian soldiers, most wearing white shirts, some half-naked, are photographed by the artist from the air. They are arranged in formation as "pixels" to depict the Pope's profile. The "white" soldiers become the "pixels" constituting the Pope's white habit, gray hair, and skullcap. The bare-chested soldiers, their dark skin barely contrasting with the ground on which they sit, become the Pope's face, forehead, chin, cheeks, and neck. Clearings in the formation represent the mouth and eyes. Given that pure white represents the Pope's cloak, hair, and cap, his white skin is paradoxically formed by the bodies of the dark-skinned soldiers. The Pope is thereby "racialized"—his *racial profile* undergoes alteration. Indeed, the John Paul II in Uklański's image was reportedly christened "Papa Mulato" by the Brazilian press, and interpreted, over and beyond the artist's intentions, as a comment on racial segregation in Brazilian society.[36]

Uklański's Pope was not only the first work purchased by the Museum for its collection. On March 16, 2005, a blown-up, billboard-sized print of it was erected on the north-east corner of Parade Square, at the intersection of

36 For a discussion of Uklański's Pope, its relationship to the Museum's collection, and as an icon of Hobbesian collective representation in Polish visual culture, see also Łukasz Zaremba, *Obrazy wychodzą na ulice. Spory w polskiej kulturze wizualnej* (Warsaw: Bęc Zmiana, 2019), 8–10, 168–78.

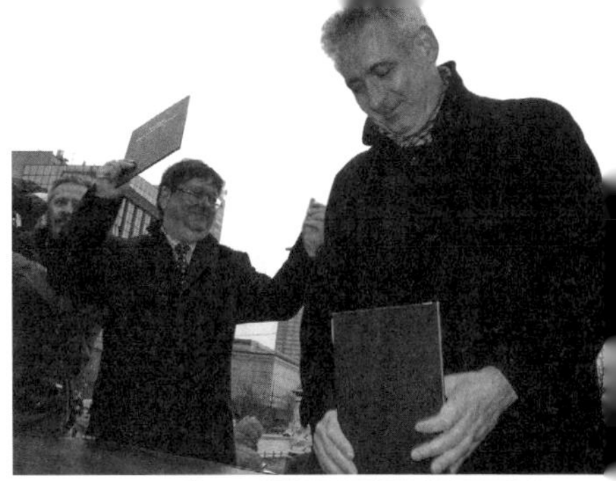

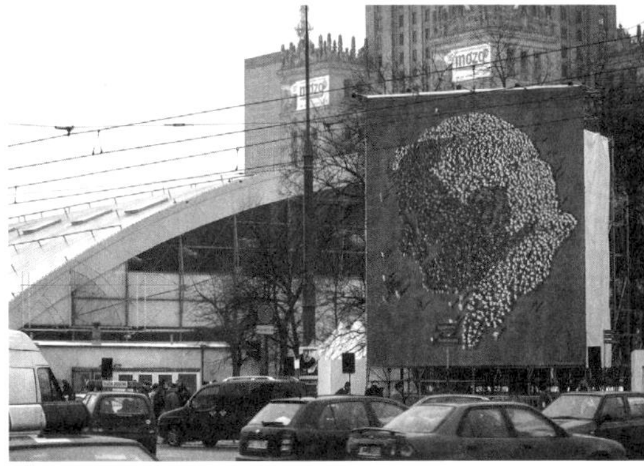

FIG. 8.1 THE SIGNING CEREMONY FOR THE CONTRACT BETWEEN THE POLISH MINISTRY OF CULTURE AND THE CITY OF WARSAW, MARKING THEIR COMMITMENT TO BUILD THE MUSEUM OF MODERN ART, MARCH 16, 2005
FIG. 8.2 THE SIGNING CEREMONY ON MARCH 16, 2005 AGAINST THE BACKDROP OF PIOTR UKLAŃSKI'S WORK DISPLAYED AS A BILLBOARD ON THE SITE OF THE FUTURE MUSEUM BUILDING

Marszałkowska and Świętokrzyska Streets, to mark the spot where the Museum was eventually to be built. In this way, Uklański's photograph served as the spectacular background against which the signing ceremony took place for the contract between the Polish Ministry of Culture and the City of Warsaw, marking their commitment to build the Museum of Modern Art [FIGS. 8.1–8.2]. As art critic Stach Szabłowski points out, the (social democratic) Minister of Culture Waldemar Dąbrowski sat next to the (Catholic conservative) Deputy Mayor of Warsaw Andrzej Urbański and signed the Museum into life on Parade Square.[37] They did so beneath a huge billboard representing the racialized profile of Papa Mulato, made up of the bodies of 3,500 Brazilian soldiers, many of them half-naked, shot by a white, New York-resident global artist while sitting in a helicopter. The signing ceremony itself appeared to take the form of a carefully curated and rather subversive piece of performance art.

It may be reductive to launch a critique of the racial or colonial imbrications and complicities of a building solely on the basis of the color of its façade. Theorists and historians of architecture and aesthetics, however, have amply demonstrated that what may be called the "chromatophobic" qualia of whiteness attached to modernist (and neo-modernist) architecture and urbanism—as well as the associated qualities of purity, hygiene, and transparency—are racialized not merely

37 Szabłowski, "Ballada o urzeczywistnieniu," 14–15.

by coincidental chromatic resemblance to white skin. In fact, modernist whiteness crystalized in tandem with and in dependence on technologies and ideologies of racial domination and control.[38] The use of a resplendent white façade to signal a gesture of newness, difference, change—or "renaissance," in Phifer's wording—should be subjected to reflection in the case of a major new museum designed by an American architect in one of the most contested spots in the capital city of a relatively poor Eastern European country. In the case of the Museum, furthermore, the foreshadowing of the relationship of blackness and whiteness between TR and MSN by the colored and white segments of Papa Mulato's face means that the building's history is marked, from its (carefully curated) inception, by such a racialized critique. Not quite twenty years after the ceremony-performance, Thomas Phifer has built not only *Letter from Milan*, but also Papa Mulato (or rather, so far, the white bit of Papa Mulato) into existence.

On April 2, 2005, two weeks after the signing ceremony-performance, John Paul II died. Uklański's billboard, however, remained in place, and—as the most visible, centrally located representation of the deceased pontiff in Warsaw—was quickly transformed into a spontaneous memorial by Varsovians, who placed candles and flowers beneath it. Not to be outdone, the Palace administration suspended another (more conventional) photograph of the Pope from the Palace's façade. At night, echoing Uklański's act of choreography, the office windows in the Palace tower were lit up in the form of a cross.[39] Six months later, an even more enormous—140 m²—print of Papa Mulato was erected, under the auspices of the municipal and episcopal authorities, in the southern Polish city of Katowice. Such a positive reaction to his artwork, its enthusiastic incorporation into the liturgy of public mourning, was by no means inevitable, opines the artist. Papa Mulato could just as easily have been interpreted "as a provocation, not a portrait"—an insulting representation of a Pope who is "too fat, not realistic and black."[40] Szabłowski observes that, in the Polish context, Uklański's work

38 See, e.g., Sharon Rotbard, *White City, Black City: Architecture and War in Tel Aviv and Jaffa* (London: Pluto Press, 2015); George Lipsitz, "The Racialization of Space and the Spatialization of Race: Theorizing the Hidden Architecture of Landscape," *Landscape Journal* 26, no. 1 (2007): 10–23; Irene Cheng, Charles L. Davis, and Mabel O. Wilson, eds., *Race and Modern Architecture: A Critical History from the Enlightenment to the Present* (Pittsburgh: University of Pittsburgh Press, 2020), especially the introductory essay; Mark Wigley, "Chronic Whiteness," *e-flux Architecture* (November 2020); Mark Wigley, *White Walls, Designer Dresses: The Fashioning of Modern Architecture* (Cambridge, MA: MIT Press, 1995); Ingrid Halland and Marte Johnslien, "'With-On' White: Inconspicuous Modernity with and on Aesthetic Surfaces, 1910–1950," *Aggregate*, no. 11 (January 2023); David Batchelor, *Chromophobia* (London: Reaktion Books, 2000).

39 Michał Murawski, "Inappropriate object: Warsaw and the Stalin-era Palace of Culture after the Smolensk disaster," *Anthropology Today* 27, no. 4 (2011): 5–10.

40 Dorota Jarecka, "Rozmowa z Piotrem Uklańskim: 'Solidarność' to pusty znak," *Wyborcza.pl*, June 15, 2007, https://wyborcza.pl/7,75410,4228967.html.

is indeed rather subversive. Poles tend to consider JPII to be "their Pope." They claim "if not the exclusive, then the greatest right" over the Polish Pope as symbol and brand. Uklański, transposing this symbol into a "tropical, postcolonial and multiracial context,"[41] seems to cast doubt on this claim to ownership. Yet, as the reaction of the faithful masses showed, in Warsaw and beyond, this act of sharing and universalizing "their Pope" elicited enthusiasm rather than anger—a sort of solidarity in mourning. Taking this association further, Uklański and curator Anda Rottenberg produced a follow-up to *Untitled (Pope John Paul II)* in 2007, in which 3,000 soldiers (this time all Polish, all white, dressed in red) spelled out the word "Solidarność" ("Solidarity") in the Gdańsk shipyard, the cradle of the movement which contested communism in Poland and of which the Pope was spiritual patron.[42]

But these trans-local connotations are not the only ones triggered by Uklański's work and its relationship to the Warsaw and Polish contexts. Says Szabłowski, "the conducting of thousands of soldiers, a human, militarized, plastic mass, from which the face of the priest is formed, unavoidably brings to mind the monumental choreography of totalitarian regimes."[43] In other words, Closed Form. Conversely, as art historian Łukasz Ronduda argues, Papa Mulato constitutes perhaps the most accomplished realization of the idea of the artwork as an "empty sign"—a notion popular among the older generation of Polish post-conceptual artists, referring to the artist's intention that it is the receiver who should endow the work with meaning. In Ronduda's interpretation, the iteration of the empty sign practiced by Uklański is populist and "radically open."[44] It consists in turning into artworks symbols or objects which are considered *meaningless* by the art world, but which on the other hand are objects of popular affect, fixation, and adoration—such as John Paul II, the Solidarity trade union, or even a sunset. In this sense, Uklański's empty sign may turn out to be compatible with Hansen's Open Form, which strove to turn architecture into a *background* for human activity.

What, if anything, did the (devoutly atheist) Hansen think of Uklański's work and its use to mark the territory of the Palace of Culture? In all likelihood, nothing good, or not very

41 Szabłowski, "Ballada o urzeczywistnieniu," 20.

42 Piotr Uklański, *Untitled (Solidarność)*, 2007, https://www.metmuseum.org/art/collection/search/682811.

43 Szabłowski, "Ballada o urzeczywistnieniu," 20.

44 Lecture "Wokół kolekcji: Łukasz Ronduda o 'Bez tytułu (Jan Paweł II)' Piotra Uklańskiego," Museum of Modern Art in Warsaw, January 20, 2009, https://artmuseum.pl/pl/doc/video-wokol-kolekcji10; Uklański also invokes the notion of the "empty sign" in an interview about his aerial artworks with Dorota Jarecka, "Rozmowa z Piotrem Uklańskim."

much. Hansen's exhibition at the Foksal Gallery Foundation (FGF), *A Dream of Warsaw*, co-curated by Joanna Mytkowska—who would take over as MSN director in 2007—closed on March 9, 2005. Hansen himself was already gravely ill with cancer, but nevertheless summoned the strength to execute his final completed work, a manifestation of his struggle with Closed Form in general and with the Palace of Culture in particular. *A Dream of Warsaw* took the form of a proposal for an anti-skyscraper, its tip somewhat resembling a UFO, to be positioned next to the Palace, realized as a cut-out affixed to the windows of FGF in Warsaw, immediately facing PKiN.[45] A major retrospective exhibition was planned for the Zachęta—National Gallery of Art in October, but Oskar Hansen (1922–2005) did not make it to the opening. He died on May 11, just over a month after Karol Wojtyła—John Paul II (1920–2005).

45 See Gola, *Oskar Hansen. Zobaczyć świat*, 102–4; Murawski, *The Palace Complex*, 226–30; and Artur Żmijewski's film *A Dream of Warsaw* (*Sen Warszawy*, 2005) documenting the exhibition.

AMPUTATING FRIENDSHIP

Alina Szapocznikow's *Monument to Polish-Soviet Friendship*, completed in 1954, is (or was, before its dismemberment) a sensuously tinged—rather tender—socialist-realist sculpture of a Polish and a Soviet worker locked in an embrace and holding a banner. From 1955 until 1992, *Friendship* stood in the entrance hall of the Palace of Culture. From 2024, it occupies a prominent location in the central staircase of the Museum of Modern Art.

Szapocznikow's own Soviet friendship—the warmth she felt for the Soviet Union, for Polish peasants and workers—was genuine and heartfelt. This is notwithstanding the fact that her later work, much better known internationally—determined by her own experience of grave illness, bodily suffering and disintegration, tuberculosis, bone and breast cancer—was far removed in terms of style and feeling. Critics have considered the extent to which the visceral viscosity of Szapocznikow's work from the 1960s and 1970s was informed by her experience of bodily illness, frailty, and the Holocaust—Szapocznikow survived the ghettos of Pabianice and Łódź, and the camps of Auschwitz, Bergen-Belsen, Buchenwald-Duderstadt, and Theresienstadt.[46] She did not talk about the war or the Holocaust in her later career, and it is difficult to accurately trace her wartime trajectory. In her socialist-realist period, however, during and just after she became ill from peritoneal tuberculosis, while the war and the camps were still fresh in her mind, she did—to a limited extent and in private—acknowledge the degree to which her ideological position—her enthusiasm for communist rule in Poland—was influenced by her experience of the Holocaust.

Szapocznikow's correspondence with her husband Ryszard Stanisławski, a grand figure in communist Poland's art world, has been published by the Museum of Modern Art.[47] Berated Ryszard: "Aluś, please do not let yourself get carried

46 Marek Beylin, *Ferwor. Życie Aliny Szapocnikow* (Kraków: Karakter; Warsaw: Muzeum Sztuki Nowoczesnej w Warszawie, 2015), 23–25.

47 Jakubowska and Szotkowska-Beylin, *Lovely, Human, True, Heartfelt.*

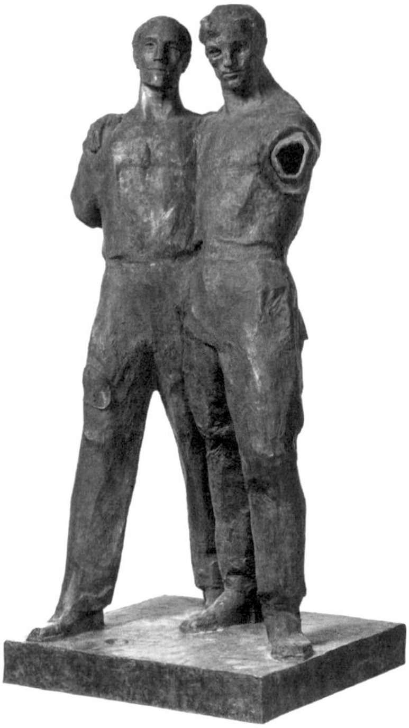

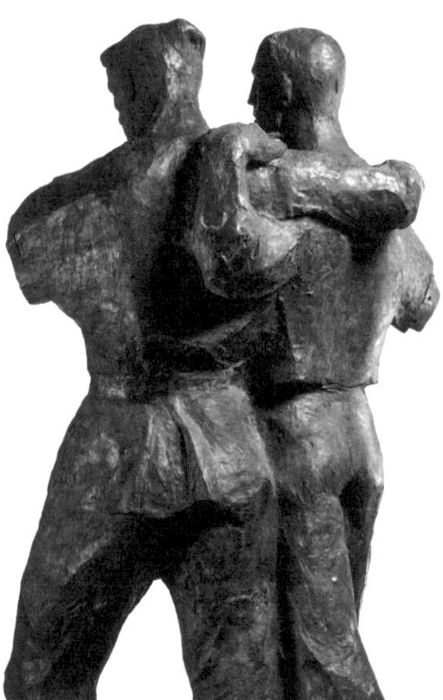

FIGS. 9.1–9.2 ALINA SZAPOCZNIKOW, *FRIENDSHIP*, 1954, PHOTOGRAPHED IN 2019

away by impulses and by the senseless enthusiasm that beats out from your letters as you speak of 'the new world' and social transformations."[48] Responds Alina,

> You simply look at certain things still in such a nice cultured, polite way. ... But the difference [between us] lies in the fact that during your formative years, over the last ten years, you did not go through that baptism of despair, all of

48 Ibid., 54.

that, all of that did not vanish all those times without a trace, as happened for me in the ghettos and the camps.[49]

She continues, "instead of 'nice, cultured, polite,' what was left [in me] was 'lovely, human, true, heartfelt.'"[50] The latter four sentiments, which also provide the title of the book of correspondence edited by Agata Jakubowska and Katarzyna Szotkowska-Beylin, might be put forward as an alternative definition of Szapocznikow's ethics and politics of friendship.

In 1992, three years following the fall of the Polish People's Republic in 1989, Szapocznikow's sculpture was unceremoniously removed from the Palace. *Friendship* was consigned to the literal trash bin by the then Director of the Palace's administration, figuring as part of a list of superfluous movable items to be cleared out of the building, alongside an old electric kettle, a fake Christmas tree, and a meat cleaver. Its arms and banner were hacked off in order to fit it through the Palace's narrow doors.[51] Happily, the sculpture was never scrapped; it stood in the garden of a suburban house outside Warsaw for nearly three decades, with several efforts to retrieve it ending unsuccessfully. Failed attempts were made to convince various Polish arts institutions to purchase *Friendship* in the 1990s; but by the time that the institutions wanted it, in the late 2000s, the owners realized its value and would not return it. The empty plinth left behind continued to stand in the hall until the middle of the 2010s.

The armless, flagless sculpture was eventually put on auction and acquired by a then-anonymous buyer—now revealed as the Poznań-based glass magnate and philanthropist Wojciech Pawłowski—for 1.7 million PLN (ca. 400,000 EUR). The buyer subsequently loaned it to the Museum for an indefinite period. Almost immediately upon being loaned, the sculpture is destined to take pride of place in the monumental central staircase of the Museum building, in the immediate proximity of the Palace of Culture. After a long hiatus, then, *Friendship* returns to Parade Square, to stand—for an indefinite period—several hundred meters away from where it stood for the first thirty-seven years of its (un-amputated) existence.

In Phifer's monumental lightwell, then, the cycle of expropriation and appropriation—mirroring the relationship

49 Ibid., 67.
50 Ibid.
51 Murawski, *The Palace Complex*, 137–40; Tomasz Urzykowski, "Słynna rzeźba z Pałacu Kultury odnaleziona po latach. Trafiła na aukcję za ogromne pieniądze," *Gazeta Wyborcza*, August 13, 2019, https://warszawa.wyborcza.pl/warszawa/7,54420,24546013,slynna-rzezba-z-palacu-kultury-odnaleziona-po-latach.html.

between the Palace of Culture and the volatile, shifting land property regimes of postwar and postsocialist Warsaw—comes full circle, mediated by acts of philanthropy. *Friendship* returns (almost-but-not-quite) home. The Museum lobby mimics and taunts the Palace lobby. The sculpture remains amputated **[FIGS. 9.1–9.2]**.

FRIENDSHIP AFTER BUCHA

Following the full-scale Russian invasion of Ukraine, the realization of the plan to install Szapocznikow's *Friendship* in the very heart of the Museum hung in the balance. Is it still possible or appropriate for this kind of "traumaphilic" gesture—a term coined by art historian Piotr Piotrowski with specific regard to museums of contemporary art, to refer to an institutional attitude to the wounds of the past that actively engages with trauma, but also runs the risk of fetishizing it—to be carried out?[52] And, in fact, to gesture—through the centrality and monumentality of its placing—toward the core of the institutional ideology of the largest new contemporary art museum in postsocialist Europe?

This trauma was already felt powerfully enough in Poland before 2022. Today, in the face of the slaughter of Ukraine, in a city co-populated by tens of thousands of Ukrainian migrants, many of whose bodies and sensibilities have been scarred and dismembered by a war fought in the name of quasi-Soviet internationalism, in the name of the Soviet ideology of "Friendship," the level of this trauma (and of the *philia* necessary to overcome it or to appropriate it) is intensified an unquantifiable number of times.

These questions are raised, in two of this book's chapters, by art historians Sarah Wilson and Agata Jakubowska, and by Ukrainian artist-activists, co-founders of the "Sunflower" Solidarity Community Center, Yulia Krivich and Taras Gembik. There is a consensus in these conversations that if *Friendship* is to remain on display, it can do so only due to the fact that it has already been amputated. Ultimately, the decision was made that it would remain in its designated place in the staircase. But, said Mytkowska, "it will be unthinkable to display this sculpture on its own, it should be counterposed by a Ukrainian artwork." At the inauguration of the new building, it will be shadowed by Nikita Kadan's *Gazelka*, made by the artist from fragments of a shot-up car recovered by him from the Ukrainian city of Severodonetsk, which pro-Russian forces attempted, unsuccessfully, to occupy and annex in 2014. In 2022, Severodonetsk was laid to waste and occupied by Russia.

52 Piotr Piotrowski, "New Museums in East-Central Europe: Between Traumaphobia and Traumaphilia," in *1968–1989: Political upheaval and artistic change*, ed. Claire Bishop and Marta Dziewańska (Warsaw: Museum of Modern Art, 2009), 148–66.

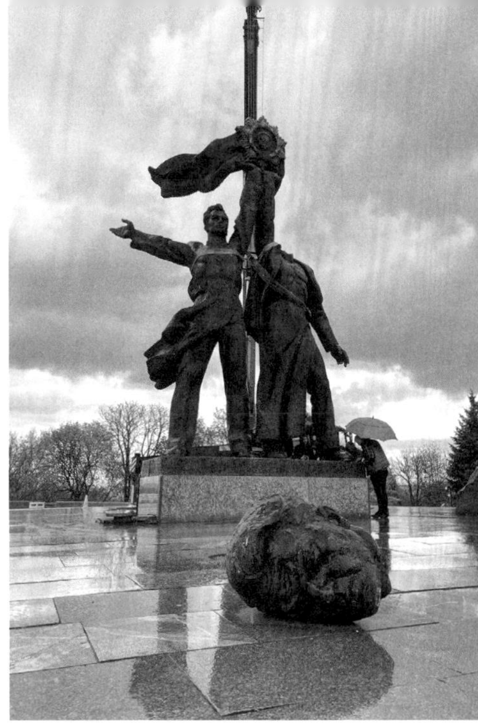

FIG. 10 THE FORMER MONUMENT TO THE REUNIFICATION OF UKRAINE WITH RUSSIA, KYIV, UKRAINE, 1982, SCULPTOR: OLEKSANDR SKOBLIKOV, ARCHITECTS: SERHII MIRHORODSKIY, KONSTANTIN SIDOROV, AND IHOR IVANOV. SEEN DURING ITS DEMOLITION ON APRIL 26, 2022 AMID RUSSIA'S INVASION OF UKRAINE

The story of Szapocznikow's *Friendship* is mirrored, although in accelerated and intensified form, in the fate of the Kyiv Arch of the Freedom of the Ukrainian People (known from its unveiling in 1982 until 1991 as The Monument to the Reunification of Ukraine with Russia, and from 1991 until 2022 as The People's Friendship Arch, but often referred to by Kyivites as *yarmo*, "the yoke," for short). Unveiled on the escarpment overlooking the Dnipro River, at the foot of Khreshchatyk Avenue, the monument consists of a late modernist steel sculpture of a rainbow enveloping a two-part neo-socialist-realist sculptural composition. One part, finally dismantled in May 2024, is a granite monument depicting the signing of the 1654 Treaty of Pereiaslav, in which Ukrainian Cossack forces loyal to Hetman Bohdan Khmelnytsky, and at the time in the throes of an uprising against the Polish-Lithuanian Commonwealth, pledged allegiance to the Tsar of Muscovy. The other section consisted (until April 2022) of a bronze statue of two extremely masculine workers—a Ukrainian and a Russian—standing alongside one another **[FIG. 10]**. They do not embrace, but their arms lock together to hold up a giant version of the Order of the Friendship of the Peoples, a state honor introduced by the USSR in 1972. In the midst of Brezhnev-era neo-Stalinist stagnation, the Order itself, and the many monuments erected in and beyond the Soviet Republics, were among the symbolic technologies through which the Stalinist ideology of Friendship was revived, ossified, and incanted during the Soviet Union's dying decades.

The bronze Friendship monument was toppled and removed in April 2022, immediately following the discovery of Russian-perpetrated mass shootings and rapes of civilians in the de-occupied Kyiv satellite towns of Bucha, Irpin, and Hostomel. Commenting on the removal, Volodymyr Klitschko (the brother of Kyiv's mayor Vitaly)—referring to the language of "brotherly nations" with which many Russians insist on framing their war on Ukraine—wrote on his Instagram and Facebook accounts: "you don't kill your brother, you don't rape your sister."[53]

There are many differences between the two Friendship monuments. In Warsaw, one worker is Polish, the other is an amorphous, nationally non-specific "Soviet" figure; in Kyiv, one worker is Ukrainian, the other is Russian. Incidental amputations occurred during both acts of iconoclasm: in Poland, the arms were removed for practical purposes; in Kyiv, the head fell off, as if by accident.[54]

"VOLUNTARY INCORPORATION," OR FRIENDSHIP'S IMPERIAL INNOCENCE

The Soviet idea of the "Friendship of the Peoples" was a circumstantial outgrowth or mutation of Soviet nationalities policy, which was consolidated following the failure of the early attempt to export the Bolshevik revolution overseas by military means; and, correspondingly, the Soviet victory against domestic and international counter-revolutionary forces in the Civil War in 1921. It was an answer to the question of how to create an ideology and practice of internationalism within a Soviet Union-in-the-making, which—multinational and multiethnic as it was—was essentially the Russian Tsarist empire after a regime change. How to promote "national" (non-Russian) cultures in the name of "national liberation" and the struggle against "great-Russian chauvinism" while keeping the empire—now called the Soviet Union—in one piece? The response of the early Soviet state was to create a hybrid, oxymoronic ideology (together with corresponding bureaucracy and resource-distribution mechanisms), which scholars have referred as an "empire of nations" or an "affirmative-action empire."[55] The idea was to overpromote the interests of the empire's "small nations" while keeping the chauvinist tendencies

53 *Facebook* / Klitschko, April 26, 2022, https://www.facebook.com/KlitschkoOfficial/posts/553697102788042/.

54 Friends in Kyiv who were present said that the head seemed to fall off unintentionally, in the process of removal. This story is also confirmed in *The Guardian*'s article about the event: Lorendo Tondo and Isobel Koshiw, "Friends no longer, Ukraine removes Russian statues and street names," *The Guardian*, April 28, 2022, https://www.theguardian.com/world/2022/apr/28/friends-no-longer-ukraine-removes-russian-statues-and-street-names.

55 Terry Martin, *The Affirmative Action Empire: Nations and Nationalisms in the Soviet Union, 1923–1939* (Ithaca: Cornell University Press, 2001); Francine Hirsch, *Empire of Nations: Ethnographic Knowledge and the Making of the Soviet Union* (Ithaca: Cornell University Press, 2005).

of the Russian majority under control. The ultimate goal was *sliianie*, or fusion. In 1916, Lenin wrote, "mankind can proceed towards the inevitable fusion (*sliianie*) of nations only through a transitional period of the complete freedom of oppressed nations."[56] The cornerstone of the "transitional period" was *koreniizatsia*, which might be translated as "rootification." The idea behind it was well expressed by Joseph Stalin in 1929: "We are undertaking the maximum development of national culture, so that it will exhaust itself completely and thereby create the base for the organization of internationalist socialist culture."[57]

This oxymoronic anti-empire was always fragile and somewhat disingenuous. It did not last long. The pressures of impending war and industrialization, the mounting grievances of Russians—who were to be, in opposition to the remaining nationalities in the USSR, de-rooted by rootification—and the resultant imperial turn in Soviet ideology and policy gained ascendancy. Historian Terry Martin wrote that, "by 1937–1938, *koreniizatsiia* was over. The Russian nationality and Russian culture were rehabilitated. The Russians and Russian culture were now made the unifying force in a newly imagined Friendship of the Peoples."[58] The ideology of Friendship, therefore, was formulated as an ersatz, Russo-centric stand-in for socialist internationalism: internationalism-in-one-country, or "domestic internationalism," in historian Brigid O'Keefe's term.[59] During World War II (known in the USSR as the "great patriotic war") this Russo-centric rehabilitation was only consolidated. The relationship to Ukraine, as Terry Martin observed, occupied the "central role in the evolution of Soviet nationalities policy throughout the Stalin period."[60] These tendencies actually intensified in the immediate aftermath of Stalin's death.

1954—the year in which plans (and competitions for) an unrealized monument to Stalin himself to be erected on Parade Square were announced, and in which Szapocznikow's *Friendship* monument was erected—played a pivotal role in fixing the contours of the ideology of what might be called the "asymmetrical Friendship" between the peoples of the USSR in the post-Stalin era; this process was also centered on Ukraine.[61] 1954 marked the third centenary of the Treaty of Pereiaslav,

56 Vladimir Lenin, "The Socialist Revolution and the Right of Nations of Self-Determination," quoted in Martin, *The Affirmative Action Empire*, 5.
57 Joseph Stalin, quoted in Martin, *The Affirmative Action Empire*, 5.
58 Martin, *The Affirmative Action Empire*, 27.
59 Brigid O'Keefe, *The Multiethnic Soviet Union and its Demise* (London: Bloomsbury, 2022).
60 Martin, *The Affirmative Action Empire*, 24.
61 An intriguing postmodern museological project for a decapitated monument to Stalin standing on and beneath Parade Square was proposed for architect and politician Czesław Bielecki's Museum of Communism. See Murawski, *The Palace Complex*, 170–71; Zaremba, *Obrazy wychodzą na ulice*, 6–7 and passim.

which saw an upsurge of Friendship propaganda throughout the Union. In particular, there was an explosion in the propaganda of "voluntary incorporation," which contended—contrary to early Soviet doctrine—that the non-Russian nationalities still inside the Soviet Union had joined the USSR "voluntarily." The tri-centenary of Ukraine's "voluntary incorporation" was marked by the so-called "gifting," initiated by Khrushchev, of Crimea from the Russian SFSR to the Ukrainian SSR,[62] and was followed by a slew of celebrations and monumentalizations of the bicentenaries or centenaries of the voluntary incorporation of dozens of territories into the Russian imperial realm, from Chechnya to Kyrgyzstan. This friendship jubilee traced the long path across time and space of Russian imperial conquests in the Caucasus, Siberia, and Central Asia in the eighteenth and nineteenth centuries.[63]

A short walk around the capital cities of most former imperial subjects of Russia reveals how tortuous, strange, and contradictory this process was. Take Bishkek (formerly Frunze). The city's oldest functioning cinema, Ala-Too, is a transitional late constructivist/early socialist-realist edifice completed in 1932. In 1963, a ceramic mosaic was added to its façade, designed by a multinational Soviet team, to celebrate the hundredth anniversary of the "union" between Kyrgyzia and Russia. A short walk away stands the Monument to Friendship, a twenty-eight-meter modernist double obelisk, ringed near its base by a frieze featuring relief sculptures of multiple pairs of Kyrgyz and Russian figures, both male and female, hands firmly interlocked **[FIGS. 11.1–11.2]**. The monument, designed by distinguished Kyrgyz sculptor Turgunbay Sadikov, was unveiled in 1974 to mark the "centenary of the voluntary incorporation of Kyrgyzia into Russia" (Sadikov's work, which often features women in heroic roles, is an exception in this essay, which is full of sculptures of men made by women). The dates are as confused as the commemoration is fraught. On the Ala-Too cinema, 1863 is presumably designated as the date of the "voluntary" union of "northern Kyrgyzia" and Russia with reference to the conquest of the northern Khoqand fortresses of Tokmok and Pishpek (today's Bishkek). 1863,

62 The relationship between the geoeconomics of the "gift" and the idea of "friendship" in Soviet public culture is noteworthy. For the case of Warsaw and the Palace, see Murawski, *The Palace Complex*, 57–69. For Soviet gift cultures, see Nikolai Ssorin-Chaikov, "On Heterochrony: Birthday Gifts to Stalin, 1949," *Journal of the Royal Anthropological Institute* 12, no. 2 (2006): 355–75; Jeffrey Brooks, *Thank You, Comrade Stalin!: Soviet Public Culture from Revolution to Cold War* (Princeton, NJ: Princeton University Press, 1999). For continuities between Russian Imperial and Soviet gift cultures, see Bruce Grant, *The Captive and the Gift: Cultural Histories of Sovereignty in Russia and the Caucasus* (Ithaca: Cornell University Press, 2009).

63 On the bicentenary of the "voluntary incorporation" of Chechnya, see Moshe Gammer, "Shamil in Soviet Historiography," *Middle Eastern Studies* 28, no. 4 (1992): 763.

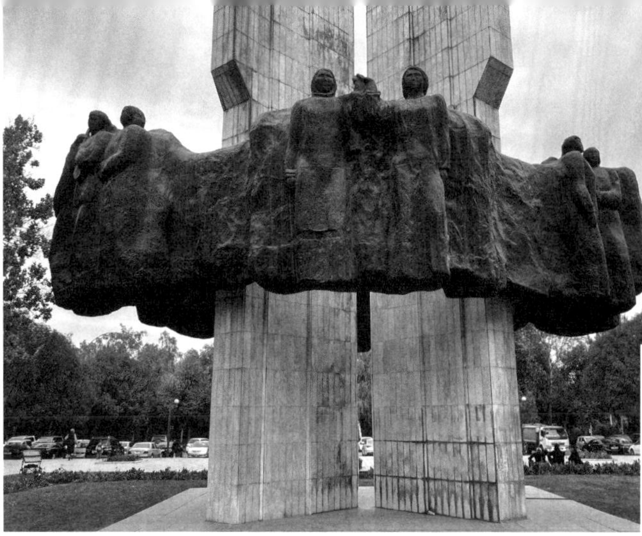

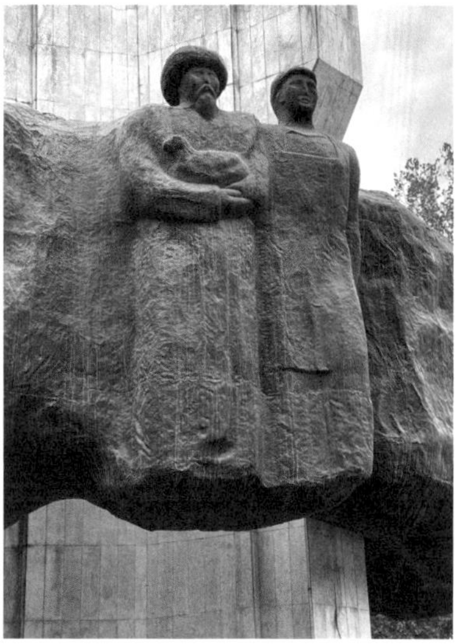

FIGS. 11.1-11.2 MONUMENT TO FRIENDSHIP, BISHKEK, KYRGYZSTAN 1974. SCULPTORS: TURGUNBAY SADIKOV, S. BAKASHEV, AND Z. KHABIBULIN, ARCHITECT: A. NEZHURIN

in fact, saw the siege, defeat, and razing to the ground of Pishpek by Russian troops, who killed its defenders and forced a surrender.[64] On the obelisk, 1874 is chosen to refer to the date of the final conquest and disintegration of the Khanate of Khoqand, which saw much of today's Kyrgyzstan fall under Russian jurisdiction. The problem being that the extermination and extinction of the Khoqand Khanate (and its replacement with the Ferghana Oblast of the Russian Empire) can under no circumstances—despite the claims of Russian imperial and Soviet historians that "the people" were relieved to be rid of the Khoqand yoke—be considered "voluntary."[65] Tens of thousands of Khoqand defenders and civilians were killed in

64 Alexander Morrison, *The Russian Conquest of Central Asia: A Study in Imperial Expansion, 1814–1914* (Cambridge: Cambridge University Press, 2020), 32–33. Prior to the Russian conquest, Khoqand was claimed by the Chinese Qing Empire. For a history of Central Asia which systematically assesses Chinese-Russian imperial rivalry, see Adeeb Khalid, *Central Asia: A New History from the Imperial Conquests to the Present* (Princeton, NJ: Princeton University Press, 2021).
65 The final date of the fall of Khoqand was in fact 1876 rather than 1874. See Morrison, *The Russian Conquest of Central Asia*, 185.

decades of fighting; Russian losses were in the dozens.[66] Details aside, the remarkable thing is quite how much energy the ideologists, artists, poets, and sculptors of the late Soviet decades expended in order to highlight, via the conduit of the "Friendship of the Peoples," the direct continuity between Soviet nationalities policy and the Russian Tsarist empire's bloody record of conquest and subjugation.[67]

In aesthetic terms, Friendship of the Peoples became one of the core subjects of expression for all spheres of Soviet socialist-realist art. In monumental sculpture, its most spectacular realization is the Fountain of the Friendship of the Peoples at the heart of the VDNKh All-Union exhibition complex in Moscow—also completed in 1954, that Friendliest of years. Following the retreat of socialist realism—more pronounced in architecture than other art forms—throughout the Soviet Bloc after 1954, the ideologies, rhetorics, and aesthetics of Friendship nevertheless persisted, and continued to manifest in architecture, monumental sculpture, and popular culture. Distinct forms of still-socialist-realist politics and aesthetics of Friendship continue to linger and metastasize in the zombie socialist orbits of Bishkek, Beijing, Pyongyang, Phnom Penh, Ulaanbaatar, Minsk, Kolkata, and beyond. Among its most spectacular realizations are the numerous, huge neo-socialist-realist monuments—many of them framed as "gifts" from the Democratic People's Republic of Korea—erected by the North Korean Mansudae Art Studio in the Middle East and Africa from the 1970s until the present day.[68]

In the Cold War context of Soviet expansionism in Eastern Europe, and of Moscow's and/or Beijing's (highly conditional) support for decolonial movements in the Global South, ideologies of intra-Soviet "Friendship" were exported globally, and garlanded with new costumes and insinuations of decolonial and internationalist solidarity. Reflecting shifting geopolitical (dis)articulations, bridges and infrastructural objects were built, hymns composed, oratories delivered, and monuments erected to honor endless configurations of hyphenated Friendship:[69] Russian-Ukrainian, Soviet-Polish, East German-Vietnamese, Libyan-Romanian, Georgian-Azeri-Armenian, Buryat-Mongol, Mozambican-German, Korean-Syrian,

66 Ibid.
67 For Chinese propaganda against Soviet "social imperialism," see, e.g., *The Ugly Features of Soviet Social-Imperialism* (Peking: Foreign Languages Press, 1976).
68 See Che Onejoon, *International Friendship: The Gifts from Africa* (Heidelberg: Kehrer, 2022).
69 Kristin Roth-Ey, "Introduction," *Socialist Internationalism and the Gritty Politics of the Particular: Second-Third World Spaces in the Cold War*, ed. Kristin Roth-Ey (London: Bloomsbury Academic, 2023), 14.

Angolan-Soviet, and so on. On Soviet-oriented terrain, for all its internationalist costume, the post-Stalinist variant of Friendship remained highly Russo-centric, racialized, centripetal-metropolitan, and indebted to the legacy of the Russian Empire.[70]

In many of the post-Soviet states, the ideologies and aesthetics of Friendship survived the fall of the Union. They reared their heads again in particularly pronounced and ugly forms following Russia's annexation of the Georgian region of South Ossetia in 2008, and following Russia's "reunification" with (annexation of) Crimea in 2014—a renunciation of Khrushchev's "gift," timed to coincide with its sixtieth anniversary. Since 2022, neo-Soviet ideologies of Friendship, kinship, solidarity, and gifthood have been revived and deployed to smokescreen processes of re-colonial expansionism and extractivism, weaponized sexual violence, and attempted genocide. At the same time, the rhetorics and aesthetics of decolonization are contested and appropriated from diverse angles. Ukrainians, Eastern Europeans, Central Asians, and indigenous activists within Russia deploy decolonial rhetorics to empower claims to liberation from Russian imperialism. Meanwhile, the Russian Federation presents itself as being engaged in a "decolonial" crusade to build a "new world order" in alliance with the "Global South" against the hegemony of the "Global North." The newly expanded BRICS (Brazil, Russia, India, China, South Africa) group is put forward as a necromantic Comecon or Non-Aligned Movement, while Russia and China's rhetorics of support for Palestine in the wake of Israel's full-scale invasion of Gaza endow their pseudo-internationalist posturing with false veneers of legitimacy. A turbo-charged neo-Stalinist (or rather neo-Brezhnevite) ideology of Friendship is today re-emerging—in a particularly brazen and absurd form—as a core component of Russia's mission to project its "imperial innocence."[71]

TOWARD AN "OPEN FORM" OF FRIENDSHIP?

Against the background of this perverted, resurgent form of zombie Russian Friendship (with a capital F), what possible future can there be for political and artistic practices based on friendship, solidarity, sisterhood, or allyship? Can politicized forms of friendship, and affective and emotional forms of politics—and their architectural and monumental embodiments—

70 Rachel Applebaum, however, provides a more sympathetic reading. See "The Friendship Project: Socialist Internationalism in the Soviet Union and Czechoslovakia in the 1950s and 1960s," *Slavic Review* 74, no. 3 (2015): 484–507.

71 See, e.g., Botakoz Kassymbekova and Erica Marat, "Time to Question Russia's Imperial Innocence," *PONARS Eurasia Policy Memo*, no. 771 (2022).

be decolonized and de-Russified? How can we continue to build political collectivities—or affective communities, in Leela Gandhi's term—based on ideas and practices of friendship and solidarity?[72] What alternatives do we have to retreating into the aesthetic-ideological security provided by the neoliberal doxa of the individualistic citizen-subject? Might we think of a differently politicized idea of friendship—grounded in the philoxenic love of strangers rather than in the xenophobic fear or hatred of others—as a capaciously "open form" of relationality, in feminist theorist Alva Gotby's phrase?[73] Can a differently politicized idea of friendship function as an ally (or an agonist) to ethics and politics of "care," encumbered as they are by institutional, biomedical, and individualistic entanglements?[74]

Jacques Derrida invested a special hope in the politics of friendship. For Derrida, a politics based on friendship offers a counterpoint to the "*familial, fraternalist* and thus *androcentric* configuration of politics" based on blood.[75] A kinship without patriarchy and without consanguinity. A politics "beyond the principle of fraternity." Fraternity, patriarchy, or *fratriarchy* nevertheless keep returning to the scene. Derrida points to the danger of "the figure of the friend, so regularly coming back on stage with the features of the *brother*."[76] In order to develop his own dialectics of friendship, Derrida has to think hard with Carl Schmitt, the Catholic Nazi jurist who inscribed the figure of the Friend into a deeply hostile, armed-to-the-teeth binary confrontation with the figure of the Enemy. But a confrontation, nevertheless, that does not rest on blood or even on culture, but on another type of affinity.

Now, it is interesting that Schmitt was developing his theory of friend and enemy in the 1930s, the years immediately preceding the moment that the ideology of Friendship (with a capital F) was taking root, under Stalin's guidance, in the Soviet Union. Indeed, the Nazi Schmitt took a keen and direct interest in Soviet political thought and practice. The "spirit of Hegel"—by which he means the agonistic energy of the dialectical method—did not "reside" for a long time in Berlin. Soon, says

72 Leela Gandhi, *Affective Communities: Anticolonial Thought, Fin-de-Siècle Radicalism, and the Politics of Friendship* (Durham and London: Duke University Press, 2006).

73 On philoxenia, see Gandhi, *Affective Communities*, 29–30, 184–89; Alva Gotby, *They Call it Love: The Politics of Emotional Life* (London: Verso, 2023). As I completed work on this essay, I learned of another recent symposium devoted to a closely overlapping theme: "What remains of the 'friendship between peoples?'" at Prater Galerie, Berlin, June 1, 2024, https://pratergalerie.de/en/prater-galerie/event/was-bleibt-von-der-voelkerfreundschaft/; and of Olga Grotova's intermedia art and research project *The Friendship Garden*, 2021–2023, https://studiovoltaire.org/whats-on/olga-grotova/.

74 For a critique of ideologies of care, see, e.g., Keti Chukhrov, "Topology for Three Power Paradigms: Pyramid, Grid, Circle," *Pirammmida.life*, August 7, 2020, https://www.pirammmida.life/keti-chukhrov.

75 Jacques Derrida, *The Politics of Friendship*, trans. George Collins (London and New York: Verso, 1997), viii.

76 Ibid., 149.

Schmitt, "Hegel wandered to Moscow via Karl Marx and Lenin. His dialectical method became established there and found its concrete expression in a new concrete-enemy concept, namely that of the international class enemy."[77]

Schmitt (and Derrida) were fascinated by the political force contained in the "absolute hostility" with which the Soviet figure of the *enemy* was invested. What he (they) did not grasp is that, at exactly the time when Schmitt was locating Hegel's enemy in Moscow, Moscow was swiftly becoming a city of *Friends*. That is, Moscow—and its empire—were overflowing with enemies, and they were being purged, show-trialed, exiled, or shot. But they were not being purged so much because of their class, but because of their foreignness or ethno-nationally specific fifth-columnhood.[78] Schmitt's vision of Moscow's absolute hostility to a class enemy was appropriate to the class militancy of the Soviet late 1920s and early 1930s, which sought to catalyze international proletarian solidarity and root out class enemies.[79] However, during this period—and in the decades before—the *brotherhood* of the peoples (*bratstvo narodov*) was the kin metaphor-in-dominance. The purpose of the campaign to replace *brotherhood* with *Friendship*—which culminated just before and during the Great Terror of 1936–1938—was intended to reorient Soviet political passions away from a negative focus on the class enemy, toward a positive affect of filial (not familial) attachment to fellow citizens (and toward Comrade Stalin). This was neither the time nor the place for brotherhood.

The centering of the friend-enemy distinction in the Soviet politics of everyday life happened in the period immediately following the publication of Schmitt's words, fawning over the "absolute hostility" to the class enemy in Soviet political discourse. It did not happen, however, in quite the way that Schmitt endorsed. Further, there was, and continues to be, a constant slippage in Soviet—and post-Soviet—political discourse between *druzhba* and *bratstvo*. Occasionally, the language of *sisterhood* (and motherhood) makes an entry, too—such as the triple-obelisked Monument to Three Sisters unveiled in 1975 on the tri-border

77 Carl Schmitt, *The Concept of the Political*, trans. George Schwab (Chicago: University of Chicago Press,1996), 62.

78 A large proportion of the victims of Stalin's Great Purge, which peaked in 1937, were killed in the so-called "national operations." Over 100,000 fell victim to the "Polish operation" alone. Many of those killed in other "sections" of the purge were also murdered on ethnic and national grounds, accused of spying for Germany, Poland, Japan, or other foreign powers, whereas certain "class" operations—such as the largest one against the kulaks—also had a hugely disproportionate effect on certain nationalities (especially Ukrainians). The hunger of the early 1930s disproportionately decimated populations of Ukrainians and Kazakhs. Brutal purges and deportations of tens of millions of members of nationalities in the Caucasus, Crimea, and Central Asia continued until the 1950s. See, e.g., Timothy Snyder, *Bloodlands: Europe between Hitler and Stalin* (New York: Basic Books, 2010); Terry Martin, "The Origins of Soviet Ethnic Cleansing," *The Journal of Modern History* 70, no. 4 (1998): 813–61.

79 Martin, *The Affirmative Action Empire*, 145.

between the Ukrainian, Belarusian, and Russian SSRs (and standing to this day).

The ethnopolitical dimension of Soviet Friendship tilted increasingly, from the late 1930s onward, toward a primordialist, essentialist understanding of ethnicity and nationality, with strong racial connotations. The friendly nations were all equal, but there were "advanced" and "backward" ones among them, and the Russian nation was, as Stalin put it, "first among equals." Visual representations of racial difference made these hierarchies crystal clear. Aleksandr Deineka's 1937 painting *Illustrious People of the Land of the Soviets*, also known as *Stakhanovites*, depicts a procession of squeaky-clean shock workers marching (or strutting) in resplendent sunshine on the parade ground beneath the (never-built) supreme building of the Soviet Union, the Palace of the Soviets. Representatives of multiple Soviet nationalities march together, arm-in-arm, all smiles. All the workers in the foreground are white-skinned, and all wear white, European-style Sunday best (with the exception of one woman in a light pink dress). By egregious contrast, all the workers (bar one) in the (rather distant) background are dark-skinned, and all of them (except the blonde woman among them) wear national dress.[80]

Whereas Stalinist Friendship of the Peoples was de facto anti-internationalist, or rather internationalist-in-one-country, post-Stalinist practice reintroduced a measure of competitive Cold War internationalism into the rhetorics and aesthetics of Friendship—most explicitly marked by the establishment in 1961 of the Patrice Lumumba People's Friendship University in Moscow. This was accompanied by a strongly articulated commitment to anti-racism (and a corollary condemnation of racism in the USA as well as the renewed wooing of black American intellectuals and public figures, among them Audre Lorde, Angela Davis, Muhammad Ali, and many others).[81] On the one hand, black visitors to the USSR gave numerous accounts, especially in public, attesting to the claim that the Soviet Union had become a racism-free society, *unlike* the United States; on the other, they also recorded numerous testimonies, especially in private diaries and correspondence, of the racist hostility and

80 For an extended discussion of *Illustrious People*, see Christina Kiaer, *Collective Body: Aleksandr Deineka at the Limit of Socialist Realism* (Chicago: University of Chicago Press, 2024), 217–31.

81 African Americans had been visiting and settling in the USSR since the 1920s and 1930s. See, e.g., David Chioni Moore, "Local Color, Global 'Color': Langston Hughes, the Black Atlantic, and Soviet Central Asia, 1932," *Research in African Literatures* 27, no. 4 (1996): 49–70; John L. Garder, "African Americans in the Soviet Union in the 1920s and 1930s: The Development of Transcontinental Protest," *The Western Journal of Black Studies* 23, no. 3 (1999): 190–201; David Featherstone and Christian Høgbsjerg, eds., *The Red and the Black: The Russian Revolution and the Black Atlantic* (Manchester: Manchester University Press, 2021).

violence they encountered during their visits. Anika Walke observes that African students in the USSR in the 1970s–1990s, many studying at the Lumumba Friendship University, experienced "forms of differential treatment in terms of housing, stipends, and even education," which created de facto institutionalized racial hierarchies.[82] Jeff Sahadeo documents the extent to which the experience of Central Asian labor migrants and students in Moscow and Leningrad directly contradicted the public myth of Friendship of the Peoples. Sahadeo's interlocutors from Central Asia and the Caucasus were regularly called *cherny* (black) or *ch---a* (literally a plank of wood, used as a highly derogatory derivative of *cherny*), terms that were initially used with reference to black people of African descent, but came to be applied to Soviet citizens of color in the 1960s and 1970s.[83]

SOCIALIST FRIENDSHIP WITHOUT SOCIALISM

In 2022 and 2023, I organized two symposia in Tbilisi and Berlin on the theme of "political friendship," its perils and potentials, with the intention of putting Szapocznikow's sculpture, its meanings and materiality, in context.[84] One discussion was held under the auspices of the Tbilisi Architecture Biennial (TAB); the second in Berlin during ICKPA (ISKRA), a Ukrainian techno festival curated since 2021 by Tbilisi's David Chikhladze and Zviad Gelbakhiani, both associated with the Bassiani club—a legendary site of political contestation, solidarity, and friendship since its foundation in 2014. Scholars, architects, and activists working on and/or hailing from numerous sites marked by socialist Friendship—Bosnia, Georgia, Korea, Kazakhstan, China, Mongolia, Poland, and Ukraine—compared notes and tried to make sense of F(f)riendship's various perfidious effects, but also its latent political potential.

We spent a lot more time on the perfidious than the potential. But the perfidious could often look very pretty, even seductive. And Friendship's perfidies almost always worked on multiple levels of interpellation, from the macro-public to

82 Anika Walke, "Was Soviet Internationalism Anti-Racist?: Towards a History of Foreign Others in the USSR," in *Ideologies of Race: Imperial Russia and the Soviet Union in Global Context*, ed. David Rainbow (Montreal: McGill-Queen's University Press, 2019), 286; Jessica Allina-Pissano and Eric Allina-Pissano, "'Friendship of the Peoples' after the Fall: Violence and Pan-African Community in Post-Soviet Moscow," in *Africa in Russia, Russia in Africa: Three Centuries of Encounters*, ed. Maxim Matusevich (Trenton, NJ: Africa World Press, 2007), 175–198.

83 Jeff Sahadeo, "Druzhba Narodov or Second-Class Citizenship? Soviet Asian Migrants in a Post-Colonial World," *Central Asian Survey* 26, no. 4 (2007): 559–79. See also Kimberly St. Julian-Varnon, "The Racist Treatment of Africans and African Americans in the Soviet Union," *New Lines Magazine*, February 17, 2023; Eugene M. Avrutin, *Racism in Modern Russia: From the Romanovs to Putin* (London: Bloomsbury Academic, 2022).

84 "Futures of Friendship: Decolonising & Demasculinising (Br)otherhood," held at Tbilisi Architecture Biennial, October 22, 2022, https://youtu.be/76fpooEMNHw?si=ppB-h92G-mcevROT4; "Political Friendship After Socialism," held at ICKPA, Berlin, June 22, 2023, https://acudmachtneu.de/events/1983/ickpa-panels/.

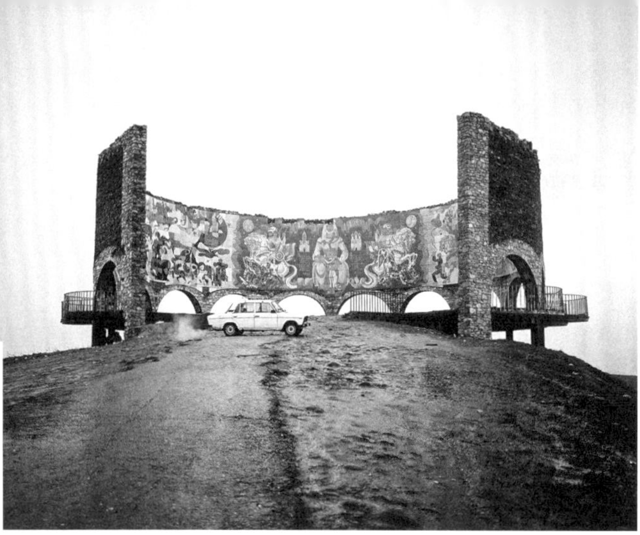

FIG. 12 RUSSIA-GEORGIA FRIENDSHIP MONUMENT, GUDAURI, GEORGIA, 1983. ARTIST: ZURAB TSERETELI, ARCHITECT: GIORGI CHAKHAVA

the nano-personal. Architect and founder of the Tbilisi Biennial, Tinatin Gurgenidze, told the story of two beautiful, if mendacious (or delusional) totems to Friendship.[85] The first is the Russia-Georgia Friendship Monument **[FIG. 12]**, erected in 1983 on the military highway leading through the mountains from Tbilisi to the border of the Russian Federation. The monument is built in the manner of a historical panorama, its inside inlaid with a gorgeous tile mural by (in)famous Georgian-Russian sculptor Zurab Tsereteli, depicting an optimistic rendering of 200 years of Russian-Georgian Friendship. It marks, in the established manner of late Soviet neo-colonial centennialism, the signing in 1783 of the Treaty of Georgievsk between Russian Empress Catherine and Georgian monarch Erekle II. In the familiar device of Soviet (counter-) historiography, Georgievsk—like Pereiaslav or the seizure of Pishpek—was supposed to historically demarcate the "voluntary incorporation" of Georgia into Russia. In reality, it sealed the submission of Georgia—an erstwhile Persian vassal—to the status of a Russian protectorate, in exchange for the (false and immediately broken) promise of guardianship against Persian retribution and domination.

The second is the Monument to the Friendship of the Youth of the Transcaucasian Republics at the Red Bridge **[FIG. 13]**, erected in 1981 on the border between Georgia and Azerbaijan, several kilometers from the border with Armenia. The monument, which Gurgenidze described as a "Tree of Life," stands on a hill on the right bank of the Chrami River, and is the work of a team led by Georgian sculptor Gia Japaridze. It mimics abstracted elements of a grape vine and a pomegranate tree, "sensitively summarising," in the assessment of artist and cura-

85 Tinatin Gurgenidze, "Soviet-Georgian Friendship," presentation at the Tbilisi Architecture Biennial, October 22, 2022.

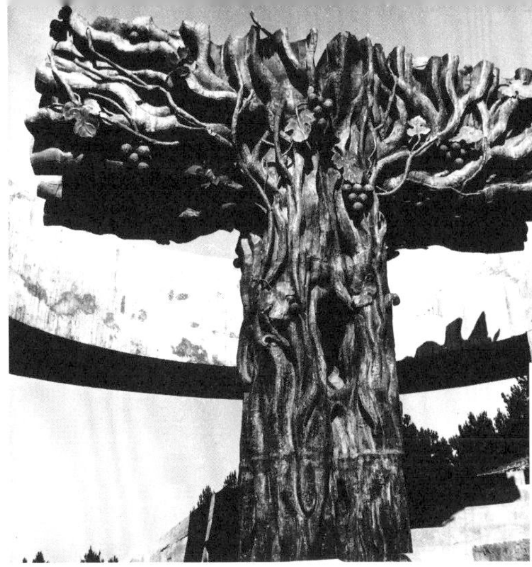

FIG. 13 FRIENDSHIP MONUMENT AT THE RED BRIDGE, GEORGIA, 1981. SCULPTOR: GIA JAPARIDZE. ARCHITECTS: VALERY BAKHTADZE, LEO BOKERIA, VLADIMER KURTISHVILI, VLADIMER TSINTSADZE. PHOTO: VLADIMER KURTISHVILI, 1981, BLACK-AND-WHITE PHOTOGRAPH, 17.5 × 17.5 CM

tor Irina Kurtishvili, "the diverse cultural traditions of three Caucasian nations," Georgia, Armenia, and Azerbaijan.[86] Erected in the immediate aftermath of successful Georgian opposition to an attempt by Moscow to remove Georgian as a state language of the Georgian SSR, Japaridze's "Tree" shows that—even amid the stagnation and repression of late Soviet life—Friendship ideology was sometimes able to bypass the Russian pivot and express itself in a relatively autonomous direction and aesthetic language. Notwithstanding its beauty and its successful invocation of a spirit of Transcaucasian harmony, its symbolism rings tragic today. "There is zero friendship" now, said Gurgenidze—speaking in Berlin in June 2023, as tension mounted ahead of Azerbaijan's September 2023 violent subjugation of the Armenian autonomous province of Artsakh. Kurtishvili, daughter of one of the monument's designers, architect Vladimer Kurtishvili, attempted to visit the "Tree of Life" in July 2024 with an international group of researchers. She discovered that not only is there now no access to the monument, but she and her companions were fined by the Georgian border force for attempting to approach it. The monument itself, in Kurtishvili's assessment, is "severely damaged," whole parts having been stripped bare, most probably stolen for scrap metal. There is currently no sign of friendship at the tri-border, says Kurtishvili, "rather mistrust, resentment, separation and isolation."[87]

Gurgenidze went on to tell how the invocation of Friendship (and/or brotherhood) by Russians toward citizens of other post-Soviet nations can itself constitute an act of violence and domination. This was historically true, all the more so following the Russian aggressions against and occupations

86 See Nini Palavandishvili and Irina Kurtishvili, eds., *Building Socialist Georgia* (Tbilisi: Goethe-Institut Georgien, 2022), 146–51.
87 Irina Kurtishvili, email to Michał Murawski, August 2, 2024.

of Georgia in 1992–1993 and 2008. Even then, and even after the Russian invasion of Ukraine in 2014, these friendships somehow endured. But after February 24, 2022, something snapped. Gurgenidze recounted:

> I quit one of my longest friendships with a Russian friend, which actually survived the war in 2008, during which she was already telling me, "I love you so much, you're my family, you're my friend." And back then, somehow, I accepted it. But when the full-scale invasion of Ukraine started in 2022, it was over. I wanted her to show solidarity, guilt, whatever, something new, but all she could talk about was "friendship." So I had to end *our* friendship then and there.

Accordingly, an important theme highlighted throughout our conversations was the significance of the *scale* of friendship. The dynamics of the connection—and dependency—between personal, micro-level friendships between individuals, and macro-level F(f)riendships between nations. Ukrainian art historian Polina Baitsym spoke about professional collaborations between Russian and Ukrainian art historians in the Stalin period, which were expected to mirror the friendship between Taras Shevchenko and his Russian collaborators.[88] In 1950s Poland, too, as art historian Agata Pietrasik shows, the friendship between the respective romantic national bards of Poland and Russia, Adam Mickiewicz and Alexander Pushkin, was framed "as a model for current Polish-Soviet relations."[89] Baitsym highlighted the slippage between Friendship and fraternity. The idea of "brotherhood of the people," the dominant metaphor during the Soviet 1920s, originated from the Bolshevik (and Second International) identification with the French Revolutionary ideology of *fraternité*. By the late 1930s, and the 1935–1938 Soviet Friendship campaign, the concept and rhetoric of Friendship arose as a "transformation, perversion, of this old idea of fraternity."[90]

Anthropologist Ed Pulford, who works on practices of friendship in the borderlands of Russia, China, and North Korea, spoke in Tbilisi about his work in Hunchun, a Korean autonomous region of north-east China, which lies

88 Polina Baitsym, "Pasts of Friendship," presentation at the Tbilisi Architecture Biennial, October 22, 2022.
89 Pietrasik, "Picking Out Paths: A Retrospective View into the 1930s," in *Was Socialist Realism Global? Modernism, Soc-Modernism, Socially Engaged Figuration*, ed. Magda Lipska and Piotr Słodkowski (Warsaw: Museum of Modern Art, 2023), 118.
90 Baitsym's arguments are developed in "Love for the Art of the Motherland," in *Entangled Art Historiographies in Ukraine*, ed. Stefania Demchuk and Ilia Levchenko (London: Routledge, [forthcoming]).

on the border with Russia.[91] Pulford referred to the tensions—but also continuities—between the types of everyday friendships and collaborations which existed between Koreans, Russians, and Chinese, and the official zombie Stalinist ideology of Friendship, which—especially in such a nodal, tri-border area—was turbocharged by the Chinese state. Hunchun, says Pulford, is one among many sites of a veritable "Friendship-industrial complex."[92] The prime infrastructural vehicle of this complex, China's Belt and Road, is rhetorically "cloaked in the language of Friendship." The dialectic between micro- and macro-friendship, which plays out from the streets of Hunchun to the pipelines and arteries of the Belt and Road, comes back down to a (larger-than-life) interpersonal scale in the figure of the "great personal friendship" between Xi Jinping and Vladimir Putin—whose joint declarations of "Friendship without boundaries" and "limitless Friendship" (the ominous wording of a communiqué signed between China and Russia at the Beijing Olympics in January 2022) mimic the elaborately performed Friendship between Stalin and Mao prior to the Sino-Soviet split of 1955.

The slippage between Friend and brother never ceases. Pulford observed that the lyrics of successive versions of the Soviet national anthem (from 1944 and 1977) referred to "Friendship of the Peoples." The post-1991 Russian anthem kept the same tune, but tweaked the lyrics to make them less overtly Soviet. Thus, "Friendship" was replaced, again, by "brotherly nations." Whichever form of *philia* or kinship was being invoked, says Pulford, the Soviet, post-Soviet Russian, and Chinese practices of Friendship and brotherhood are all "founded on a fundamental structure of otherness," which is concerned with classification, taxonomy, and the fetishization of difference. Friendship becomes a form of "cultural essentialism" which comes into sharp relief at boundary sites, especially multiboundary sites such as Hunchun.

Historians have observed that Soviet nationalities policy, whose chief ideological cog was friendship, was in principle opposed to race theory. In practice, however, the constant reiteration of difference—reinforced through practices such as the identification of a single "nationality" in Soviet passports—ultimately reinforced a racialized idea of

91 Ed Pulford, "The Friendship-Industrial Complex," presentation at the Tbilisi Architecture Biennial, October 22, 2022. Pulford's arguments are developed in "Differences over Difference: Sino-Russian Friendship at Interstate and Interpersonal Scales," *Comparative Studies in Society and History* 63, no. 3 (2021): 685–721; and his monograph, *Past Progress: Time and Politics at the Borders of China, Russia, and Korea* (Stanford: Stanford University Press, 2024).
92 Pulford, *Past Progress*, 115.

ethnicized, primordial nationality. Most people understood their nations in a racialized way. If, as Ghanian philosopher Kwame Anthony Appiah observes, nationality has a "racial essence," migration historian Jeff Sahadeo points out that in the Soviet context this racialization was uncommonly pronounced.[93] Socialist friendship simultaneously obfuscated and aggressively reinforced the hierarchy, asymmetry, and Russocentrism built into it.

Architectural historian Da Hyung Jeong hinted, in his contribution to the Tbilisi panel, at other axes of friendship which bypass—like Japaridze's "Tree of Life"—the Russo-centric directionality written into the doctrine.[94] Notwithstanding the non-aligned (i.e. non-Soviet) roots of Afro-Asiatism—codified by Algerian philosopher Malek Bennabi in his book on the Bandung Afro-Asian Conference of 1955—its ideological impulse was swiftly incorporated into (and appropriated by) the lexicon and practice of Soviet "Friendship assistance" to decolonized and decolonizing African and Asian states.[95] Correspondingly, Afro-Asiatism acquired a distinctive architectural form, discernible in the striking affinity between Soviet-built structures in distinct places by different architects, such as the Conakry Polytechnic Institute, Guinea, completed in 1962, and the Kabul Polytechnic Institute, Afghanistan, completed in 1963. This resemblance, argues Jeong, was not due to prefabrication or mindless copy-pasting—it was also an effect of the profound impact that Afro-Asiatist ideas, formulated at and following Bandung, exerted on Soviet design, ideology, and praxis. The USSR, says Jeong, did not merely export influence, expertise, technology, and architectural aesthetics to Africa and Asia—it was also "on the receiving end of a discursive exchange," and it "subscribed and made policy in accordance with Afro-Asiatism." Whereas what Jeong calls "Soviet architectural Afro-Asiatism" shows that Soviet Friendship ideology was capacious enough to absorb influences from its asymmetric beneficiaries, this absorption constituted an act of appropriation carried out for strategic gain.

Soviet-coalesced aesthetics of Afro-Asiatism nevertheless survived the collapse of the Soviet Union. As Jeong pointed out in his talk,

93 Sahadeo, "Druzhba Narodov," 506.

94 Da Hyung Jeong, "Soviet Architectural Afro-Asiatism," presentation at the Tbilisi Architecture Biennial, October 22, 2022.

95 Ibid. See also Da Hyung Jeong, "Soviet Architectural Presence in Southeast Asia," *PostMoMA*, November 18, 2020, https://post.moma.org/soviet-architectural-presence-in-southeast-asia/.

> over three decades since the collapse of the Eastern Bloc, such monuments continue to be built, notably by the North Korean Mansudae Art Studio, which has been perpetuating the idea of *socialist Friendship in the absence of socialism*, or Afro-Asiatist Friendship in a new era of Afro-Asiatism [emphasis added].

Jeong points to the specific example of the African Renaissance Monument in Dakar, Senegal, built by the Mansudae Art Studio and completed in 2010 **[FIG. 14]**; whose "dynamic composition clearly takes after" the Chollima Statue in Pyongyang, completed in 1961 **[FIG. 15]** and dedicated to the "Chollima speed" of the DPRK's Chollima shock worker movement; which in turn is modeled on Vera Mukhina's famous 1937 Monument to the Worker and Kolkhoz Woman **[FIG. 16]**, first displayed at the Exposition Internationale in Paris in 1937, prior to its relocation to the main entrance of the All-Union Agricultural Exhibition, rechristened in 1959 as the Exhibition of Achievements of National Economy (VDNKh). Centripetal and Russo-centric (and Yugo-centric, and Sino- or Han-centric) as it is, its temporalities and directionalities are multiple and, for better or worse, a form of socialist friendship lives on—along with the affective bonds and tensions it creates, and the infrastructural-industrial complexes it cements.

It lives on, and yet it does not. In some places, ideas of Friendship (delusional or mendacious as they may have been) have been expunged in substance and persist only as nostalgia. Yugoslavia's socialism developed independently of the Soviet model; Friendship was present in (geo)political discourse, but it did not become the guiding metaphor. Instead, as Bosnian-born, Austrian-based theorist of architecture Anela Dumonjić observed during her contribution to the Berlin seminar, the World War II communist partisan slogan of "brotherhood and unity" became the guiding metaphor for the Yugoslav variant of internationalism-in-one-country (although it also trickled through to the rhetoric of the Non-Aligned Movement).[96] Yugoslav nostalgics, Dumonjić observes, still appear to be fascinated by this slogan, "but I don't see how much brotherhood we had when we butcher each other's brothers and sisters, when there's mass sexual assault, when some people have everything and others have nothing."

96 Anela Dumonjić, contribution to the "Political Friendship After Socialism" seminar, ICKPA Festival, Berlin, June 22, 2023; see also Paul Stubbs, "Yugocentrism and the Study of the Non-Aligned Movement: Towards a Decolonial Historiography," *History in Flux: Journal of the Department of History, Faculty of Humanities, Juraj Dobrila University of Pula* 3, no. 3 (2021): 133–55.

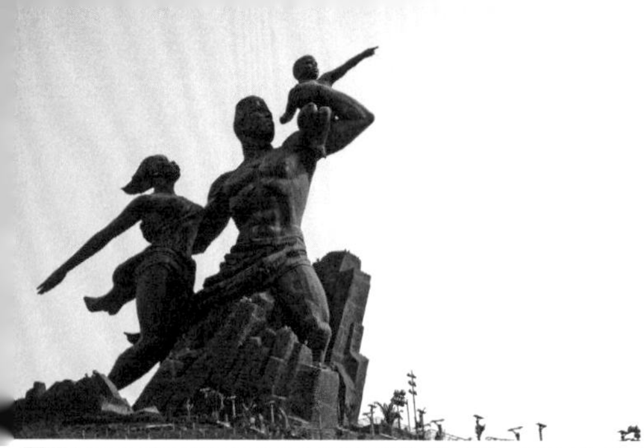

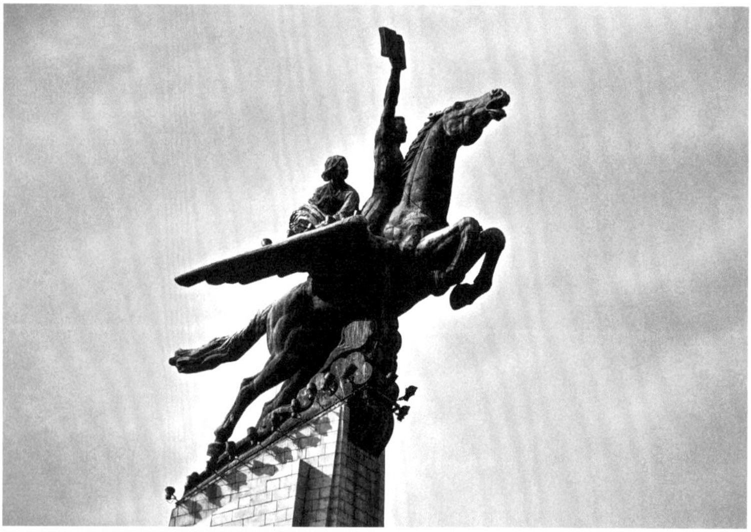

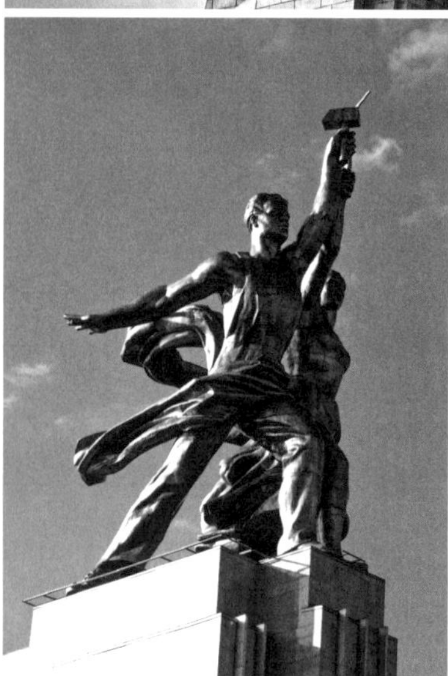

FIG. 14 AFRICAN RENAISSANCE MONUMENT, DAKAR, 2010, SCULPTOR: OUSMANE SOW (WITHDREW FROM THE PROJECT), ARCHITECT: PIERRE GOUDIABY, EXECUTED BY THE MANSUDAE ART STUDIO
FIG. 15 CHOLLIMA STATUE, PYONGYANG, 1961, SCULPTORS: O SONGSAM AND CHO WONSOK, EXECUTED BY THE MANSUDAE ART STUDIO
FIG. 16 WORKER AND KOLKHOZ WOMAN, 1937, PARIS AND MOSCOW, SCULPTOR: VERA MUHKINA, ARCHITECT: BORIS IOFAN

Following the Yugoslav Wars, however, the Muslim-majority former Yugoslav countries, Bosnia and Kosovo, became quasi-colonial protectorates co-governed and occupied by Western-appointed viceroys.[97] The subject of brotherhood and unity was replaced,

97 The word "viceroy," the English term for the colonial governor of India, was regularly used with reference to the UN-appointed High Representative for Bosnia-Herzegovina; see, e.g., "The viceroy rules, OK? Not everyone thinks so," *The Economist*, July 24, 2003, https://www.economist.com/europe/2003/07/24/the-viceroy-rules-ok-not-everyone-thinks-so.

said Dumonjić, by an eviscerated, neoliberalized "post-Yugoslav subject," whose infrastructure of community has been taken away and replaced by a "radical depoliticization" and "self-responsibilization." At the same time as post-Yugoslav subjects are expected to take responsibility for their own fate, pull themselves up by the bootstraps, the hegemonic "Western savior complex" presents them as "ostracized individuals who cannot ever possibly even have a conversation with someone of a different ethnic, national, or religious background." This parallel, and utterly contradictory neoliberal self-responsibilization and infantilization is especially severe, Dumonjić asserts, in the multiethnic space of Bosnia, functioning as a sort of "mini-Yugoslavia," in which the coming-together of different peoples under the slogan of brotherhood and unity was articulated with special emphasis. It is in sites like this, where the withdrawal of the infrastructure of socialist welfare is painfully felt, but where the iteration of brotherhood and unity lingers in the form of vacuous, Yugo-apologetic (Serb-centric) nostalgia, that the space for a rearticulation of political friendship coalesces.

We had amply demonstrated the *perils*, while also—in the case of Gurgenidze, Jeong, and Dumonjić—haltingly attempted to articulate the *potentials*. The questions from the audience, however, were, both in Tbilisi and Berlin, concerned with the latter rather than the former. One (Georgian) member of the audience in Berlin asked panel members to speculate about the future of F(f)riendship between non-Russian nationalities formerly incorporated into the USSR: "How is it possible to make friendship between us, between nations, after Stalinist *druzhba narodov*, in a decentralized, not in a centralized way?" In Tbilisi, another audience member objected to the notion that socialist friendship constituted a "perversion." Friendship between Georgia and Ukraine, they pointed out, was "forged in the Soviet Union; that's when the Ukrainians and Georgians really got to know each other." Echoing Gurgenidze's and Jeong's presentations, they also indicated the infrastructural-architectural manifestations of Friendship which bypass the Russian orbit, such as the mosaic monument to Georgian-Ukrainian Friendship in the village of Shroma, in western Georgia's Guria region.[98] They continued:

> Since I was born I hear about "fake friendship" or "perverted friendship." Like nothing [that we know] has ever really even existed, and even if it did it was just created by force from Moscow. So, for me, this idea of "fake friendship" was introduced by neoliberal forces in the post-Soviet space to dismantle the very idea of solidarity between nations after the fall of the Soviet Union.

98 The mosaic in Shroma (date not ascertained) is based on a monument to Georgian-Ukrainian Friendship erected in Henichesk in Ukraine's Kherson Oblast (under Russian occupation since 2022) in 1969, on the thirtieth anniversary of a twinning arrangement between two collective farms. Relations between Henichesk and Ozurgeti, capital of the Guria region, fizzled out after the fall of the USSR, but were renewed in 2020. According to the authors of a Henichesk blog, this ongoing friendship is proof that "even banal internationalist-proletarian initiatives of the regime ... could be transformed into something really, truly good, kind and authentic." Namori, https://namori.com.ua/blog/genichesk-i-ozurgeti-drujba-proverennaya-vremenem. With sincere thanks to Tinatin Gurgenidze for her help in clarifying information about the Henichesk and Ozurgeti monuments.

PART III

BATTLE

AFTER THE BATTLE

The battle in the title of this essay refers to the Battle of Parade Square in Warsaw, which took place on July 21, 2009. Several hundred traders—the last surviving veterans of the huge open-air bazaar which sprouted up on the Square in June 1989, as the Polish People's Republic tumbled out of existence—barricaded themselves inside a huge hangar. Three such outsized sheds had been erected over the course of the 1990s by Warsaw's city authorities, in an attempt to tame the emergent chaos of the Parade Square bazaar. Two of the hangars were dismantled in 2005 and 2008 respectively, but the largest one—the so-called Merchants' Department Store (KDT—Kupieckie Domy Towarowe) remained. After their lease expired in 2009, the traders hung on and refused to vacate the site ahead of the bailiff's arrival. The bailiff did not come alone—he brought a lot of friends with him: an entire unit of riot police, equipped not just with helmets and shields, but even horses and water cannon. A proper battle broke out. Water cannon had seldom been used in Poland since the fall of the Polish People's Republic (PRL—Polska Rzeczpospolita Ludowa). The scene brought to mind the police violence of the PRL period, and in particular the role of the infamous ZOMO riot police therein. The Battle of Parade Square, in fact, broke something of a taboo. Water cannon came into regular use again in Poland during the 2010s and 2020s, most frequently against protesting farmers, nationalists, or football hooligans. Notoriously, water cannon were used against freezing and starving migrants, many of them from Syria, Iraq, and Afghanistan, protesting on the Belarusian-Polish border in November 2021.

The merchants directly invoked ZOMO, martial law, "communists," and other detested specters ("Jews," "faggots") in their chants of contestation. I was there that day, and talked to many of the protesters. So was filmmaker and artist Artur Żmijewski, who produced a vivid film record, *Eviction of Traders from the KDT Traders' Hall*, of the day's events. A selection of stills from the film constitute **CHAPTER 2** of this book. Although many of the Polish protesters chanted nationalistic and antisemitic

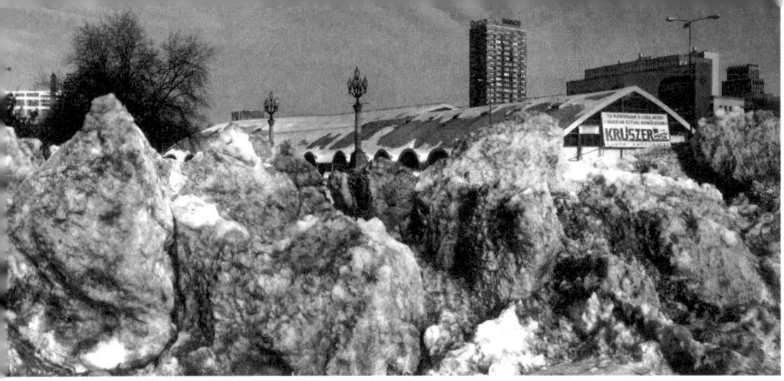

FIG. 17 JAN SMAGA, *HERE IT SHALL RISE*, 2010, COLOR PHOTOGRAPH, PRINT ON PAPER, 113 × 234.5 CM

slogans ("Poland for the Poles, Jews go home"), not all of those throwing projectiles at the police were Polish—among them were several migrant workers. A significant proportion of the KDT merchants were migrants from the Caucasus, Central Asia, and the Middle East—although, in all likelihood, a smaller proportion took part in the violent resistance against the siege of KDT, not wanting to risk deportation or other severe consequences. Many protesters among those I spoke to also pointed out that the city was seizing what they saw as their land and property, and that the ultimate fruit of this landgrab, executed by the "elites" against the ordinary citizens of Warsaw, would be the Museum of Modern Art, which was set to be built on the same site. Some of my interlocutors expressed doubt that the Museum would be built, insinuating that there are other factors at play, and that the Museum is merely a front for private capital.[99] The final shot in Żmijewski's film, taken some months after the riot, featured an infamous billboard erected on the site of KDT by the firm whose job it was to dismantle the merchants' hangar. It read: "On this site the second line of the Warsaw Metro / and the Museum of Modern Art will be built." The firm's name was KRUSZER **[FIG. 17]**.

The Museum was thus directly implicated, in fact and in people's consciousness, in the violence of the battle. Now, the institution has since done much to address and acknowledge its entanglement in processes of gentrification and social cleansing in Warsaw, foregrounding a reflection on issues of land ownership and class into its collection and public program. It has done so, in particular, through the agonistic and participatory device provided by the WARSAW UNDER CONSTRUCTION (WWB) festival, organized every year since 2009 by MSN in collaboration with other institutions, notably the Museum of Warsaw as the main partner since 2013, as well as numerous activist and interest groups (more on WWB in this text's concluding section).

99 See Murawski, *The Palace Complex*, 242.

Further, the Battle of Parade Square was far from being the sole act in the process of slow violence to which Warsaw has been subjected in the decades following the fall of the Polish People's Republic. It was one of the peak moments in this long condition of ordinary violence. The other was the murder of Jolanta Brzeska, a tenants' rights and anti-repossession activist, whose charred remains were discovered in a forest outside Warsaw in March 2011. The perpetrator was never identified. Many suspect that Brzeska was killed by people connected to Warsaw's so-called "reprivatization" (*reprywatyzacja*) or restitution mafia. I will use the term "reprivatization" in this text in recognition of the fact that "restitution"—as housing activist Antoni Wiesztort attests in conversation with MSN curator Szymon Maliborski—is a euphemism, "newspeak" working to legitimate the process of wild property reaccumulation.[100]

Warsaw's (long, flawed, unfinished) experience of property reprivatization is a process, condition, and reality of foundational importance to the history of MSN, both as an institution and a building, and to the history of Warsaw writ large. In fact, for the Museum, it was a process with consequences that were not only formative, but very nearly terminal—property reprivatization almost stopped MSN from coming into being at all. To over-simplify: in 1945, all private land in Warsaw was nationalized on the strength of the so-called Bierut Decree, named after Bolesław Bierut, who was then head of the State National Council, the de facto Polish government. People were allowed to submit compensation claims and appeals, but none were honored during the PRL period. After 1989, many other ex-socialist countries in Eastern Europe passed reprivatization laws, regulating the manner in which plots were either returned to their former owners or the process of awarding them compensation. In Poland, no such reprivatization law was passed until 2016, and no reliable mechanism for compensation existed. The lack of a sound legal framework meant that, in the 1990s, many postwar descendants sold their ownership claims (or had them extorted) to third parties. Speculators—or just gangsters—bought up these claims (sometimes traveling around the world to track down former owners), with the intention of securing prime real estate in the process.

During the 2000s, and especially following the accession of Poland to the EU in 2004, reprivatization gathered pace, and the era of so-called "wild reprivatization" (*dzika*

100 Tomasz Fudala, ed., *Spór o odbudowę Warszawy: od gruzów do reprywatyzacji* (Warsaw: Museum of Modern Art, 2016), 277.

reprywatyzacja) began in earnest. In the case of residential plots, the new owners needed to force out existing tenants so that they could knock down buildings (many of them containing communal flats, or in a state of disrepair); or renovate, raise value, and socially cleanse them. In order to do so, they had to find their way around still-extant tenant protection laws. Oftentimes they resorted to hiring thugs, cutting off electricity supplies, even setting fire to buildings, in order to coerce tenants into submission. This is where activists like Brzeska stepped in. Brzeska was so tireless, fearless, and effective that, in the end, she suffered the same fate as the buildings whose tenants she was trying to protect.[101]

Parade Square was different. No one lived there, but its plots were the priciest in town. Before the eventual passing of two partial reprivatization laws in 2017 and 2021 (both largely restricted to Warsaw in terms of their jurisdiction), if the city needed a chunk of land for something like a public investment (such as the Museum), it had to buy up plots from their (new) owners at the market rate. This was a hugely costly and fraught process. As Museum Director Joanna Mytkowska acknowledges, "the museum construction was torpedoed for many years by property claims," and reprivatization constituted one of the ultimate reasons for the failure of the Kerez project (by the time Phifer came on board, most of the plots had already been bought up by the city). Sometimes, the owners refused to sell up, blocking investments in the hope of obtaining more buck for their bang.

"Wild reprivatization" found vivid material and aesthetic expression on the terrain of Parade Square. Among the only plots of land held by a *bona fide* descendant are numbers 23/33 and 23/36, which were reprivatized to Tadeusz Koss, the grandson of their prewar owner. Koss fought multiple legal battles with the city, and finally succeeded in regaining ownership in 2008 following a lengthy court battle at the European Court of Human Rights. On acquiring his plots, which stood in the north-east corner of Parade Square, adjacent to the Museum construction site, Koss immediately proceeded to try to make as much money from them as possible, in anticipation that he would one day be evicted. In his own words, "I want to make this site as hideous as possible for the city, who are refusing to honor

101 For more on the case of Brzeska, see Fudala, *Spór o odbudowę Warszawy*, 258-75; Beata Siemieniako, *Reprywatyzując Polskę. Historia wielkiego przekrętu* (Warsaw: Wydawnictwo Krytyki Politycznej, 2017); Piotr Ciszewski and Robert Nowak, *Wszystkich nas nie spalicie* (Warsaw: Trzecia Strona, 2016).

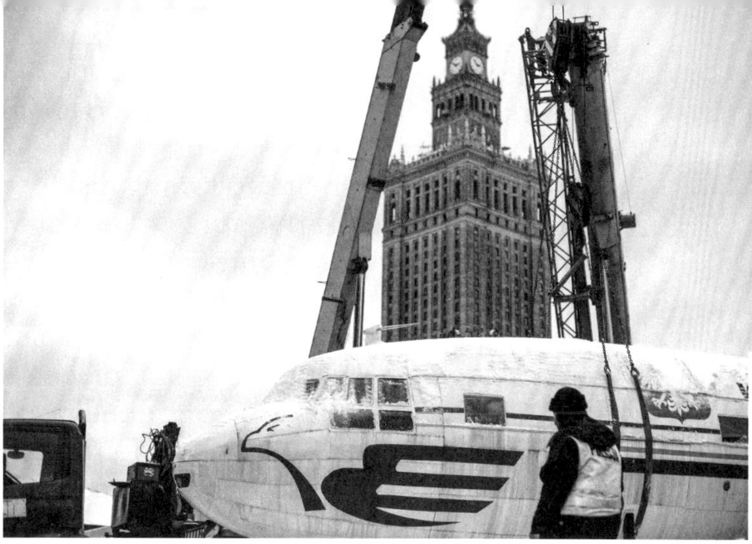

FIG. 18 ILYUSHIN IL-14, A SOVIET PASSENGER PLANE FROM THE 1950S, INSTALLED NEAR PARADE SQUARE IN 2017–2018

my property rights."[102] Bypassing planning regulations forbidding property owners from making commercial use of plots destined for public investments, he recruited an elaborate nested pyramid of contractors and subcontractors, who unleashed an eclectic array of horrors onto the site.

First came a series of huge billboards, obscuring the view of Swiętokrzyski Park from the street. In July 2017, an Ilyushin Il-14, a Soviet passenger plane from the 1950s—but amputated, wingless—"landed," seemingly from nowhere, on Koss's plot **[FIG. 18]**. Painted in the colors of the Polish flag (with a Polish and at one point also a Palestinian flag fluttering from the cockpit), Koss's amputated Ilyushin was also eerily reminiscent of the Polish government plane—another Soviet model, the Tupolev TU-154—which crashed in Smolensk in western Russia in 2010, killing 96 people, including Polish President Lech Kaczyński and dozens of VIP passengers. The Ilyushin reportedly operated for several months as a restaurant, an extension of the fast-food hut next to it (also standing on Koss's plot). The Smolensk connotation was accentuated in February 2018, when—on the day that the Ilyushin was to be dismantled on the order of the Warsaw Construction Inspectorate—the food hut was set alight in protest by its Palestinian-born manager, who was leasing the plot from Koss via an intermediary. A huge plume of black smoke spread over Parade Square. The Ilyushin stood alongside the smoldering wreck of the food hut before its dismantlement. The Palestinian manager, a resident of Warsaw for nearly a decade, was arrested, prosecuted, and jailed for three

102 Piotr Barejka, "'Chcę im ten plac zohydzić'. Samolot nie zniknie z centrum Warszawy," *WP*, August 1, 2017, https://wiadomosci.wp.pl/chce-im-ten-plac-zohydzic-samolot-nie-zniknie-z-centrum-warszawy-6150192665323649a.

months for his involvement in the matter.[103] Koss and his lawyer-cum-fixer Michał Kłos walked away unscathed.

There's more. In August 2021, Koss's plot (now owned by his heirs, following his death in 2020) was sublet to the operator of the Warsaw Park of Miniatures,[104] a traveling exhibit comprising intricate scale models of numerous Warsaw monuments not rebuilt following their destruction in World War II (among them the nearby Saxon Palace and the Warsaw Great Synagogue).[105] Events taking place on plots 23/33 and 23/36 seemed destined to continually troll history-in-the-making, first by re-enacting the national trauma event of Smolensk, then by erecting nostalgic replicas of prewar architectural landmarks on Parade Square **[FIG. 19]**. With the latter act, this tiny, disputed scrap of land in the north-eastern corner of Parade Square provided the stage for a sort of scornful meta-commentary on the obstacles and failures faced by all previous attempts at executing the Parade Square masterplan and erecting new structures on the site.[106]

The museum of *schadenfreudliche* miniatures soon shared the fate of the Ilyushin and became derelict after less than a year, wrecked by vandals and the elements, and covered in graffiti **[FIG. 20]**. As one journalist put it, by spring 2022, the park of miniatures resembled "a replica of the ruins of Warsaw" as they may have appeared in 1945.[107] In summer 2023, my attempt to climb through a hole in the fence to take a closer look was sabotaged by the scurrying of one living rat, and the decomposing corpse of another. It is not clear whether the now derelict miniature park, infested with vermin and human feces, constituted the last piece of vernacular performance art staged on plots 23/33 & 23/36 on Parade Square. What is clear, however, is that this two-decades-long process of life imitating post-conceptual art was inaugurated in 2005, when MSN—in its very first public act as an institution—erected Uklański's Papa Mulato in the north-east corner of Parade Square; and signed itself into being on a site that was then still in municipal ownership, but would soon be reprivatized to Tadeusz Koss.

103 Kamil Siałkowski, "Fadi M. podpalił budkę z kebabem. W środku było dziesięć butli z gazem. Jest zarzut i wniosek o areszt," *Wyborcza.pl.*, February 7, 2018, https://warszawa.wyborcza.pl/warszawa/7,54420,22995985,fadi-m-podpalil-budke-z-kebabem-w-srodku-bylo-10-butli-z-gazem.html.
104 *Facebook* / Park Miniatur, https://www.facebook.com/parkminiatur/.
105 Writing in 2016, in the catalog to the WARSAW UNDER CONSTRUCTION festival devoted to restitution, MSN curator Tomasz Fudala gave the miniature park's earlier incarnation, then in an art nouveau former bank building, as an example of the fetishism of property built into the nostalgia for prewar Warsaw felt by many in the city today. Little did he know the miniature park would end up, *in ruins*, on Parade Square itself; see Fudala, *Spór o odbudowę Warszawy*, 19.
106 Murawski, *The Palace Complex*, 136–98.
107 Aleksander Sławiński, "Miasteczko jak z horroru w samym centrum Warszawy. Park Miniatur miał być atrakcją, teraz straszy przechodniów," *Wyborcza.pl*, December 4, 2022, https://warszawa.wyborcza.pl/warszawa/7,54420,29214445,park-minatur-jak-scenografia-z-horroru-miasto-bezradne-w-sprawie.html.

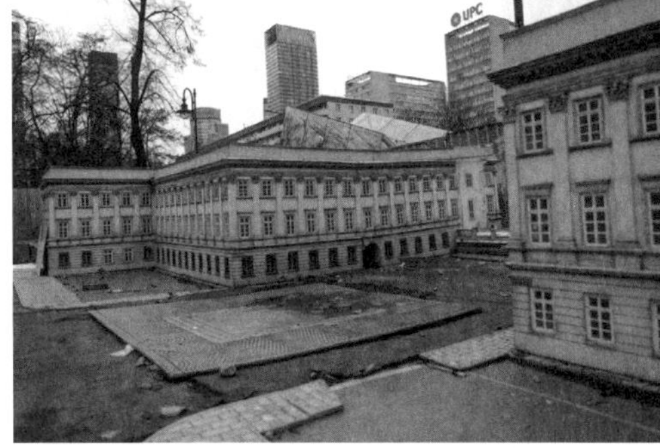

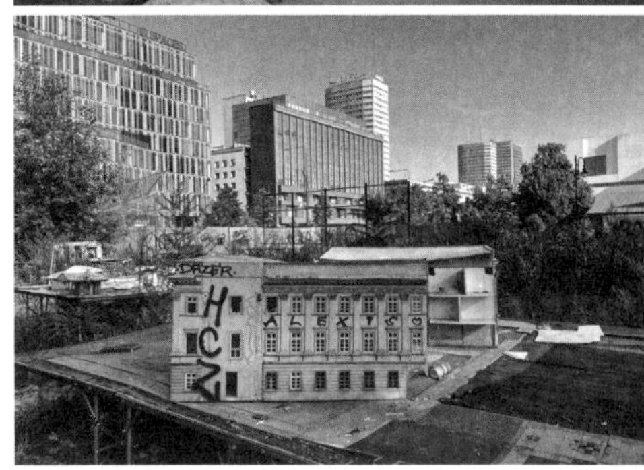

FIG. 19 NOSTALGIC REPLICAS OF PREWAR ARCHITECTURAL LANDMARKS ON PARADE SQUARE SEEN IN 2022
FIG. 20 THE PARK OF MINIATURES IN ALL OF ITS DERELICTION

AFTER WHICH BATTLE?

The complex, unpredictable, and deadly political economy of property in Warsaw—and its material and symbolic manifestations—is indexed with great clarity by the wanderings and mutations of Szapocznikow's *Friendship*. Thirty-seven years (1955–1992) in the Palace; amputation (1992); twenty-seven years in a Józefów yard (1992–2019); auctioned and sold (2019); five years in warehouses (2019–2024); finally, the return to Parade Square (2024), to occupy a pivotal location in the new Museum, facing its former home across the Square. Says Zygmunt Borawski of A-A Collective, "this sculpture, like the square, is a calque of our history" **(CHAPTER 5).**

The Museum and the square on which it stands witness multiple processes of violence—and of resistance. The Battle of Parade Square was merely an epiphenomenon of the slow, unfinished violence of the possession and dispossession of property in postsocialist Warsaw. Beyond that, Parade Square has been a site of violence, contestation, and even sacrifice multiple times since the fall of communism in 1989. On October 19, 2017, fifty-four-year-old chemist and educator Piotr Szczęsny set himself on fire next to the Tribune of Honor—built for communist leaders to wave at May Day crowds from—in protest at the politics of the Law and Justice government. He suffered severe burns and died in hospital ten days later. A spontaneous memorial to Szczęsny was maintained for four years by the municipality of Warsaw **[FIG. 21]**, but it has been disassembled (in theory, temporarily), in order to make way for the construction of the

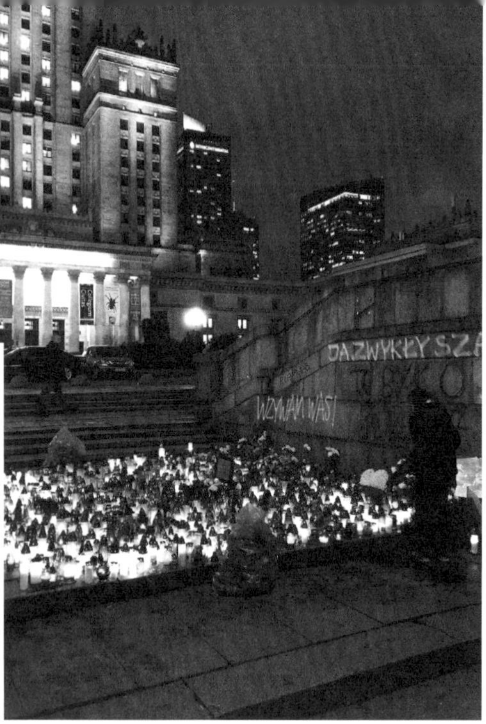

FIG. 21 A SPONTANEOUS MEMORIAL TO PIOTR SZCZĘSNY, WHO COMMITTED SELF-IMMOLATION ON PARADE SQUARE ON OCTOBER 19, 2017

(as yet unnamed) Warsaw Central Square, designed by A-A Collective. Most urgently, since Russia's first invasion of Ukraine in 2014, and its full-scale invasion in 2022, the Museum—as institution, as building, and as construction site—has also been directly involved in and affected by the overdetermining reality of that war and its numerous geopolitical, local, and personal entanglements and ramifications.

Notions of possession and dispossession, seizure, enclosure, and occupation, refer not just to the shifting of property regimes, but also to military confrontation. Warsaw's "liberation" from Nazi German occupation by the Red Army, and Poland's subsequent proxy "occupation" by the Soviet Union, were the conditions of possibility for the expropriation of private property in Warsaw by the state, and the consequent construction of Parade Square and the Palace. The transformation of Warsaw into some sort of "capitalist" city (albeit of a path-dependent, postsocialist sort) would not have happened without the disintegration of the Warsaw Pact and the withdrawal of the last Red Army troops from Polish territory in 1992–1993.

CONCLUSION: FORMS, STRUCTURES, AND COLORS OF SOLIDARITY

To end, some reflections on the relationship between friendship, form, color, and solidarity. What geographies of solidarity are within the Museum's purview? How can the edifice maximize the friendship-making and solidarity-creating potential of the institution? What is the role of whiteness therein? Not merely that of the building's façade, but also the conundrum of whiteness, which complicates attempts to plug Eastern Europe, and even the broader postsocialist space, into intersectional and decolonial conversations.

And what about solidarity? Another capacious, contested concept—especially in Polish context. In the aftermath of Russia's full-scale invasion of Ukraine, German-Cameroonian curator and then-incoming Director of HKW Berlin, Bonaventure Soh Bejeng Ndikung, expressed his support for Ukraine in a text in *e-flux*. I engage here with Ndikung's text, because it is penned by the head of a major publicly funded contemporary art institution, not unlike MSN in that sense, which aspires to a decolonial praxis while navigating multiple pressures and limitations along the way.

Writes Ndikung, "My solidarity, empathy and support goes to the Ukrainian people as they go through these unbearable times."[108] At the same time as expressing this solidarity for Ukraine, not in spite of it, Ndikung's text gave voice to some of the victims, on whose behalf he has never been petitioned. Art world colleagues who were beseeching solidarity for Ukraine, Ndikung points out, were silent when predominantly Muslim Syrian, Iraqi, and Afghan refugees "were beaten up, maltreated, shot at by the border police" at the Belarusian border; when Ukrainian and Polish border guards and officials refused passage to or detained black and brown Ukrainians and Ukrainian residents trying to leave the country; when Ethiopian armed forces perpetuated genocide in Tigray; and when Anglophone Cameroonians were massacred and displaced by government and government-allied forces. They were silent about Myanmar and Mexico, Congo and the Mediterranean Sea. Gaza and Palestine were notably absent from Ndikung's list. Indeed, since the text was published, German publicly funded cultural institutions—HKW among them—have also chosen, or been forced, to withdraw open solidarity for Palestine, in the face of unprecedented pressure from their state and municipal sponsors. Any foregrounding of one victim necessarily backgrounds another. Solidarity—especially when practiced by a large public arts institutions—is always selective.

"Solidarity," writes Ndikung,

> is not a one-way street, solidarity must be multidimensional and multidirectional, solidarity is not coloured white and must also apply to

108 Bonaventure Soh Bejeng Ndikung, "A Means to Render Our Lives Believable: Of Solitude and Solidarity, or the Whitewashing of Solidarity," *e-flux Notes*, March 21, 2022, https://www.e-flux.com/notes/456685/a-means-to-render-our-lives-believable-of-solitude-and-solidarity-or-the-whitewashing-of-solidarity.

> the "darker than blue" of the world and solidarity cannot be a racialized practice.

This does not mean that solidarity should not be practiced. It means that it should be about more than the mass co-signing of Google Doc protestations. That processes of foregrounding and backgrounding must trigger reflection rather than denial. And that solidarity cannot be *whitewashed*. Ndikung continues:

> How can we build *structures of solidarity* that go beyond the power gradients imposed by coloniality? How do we conceive solidarity on a basis that transcends our skinfolds and kinfolks? What is a solidarity unplagued by whiteness? Can we afford a cherry-picking solidarity in which some humans are more equal than others? [emphasis added]

Taras Gembik and Yulia Krivich, who are among the founders of the "Sunflower" Solidarity Community Center at the Warsaw Museum of Modern Art, which will also retain an institutional presence in the new building, proffer some possible answers to these questions. In reference to Szapocznikow's *Friendship*, they point out that the Sunflower was founded precisely on friendship—by a group of friends who came together in the time of upheaval which immediately followed Russia's full-scale invasion of Ukraine (**CHAPTER 4**). The Sunflower grew out of strong interpersonal friendships; but it also depended on the *hospitality* that the Museum has consistently and reliably afforded to it since inception. Both friendship and hospitality were not without hiccups, uncertainties, or tensions, but they drew on the consistent labor that friends, hosts, and guests (these figures were not always distinguishable from each other) were willing to put into their maintenance. As Sarah Wilson pointed out in her conversation with Agata Jakubowska about Szapocznikow's sculpture (**CHAPTER 3**), "you actually have to *work* at friendship." In the case of the Sunflower-in-the-Museum, that labor was done and shared to the point where boundaries and hierarchies became blurred. But this collective, shared labor was not something random or uncoordinated. It was done with a view, in Gembik's words, which mirror Ndikung's, "to come up with a certain *form*, a certain *structure* that would enable us to continue operating sustainably."

Krivich and Gembik have an ambivalent relationship to the idea of placing Szapocznikow's *Friendship* at the center of the Museum building. They, like Wilson and Jakubowska, agree that to do so is to drench the Museum irreversibly in post-Sovietness. We joked, on the margins of our conversation, about whether the Museum would sell mini replicas of *Friend-*

ship in the gift shop, perhaps also busts of Stalin or hammer and sickle trinkets. Nevertheless, Krivich and Gembik agree that it is desirable to appropriate and build on certain dimensions of socialist and/or Soviet heritage. The past can be shown, like Szapocznikow's sculpture, in a discernible but dismembered form, with the wounds—the traumas—it generated visible to the naked eye, but "it cannot," in Gembik's words, "be erased."

The idea of the "Palace" or "House" of Culture—which is present in the Polish and Ukrainian names of the Sunflower (as "House of Culture")—has a Soviet lineage, too. Says Krivich, "I feel sentimental about the institution of the House of Culture, and I like the fact that it is possible to somehow use this aspect of the Soviet legacy, changing its meaning to move away from the painful or traumatic experiences of the past." The voices brought together in this book are unanimous on this matter of non-erasure. In the words of former City Architect of Warsaw Marlena Happach, speaking to architectural historian Dorota Jędruch and architect Zygmunt Borawski, "We no longer have to erase anything from the history of the city. We don't have to force the Palace into a new environment and pretend that it is something it is not.... We can use the Palace and the square for various purposes, including completely new ones."

Gembik and Krivich invoke Ukrainian curator and theorist Olexii Kuchanskiy's idea of the "trans-Soviet," a condition that goes beyond the post-Soviet but does not negate it or pretend it never existed. Kuchanskyi argues that Ukrainian artists (video artists in particular), have—since roughly 2014—begun to operate in a "trans-Soviet" idiom, whereby they *explore* Soviet (and post-Soviet) legacies, even defend them in some instances, but are not beholden to or overdetermined by such legacies and their ideological and aesthetic accoutrements. What Kuchanskyi calls the "exodus" from the post-Soviet condition is "rather trans- [than] anti-Soviet—it requires a critical observation of [the] post-Soviet condition, just [like] taking a close look at minor traces of Soviet culture—unfinished or upcoming ones, which may become platforms of further assemblings."[109] I make a commensurable argument in another text, published more or less at the same time as Kuchanskyi's, about a "trans-socialist" project, for which "socialism's tangible and intangible legacies provide an infrastructural 'scaffold'" onto which new forms of progressive political and aesthetic practice may be able to hoist themselves.[110]

109 Olexii Kuchanskyi, "Exodus from the post-Soviet Condition," *Soniakh*, 2022, https://soniakh.com/index.php/2022/11/24/exodus-from-the-post-soviet-condition/.

110 Michał Murawski, "Locating Trans-Socialism: Communism, Putinism, and Human Nature," *e-flux Notes*, June 27, 2022, https://www.e-flux.com/notes/476507/locating-trans-socialism-communism-putinism-and-human-nature. The term "scaffold" is Kimberly Elman Zarecor's. See "What Was So Socialist about the Socialist City? Second World Urbanity in Europe," *Journal of Urban History* 44, no. 1 (2018).

The mission of the Sunflower, say Gembik and Krivich, is to "forge trans-local solidarity in spite of evil," a "multidirectional solidarity." They identify Warsaw as a propitious terrain for a form of trans-local, trans-socialist solidarity to coalesce: "Poland is a great place where many trails converge." As they observe, and as any visitor to Warsaw will quickly discern, in recent years, an increasing number of migrants not only from Ukraine, but also from the Caucasus and Central Asia (as well as from South, South-East, and West Asia, and from Africa) have made their way to Warsaw, and have taken up work in numerous sectors of the economy. These migrations are not incidental—the trajectories and conditions according to which they take place are themselves the products of war, upheaval, racism, and, particularly in Poland, brazen profiteering.[111] Poland's Ukrainian community mushroomed after the annexation of Crimea and the occupation of parts of Donbas in 2014, and increased further following the full-scale invasion of Ukraine. At the same time, over 100,000 Ukrainian men returned home, to fight or support their homesteads, following the full-scale invasion. Many Ukrainian laborers and specialists worked on the construction of the Museum, and their sudden departure contributed to delays in the completion of the building. In turn, hundreds of thousands of Ukrainian women (and children) entered Poland after 2022—those who stayed took jobs in overlapping but not identical sectors of the economy. Some of the gaps in the labor market left by departed Ukrainian men have been filled by newcomers from Central Asia and the Caucasus.

Some of the citizens of Georgia, Armenia, Uzbekistan, and Kazakhstan who live in Warsaw had formerly migrated to the big cities of Russia for work. My own conversations with some of these migrants suggest that they were driven out of Russia by the vicious upsurge in racism and xenophobia in recent years. Since the full-scale invasion of Ukraine, they are all the keener to avoid Russia due to the risk of being illegally drafted into the army or into private military companies and forced to fight in Ukraine,[112] as well as by the volatile ruble exchange rate, which impacts their ability to send remittances home. Many of

111 In Poland, the mass exploitation of migration, conducted by actors who proclaim anti-immigrant rhetoric, has reached brazen new heights. Up to 350,000 visas may have been illegally issued by the Polish Ministry of Foreign Affairs from 2021 to 2023 in multiple African and Asian countries in exchange for travel documents. The "cash for visas" scandal played a role in the downfall of the (anti-immigration) Law and Justice government in 2023.

112 There are multiple reported instances of migrants not only from Central Asian countries, but also from India, Nepal, Zambia, and other countries far beyond the post-Soviet orbit, being either drafted on site or lured to Russia to join the army. Over 10,000 migrants have recently obtained citizenship, as have thousands more who have been drafted illegally. See, e.g., Kimberly St. Julian-Varnon, "Russian hypocrisy and the death of a Zambian Student in Ukraine," *Al Jazeera*, January 3, 2023, https://www.aljazeera.com/opinions/2023/1/3/is-russia-really-africas-friend; Marina Baranovskaya, "How Russia drafts migrants to fight in Ukraine," *Deutsche Welle*, December 9, 2023, https://www.dw.com/en/how-russia-drafts-migrants-to-fight-in-ukraine/a-66792405.

these new-ish migrants live in workers' hostels on the outskirts of the city, where living conditions are often miserable. Poland, which until some years ago may well have been (and may still be) Europe's whitest and most homogenous society, has benefited from this influx of migrants, and gained in diversity, precisely because of the tragedy of war. The roots of diversity are in themselves traumatic, but they place the Museum—as a site of solidarity—in a place and position of critical responsibility.

Gembik and Krivich call for "solidarity with all countries that are trying to gain independence from Russia, as well as with all countries and groups that are fighting a decolonial struggle." How to maintain solidarity not only through words and symbols, but also through *forms* and *structures*? MSN's own WARSAW UNDER CONSTRUCTION festival has a strong track-record of working with activist groups and highlighting issues that are uncomfortable for the city administration. In 2011, the curators of WWB showed a map of property claims as part of the public exhibition accompanying the festival. In 2015, the entire festival and exhibition—curated by Tomasz Fudala and Szymon Maliborski—was devoted to the complex relationship between the communalization of urban property in Warsaw in 1945, the postwar reconstruction of the city, and the specter and process of "wild reprivatization." Wild reprivatization finally gained the status of political scandal in 2016, the year after WWB was organized in collaboration with activists from the Warsaw Tenants' Movement and Syrena (Mermaid), a syndicalist anti-eviction collective, who curated the section of the exhibition devoted to reprivatization, its victims, and resistance to it.

A relief metal sculpture of Jolanta Brzeska **[FIG. 22]**, captioned with one of her best-known slogans, "You have to do something!" ("Musicie coś zrobić"), was hung from one of the walls of the exhibition venue, a modernist school building, from which the school had recently been evicted after the municipal authorities made an unsuccessful attempt to sell the plot of land on which it stood to a property developer. In an interview with curator Szymon Maliborski, Antoni Wiesztort emphasizes that the role of the ally-(or friend-)institution should be "to provide a framework, an infrastructure" to foreground grassroots movements, stories, and symbols. The role of the institution is to provide the instruments and means through which marginalized, subjugated communities—commensurable in the Warsaw context to what Fred Moten and Stefano Harney call the "undercommons"—can render visible and legitimate their demands and rise

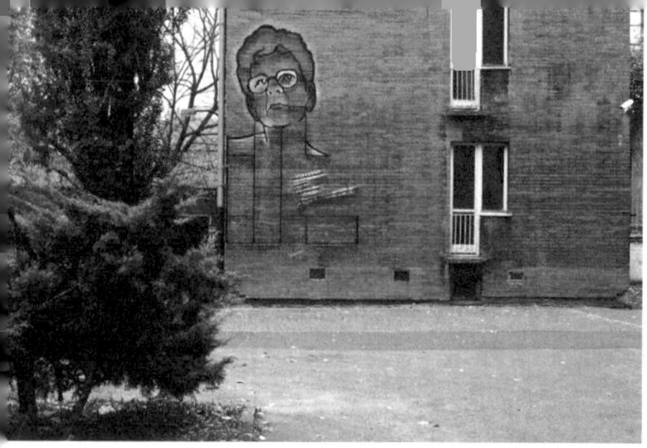

FIG. 22 VIEW OF THE EXHIBITION *RECONSTRUCTION DISPUTES*, 7TH EDITION OF THE WARSAW UNDER CONSTRUCTION FESTIVAL IN 2015, FEATURING A RELIEF METAL SCULPTURE OF JOLANTA BRZESKA CREATED BY RAFAŁ JAKUBOWICZ

to the surface.[113] But institutions, says Wiesztort, must "take responsibility for the dramatic events about which they tell stories." Institutions can choose between being "a temporary animator, a naive ally, or an impactful element in a process of resistance."[114]

If MSN possessed any kind of infrastructure (for resistance) then, it has it in droves now—20,000 square meters of it. A monumental staircase. A cutting-edge and diverse international collection (although driven by thoughtful and rigorous regional focus). The world's attention. The distinction of being the first building which managed to break the "curse" or "complex" of the Palace of Culture. An elegant façade made of shimmering white concrete. Because of, or in spite of its twenty years of activity, the Museum-as-institution still, for now, remains scrappy, radical, and rooted enough to retain and nourish its connections and commitments to the "projectariat,"[115] to tenants, migrants, and racial others. And to the broader undercommons, which in the Polish incarnation also includes women and queer and trans people, who are marginalized more there than anywhere else in the European Union.[116] In a vision of institutionality which is, in sociologist and activist Rodrigo Nunes's phrase, "neither vertical nor horizontal," the Museum is the vertical scaffolding onto which the horizontal axis of activism and resistance may attach itself. In this sense, the Museum is *rooted* in contextual specificity, but it nurtures the upward growth from that root.[117]

The word "radical" has its stem in the Latin *radix*—meaning "root." In this transversal understanding, in its alliance with activist groups, MSN possesses an institutional history, a present infrastructure, and a sharp ethic of responsi-

113 Fred Moten and Stefano Harney, *The Undercommons: Fugitive Planning and Black Study* (Wivenhoe: Minor Compositions, 2014).
114 Fudala, *Spór o odbudowę Warszawy*, 264.
115 Kuba Szreder, *The ABC of the projectariat: Living and working in a precarious art world* (Manchester: Manchester University Press, 2021).
116 Despite the defeat of the conservative nationalist Law and Justice Party in October 2023 and its replacement by a liberal government, Poland was ranked the worst country in the European Union for LGBTQI+ people for the fifth year running by the ILGA Rainbow map. Ukraine scores one place above Poland in the Europe-wide list, and Russia is last. See www.rainbowmap.ilga-europe.org.
117 Rodrigo Nunes, *Neither Vertical nor Horizontal: A Theory of Political Organization* (London: Verso, 2021).

bility, moving it to function not merely as a "critical" but a substantively "radical" institution.[118] At the beginning of the 2010s, wrote Piotr Piotrowski, MSN appeared to be heading in an institutional direction which is neither traumaphilic nor traumaphobic, but something else. Perhaps this is because historical trauma may in fact not be the institution's primary concern. Instead, the Museum may be more driven to function as an infrastructure for the social context within which it exists, a bridge between the horizontal and vertical axes. Even better, a Trojan horse which assists the horizontal to infiltrate the vertical. To turn Nunes's concept around—*both horizontal and vertical.* Both friend and ally, both (or neither?) brother and sister. Both open (to friends) and closed (to oppressors).[119] Both civilian and partisan.

A word about roots, resistance, and the imperative to delineate the scope of the trans-local. Gembik and Krivich highlight the commitment to trans-local solidarity. Ndikung argues that solidarity cannot be whitewashed. Gembik and Krivich articulate a geopolitics of trans-locality, and an ethics and politics of friendship and solidarity, which is global, but not in an arbitrary way. This trans-locality is positioned within flows and along axes that are pertinent to its location's recent past, uncertain present, and volatile future. The Museum's employees, artists, and audiences have expertise and experience that can shed light on processes and phenomena of local extraction, but global relevance. To list merely a few possible directions, of varying scale and scope, stemming from some of the themes touched on in this essay: the political economy of property and the human dramas it necessitates; the politics of migration in Eastern Europe, Central Asia, North Eurasia, and the Caucasus; the deaths of migrants illegally pushed back to Belarus by Polish border guards in the Białowieża Forest; the historical and contemporary trajectories of Poland's own relationship of extractive coloniality with relation to its eastern "borderlands" and beyond;[120] the escalating climate emergency and the multiple ecological crises in which Poland—as one of Europe's dirtiest and most carbon-intensive economies—is damningly implicated.

118 See also Piotr Piotrowski and Katarzyna Murawska-Muthesius, *From Museum Critique to the Critical Museum* (London: Routledge, 2015).
119 An illustrative example of a structure which is welcoming to friends but foreboding to oppressors is the recreation of the Snake's Walls (*Zmiievii Valy*), ancient earthen fortifications around Kyiv, designed and built by FORMA as part of the Ukrainian pavilion at the 2023 Venice Biennale of Architecture in Giardini. See Iryna Miroshnykova, Oleksii Petrov, and Borys Filonenko, *Before the Future*, catalog of the Ukrainian pavilion at the 18th Venice Biennale of Architecture (Kyiv: IST Publishing 2024).
120 On Poland's coloniality, see, e.g., Bogusław Bakuła, "Colonial and Postcolonial Aspects of Polish Borderlands Studies: an Outline," trans. Anna Warso, *Teksty Drugie* 1, Special Issue (2014); on Poland's unsuccessful ambitions to acquire African colonies in the interwar period, and the racial dimension of this campaign, see Bolaji Balogun, "Polish *Lebensraum*: the colonial ambition to expand on racial terms," *Ethnic and Racial Studies* 41, no. 14 (2018): 2561–79; and, idem, *Race and Colour-Line: The Boundaries of Europeanness in Poland* (London: Routledge, 2024); Dorota Michalska and Marta Zboralska, eds., *Art, Race, and Coloniality in Eastern Europe* (London: Routledge, 2025).

A word on whiteness, on its ecological, racial, and proprietorial imbrications. Architectural historian Lidia Klein asked Tom Phifer whether he thought it would be difficult to maintain the whiteness of the Museum's façade. He responded optimistically: "I think it'll be easy to clean, you'll just have to go up there with a powerwash."[121] Mark Wigley reminds that "white is never a given. It is a permanent labor—an ongoing repetitive work of exclusion."[122] Indeed, while the Warsaw Museum will not need to be treated with Ripolin, continually powerwashing a building of its size is a questionable use of water and electricity in the midst of a climate emergency gathering momentum. The whiteness of architecture co-depends on intersecting domains from ideology to technology, ecology to economy, race to property. In legal philosopher Cheryl Harris's influential analysis, modern understandings and institutions of whiteness and private property emerged in tandem.[123] Quite literally, white skin functions as a form of entitlement to the ownership of property (whether of other human beings in the form of chattel slavery, land, or commercial shares). The idea that race is natural rather than contingent, produced, or performed is inextricably connected to the doxa that private property is the only normal form of human relation to land and things. Poland's (ongoing, unfinished) saga of reprivatization has engendered a shift in attitudes to private property as a god-given right. So what are we to make of the manifest whiteness of a Museum, situated in the very center of a city which, for the first time since the Holocaust, is reconstituting itself through an assimilative encounter with national, ethnic, and racial others?

The whiteness of buildings—especially public ones, all the more so museums—is a matter not only of color and materiality, but also of race. And the glaring whiteness of the MSN edifice may be apprehended as an opportunity to confront the predicament of whiteness and coloniality within which Warsaw, Poland, and Eastern Europe are (unevenly, differentially) entangled. To name but a few of these (differential but commensurable) predicaments, Eastern Europe is postcolonial (and postsocialist), but still (mostly) white. Almost all of Eastern Europe is formerly or presently colonized, but, in some cases (Poland, Lithuania, Hungary, Serbia, not to speak of Russia), it was once (or is still) engaged in projects of empire-building and the subjugation and colonization of its neighbors. Eastern Europe

121 Lidia Klein, interview with Thomas Phifer.
122 Wigley, "Chronic Whiteness," 11.
123 Cheryl Harris, "Whiteness as Property," *Harvard Law Review* 106, no. 8 (1993): 1707–91.

is poor, but parts of it are getting richer and arming themselves to the teeth (Poland in particular). Other parts are not only still poor, but are also at war (Ukraine) or under (partial or total) Russian occupation (Ukraine, Georgia, Chechnya-Ichkeria, Moldova). Notwithstanding this dire predicament, Ukrainians—despite ten years of invasion and obliteration by Russia, and centuries of colonial subjugation—are still barred, by many on the Western decolonial left, from a position of ethical equivalence with other victims of war and colonized peoples. Ukraine, most egregiously, is haunted by what Darya Tsymbalyuk calls the "colonial trap" of proximity to hegemonic whiteness, whether of the Euro-American or Russian-Slavic sort.[124] This conundrum of whiteness—or colonial trap, or decolonial handicap—on the one hand lubricates Ukraine's efforts to wrest (conditional, limited) support for its resistance—emotional, material, martial—from "the West." On the other, it seems to drive wedges between (predominantly white) Ukrainians (and their Eastern European allies) and other (disproportionately black and brown) subjugated peoples, subjected to and resisting imperialist aggression the world over.

So, whereas we cannot judge the Museum purely on the basis of its color, and we cannot reduce its color purely to race, can we find a way to deploy the Museum's whiteness as a surface upon which to trigger intersections, bridge chasms, shift wedges, and nourish trust between postsocialist and decolonial conversations? Might these conversations grow, in time and with labor, into new structures of solidarity and forms of friendship? And what impact, if any, might these conversations have on the Museum building itself? Will the Museum commit itself to the permanent labor of powerwashing? Or will it allow its façade's palette to shift with time? Or, perhaps, to function as a canvas, screen, or monitor onto which cries for change can be broadcast? On which attempts to maintain or defend reactionary doxa—whether of race, sexuality, gender, class, property, ecology, or nationality—can be contested and unmasked?

Let this labor—not of powerwashing, but of friendship-forming—be a long-term commitment. As it unfolds, perhaps the figure of Jolanta Brzeska—or another form, figure, critic, or friend—can look down from the edifice of the Museum

124 Darya Tsymbalyuk, "Ukraine and the Traps of Proximity to European and Russian Slavic Whiteness," *The Funambulist*, June 22, 2023, https://thefunambulist.net/magazine/fifty-shades-of-whiteness/ukraine-and-the-traps-of-proximity-to-european-and-russian-slavic-whiteness. Tsymbalyuk comments that, according to the logic of the "white war," "if Ukraine is only supported because it is seen as white and European, it means that by supporting Ukraine one perpetuates the ordering of life according to white supremacy." This logic, she comments, "results in direct or indirect suggestions of reducing and denying support for Ukraine's anti-colonial struggle." See also remaining contributions to this special issue of *The Funambulist* devoted to countering "hegemonic" norms of whiteness.

at the city. For how long? Forever, maybe. Until Brzeska's murderers are found and sentenced, until Poland institutes a real social housing program, until Poland acknowledges and addresses its disavowed inheritance of colonial violence, until Ukraine regains its sovereignty, until migrants cease to be killed or left to die at the Polish-Belarusian border, until Palestine is free, until the Russian Federation is defeated (and decolonized). And through this long (perhaps infinite) labor, may new (and unexpected) forms, structures, and colors of political friendship take root.

EVICTION OF TRADERS FROM THE KDT TRADERS' HALL

On July 21, 2009, several hundred vendors from the KDT Traders' Hall (Kupieckie Domy Towarowe–Merchants' Department Store) barricaded themselves inside the building they were due to be evicted from that day. A street battle ensued, involving mounted police, water cannon, paving stones, burning tires, and tear gas. Several dozen traders and their supporters, police and private security guards, were seriously wounded. KDT stood on a section of the site designated for the construction of the Museum of Modern Art. The events of the day were documented in the film *Eviction of Traders from the KDT Traders' Hall* (11:28) by artist and filmmaker Artur Żmijewski, which forms part of his *Democracies* series of twenty documentary videos (2009).

Artur Żmijewski, graduate of the Faculty of Sculpture at the Academy of Fine Arts in Warsaw with a diploma in 1995 from the studio of Prof. Grzegorz Kowalski. Creates films, photographs, paintings, and sculptures. His work *Repetition* was shown at the Polish Pavilion during the 51st Venice Biennale. His film *Them* (2007) was shown at documenta 12 in Kassel. Active also as a critic and curator, including of the 7th Berlin Biennale. In 2010, awarded the Ordway Prize by the New Museum in New York and Creative Link for the Arts.

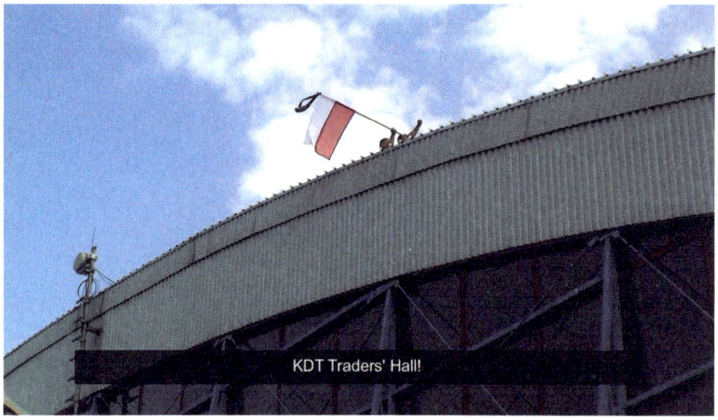

0:22

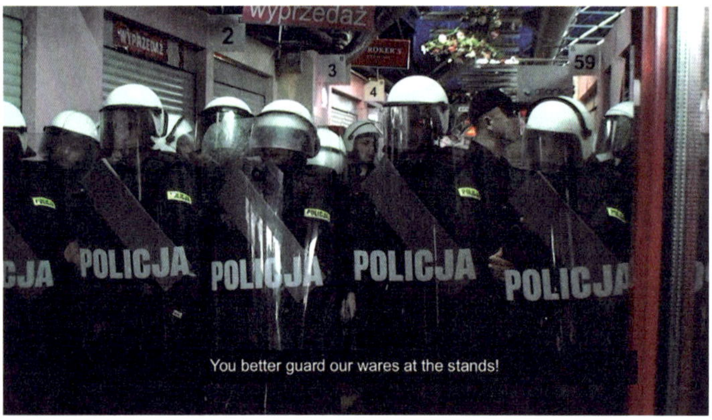

0:40

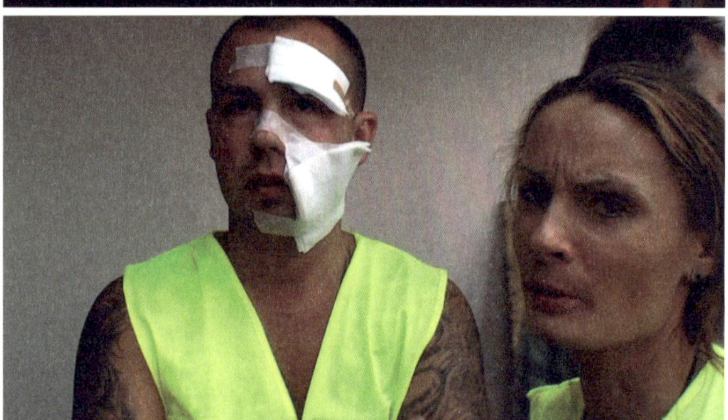

0:57

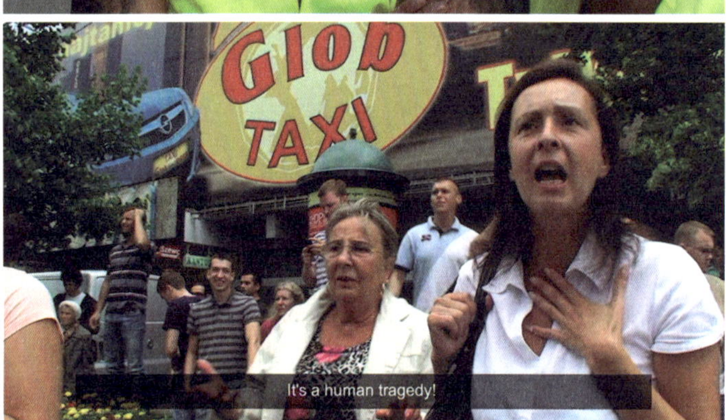

1:45

2:37

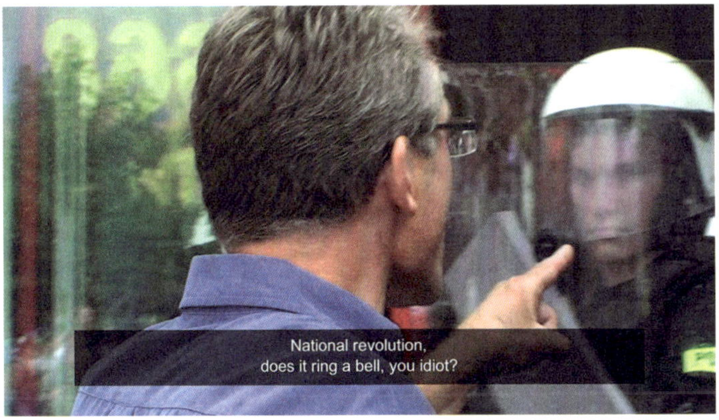

3:22

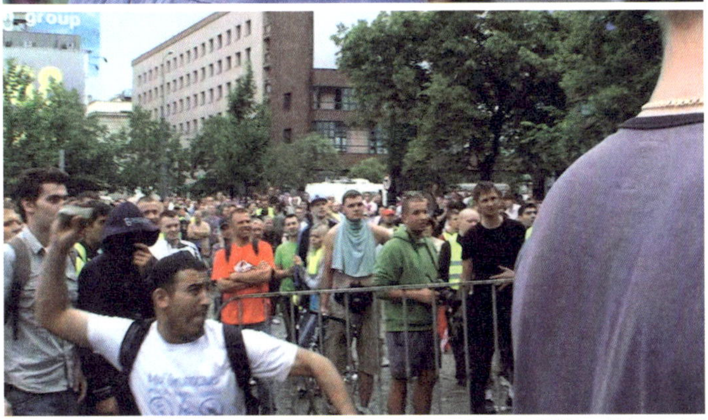

4:11

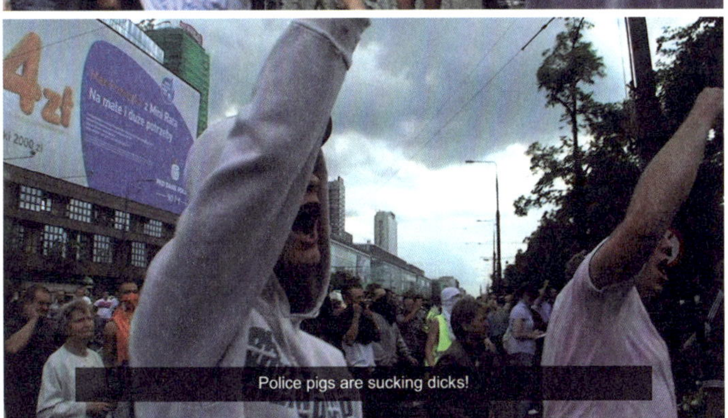

4:34

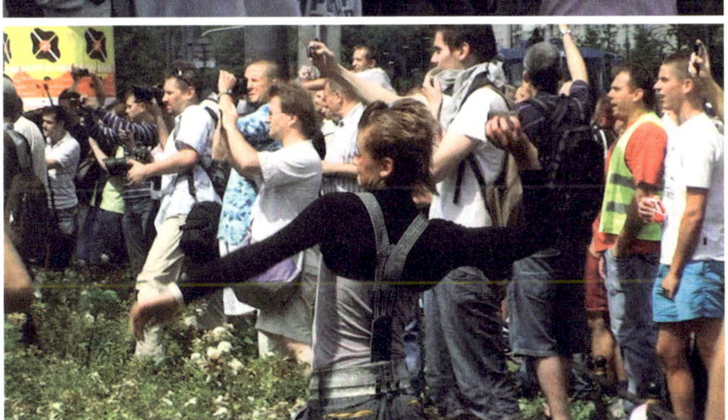

4:52

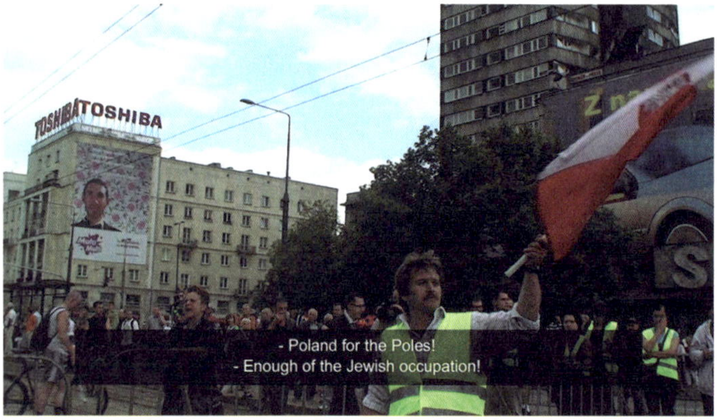

5:44

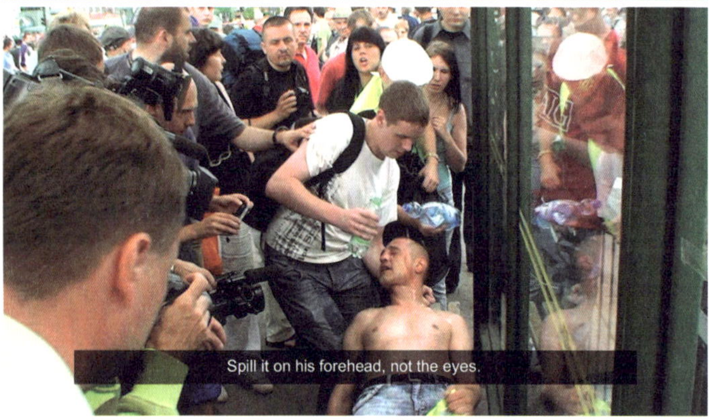

6:19

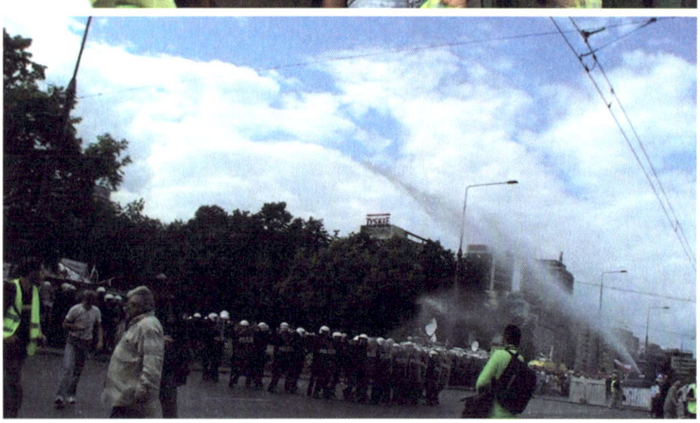

7:08

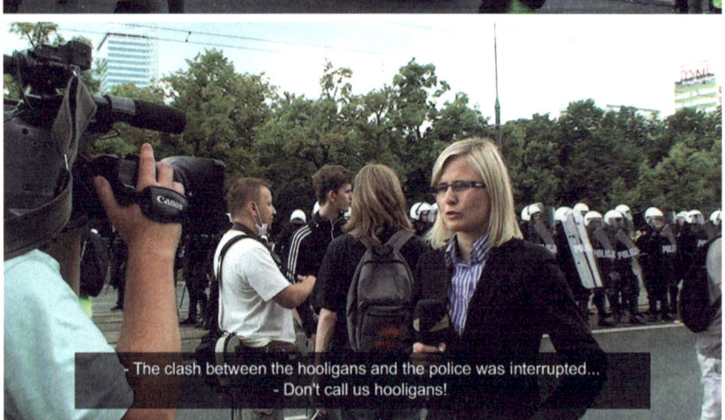

8:45

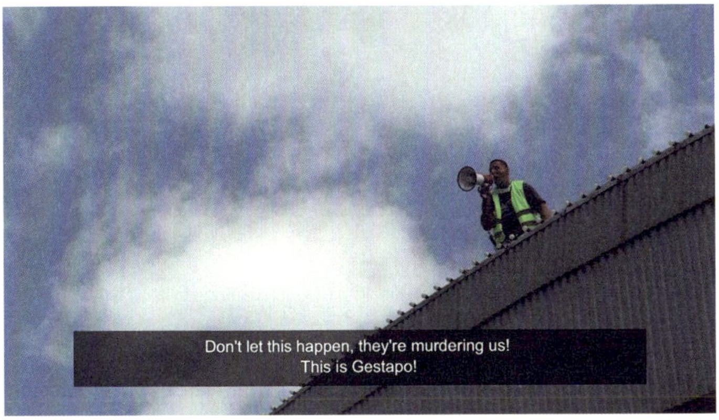

8:54

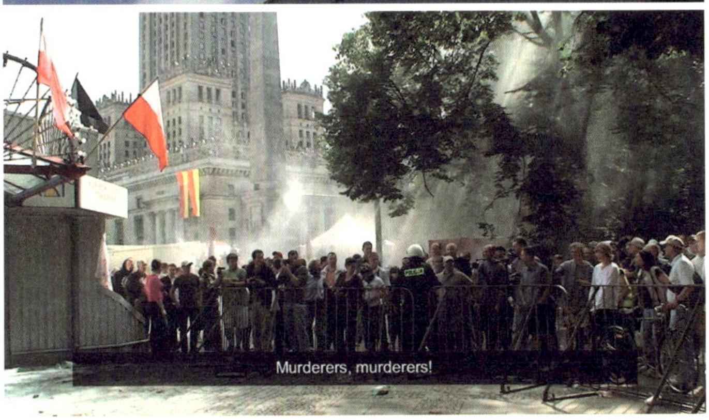

9:59

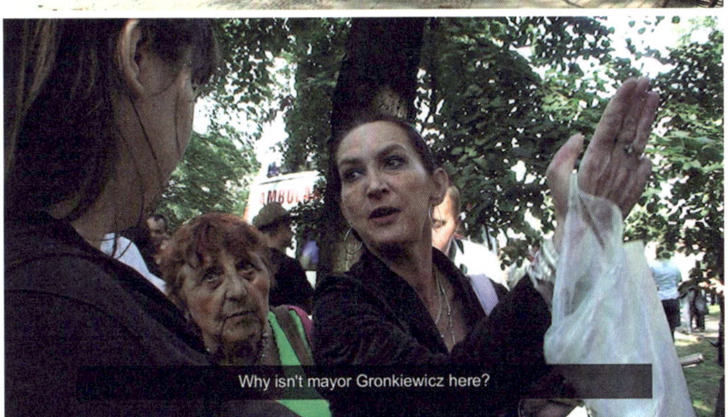

11:13

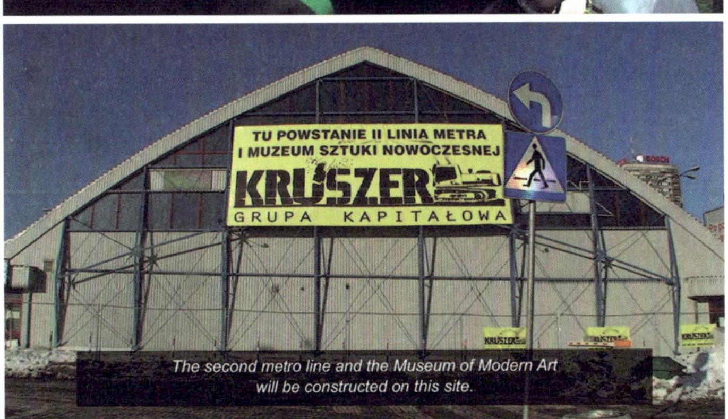

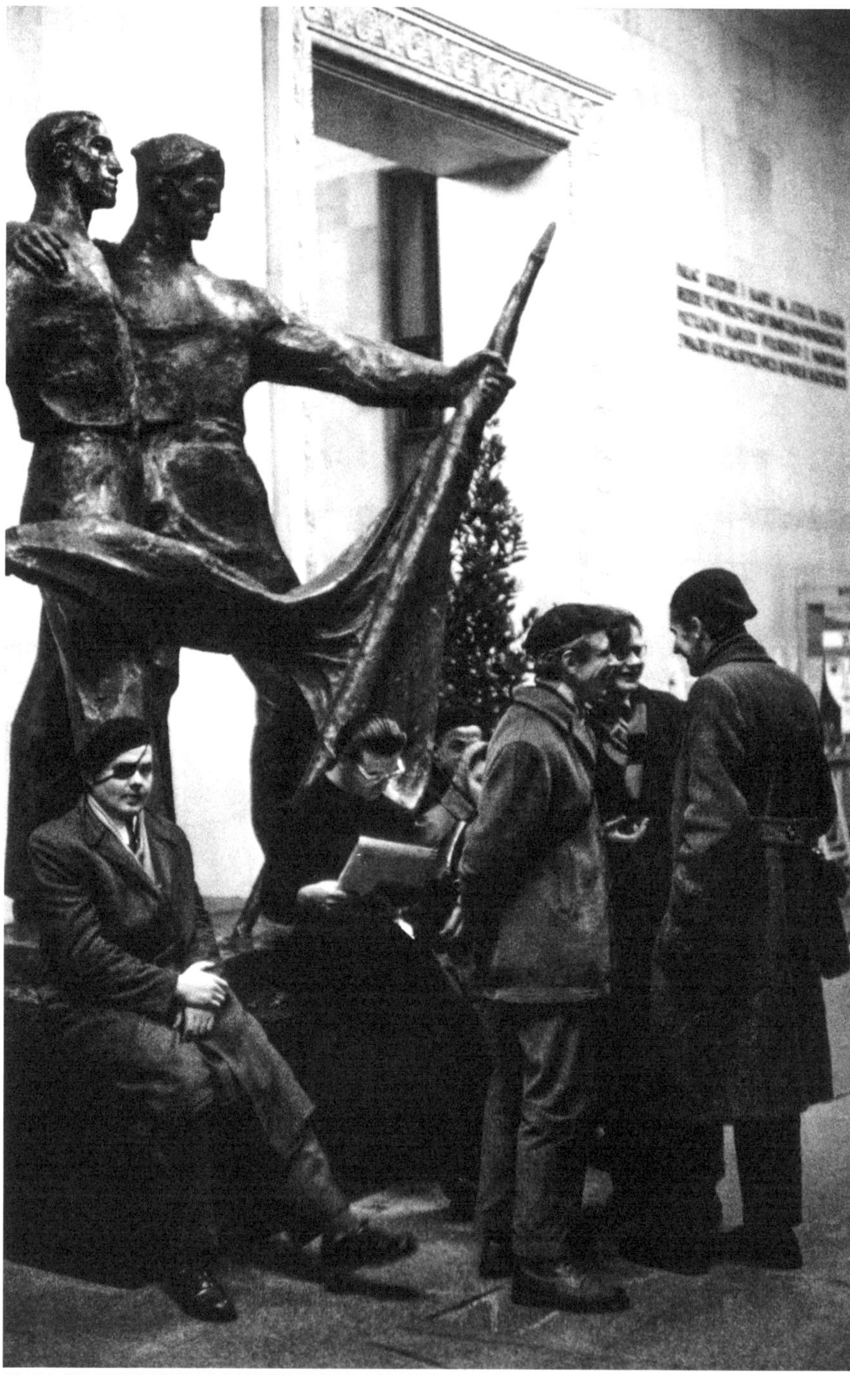

ALINA SZAPOCZNIKOW'S SCULPTURE *MONUMENT TO POLISH-SOVIET FRIENDSHIP* IN THE MAIN HALL OF THE PALACE OF CULTURE AND SCIENCE IN WARSAW, 1956

AGATA JAKUBOWSKA,
SARAH WILSON,
AND MICHAŁ MURAWSKI

BARE FRIENDSHIP, FUTURE FRIENDSHIP

This conversation, focusing on Alina Szapocznikow's sculpture *Monument to Polish-Soviet Friendship*, took place on February 17, 2022, seven days before Russia's full-scale invasion of Ukraine on February 24, 2022. The sculpture's display in the new building of the Museum of Modern Art in Warsaw is explained in the following note by Sebastian Cichocki from the catalog of the Museum's collection exhibition in 2025: "In front of the entrance to the exhibition, on the first floor of the Museum, there is a damaged sculpture: two men in an embrace, each missing an arm, carrying a burden that is no longer present. This is Alina Szapocznikow's *Friendship* from 1954, a monument glorifying brotherly Polish-Soviet relations. For almost half a century, *Friendship* stood in the lobby of the Palace of Culture. After the decision to scrap it as a communist relic, the men's arms and the banner they held were removed so that the sculpture could be carried out the door. Following Russia's full-scale invasion of Ukraine in 2022 (and its earlier annexation of Crimea in 2014), the postwar order has once again fallen to pieces. Near the Szapocznikow sculpture "flutters" *Gazelka*—a steel sculpture of a flag made by Ukrainian artist Nikita Kadan. It is made from parts of the body of a shelled car found by the artist in the city of Severodonetsk, seized by pro-Russian military forces in 2014."

Agata Jakubowska, Professor at the Institute of Art History, University of Warsaw. Author and editor of numerous books on women's art, devoted to such figures as Alina Szapocznikow, Zofia Kulik, and more recently Polish sculptor Maria Pinińska-Bereś. Co-editor of *All-Women Art Spaces in Europe in the Long 1970s* (with Katy Deepwell, 2018), and *Horizontal Art History and Beyond. Revisioning Peripheral Critical Practices* (with Magdalena Radomska, 2022). Editorial team member of Avant-Garde Critical Studies (Brill) and of the international TEAM initiative led by AWARE (Archives of Women Artists Research & Exhibitions).

Sarah Wilson is Professor of the History of Modern and Contemporary Art at The Courtauld, University of London. As principal curator of *Paris, Capital of the Arts, 1900–1968* (Royal Academy of Arts, London; Guggenheim Museum, Bilbao, 2002–2003), she showed Alina Szpocznikow's work for the first time in Britain and Spain. She has published extensively, including in Polish, and was appointed Chevalier des Arts et des Lettres for services to French culture in 1997. In 2015, she was a co-curator of the 1st Asia Biennial / 5th Guangzhou Triennial, and was awarded the International Association of Art Critics prize for her distinguished contribution to art criticism. More is available on her personal website www.sarah-wilson.london.

AGATA JAKUBOWSKA We are talking about the idea of putting Alina Szapocznikow's *Friendship* in the hall of the Museum. Szapocznikow made the sculpture in 1954, and it was installed in the Palace of Culture and Science in 1955, when the building was opened. The sculpture stood in the main entrance hall as the *Monument to Polish-Soviet Friendship.*

SARAH WILSON I didn't really think about the fact that she made the sculpture the year after Stalin's death. So how was it impacted by the death? I've just realized that this is a posthumous project, and yet it's just before the 20th Congress of the Communist Party of the Soviet Union, meaning that it was created *after* Stalin died. It's an interesting in-between moment.

AJ I would say that Stalin died, but Polish-Soviet friendship did not. And the death of Stalin influenced the history of another work by Szapocznikow—the monument to Stalin. It was planned to be erected outside the main entrance to the Palace, and there was a competition for the monument **[FIG. 1]**. But ultimately the decision was made not to erect it. Indeed, it was at a very specific moment, just before 1956.[1]

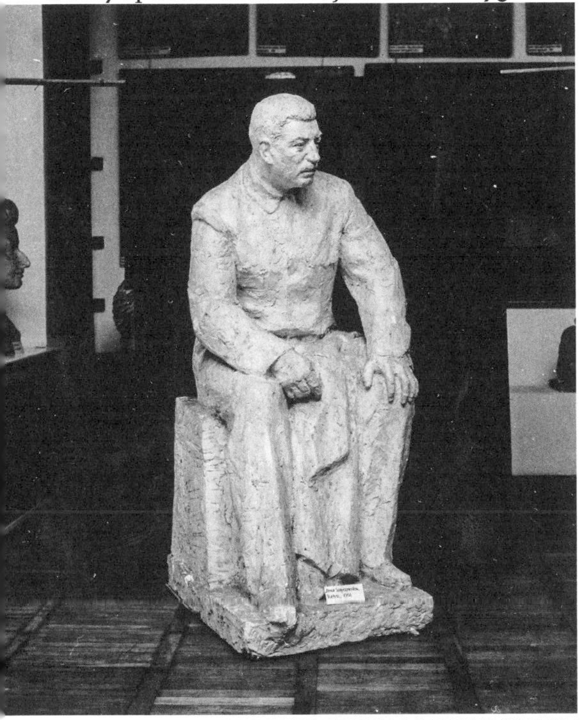

FIG. 1 ALINA SZAPOCZNIKOW, STATUE OF JOSEPH STALIN, 1953

1 1956 saw the beginning of de-Stalinization in Poland, coinciding with the thaw in the Soviet Union. Its epoch-marking event was the speech by Władysław Gomułka, First Secretary of the Polish United Workers' Party (PZPR), delivered from the Tribune of Honor on Parade Square in front of an audience of up to half a million people. See Michał Murawski, *The Palace Complex: A Stalinist Skyscraper, Capitalist Warsaw, and a City Transfixed* (Bloomington: Indiana University Press, 2019), 85–90.

MICHAŁ MURAWSKI It was a liminal time. And already then, Polish architecture was moving away from socialist realism. In the same year that the Palace was opened, the 10th-Anniversary Stadium was also opened,[2] which was much more of a modernist project than the Palace. So it was an in-between time, and yet the Palace of Culture was still formally named after Stalin. The full name is carved into the stone above the entrance. It says "Palace of Culture and Science." And underneath it, it adds "in the name of Joseph Stalin." But after 1956, they just covered this up very awkwardly with a thin piece of metal. And it's still there. And, of course, Alina Szapocznikow was also working on her own Stalin.

AJ I must admit that this part of her history is unclear to me and to other researchers. We don't know why she actually did the Stalin, because she was not invited to take part in the competition for the monument; her name is not mentioned in the documents. Most people thought that Xawery Dunikowski would make the Stalin.[3] She did her project anyway. Maybe she hoped that it would be noticed and recommended by the commission or something like that.

AGATA JAKUBOWSKA

" She wanted to have commissions. It was the easiest way to do something important in terms of sculpture at the time—to have commissions for monuments. "

2 Co-designed by architects Jerzy Hryniewiecki, Jerzy Sołtan, and Zbigniew Ihnatowicz, the stadium can be seen as a proto-modernist contemporary of the Palace and a harbinger of change. In 1989, the stadium became the site of Europe's largest open-air bazaar, Jarmark Europa; in 2011, Poland's new national stadium was opened atop the structure of the old one. See: Joanna Warsza, ed., *Stadium X: A Place That Never Was* (Warsaw: Bęc Zmiana, 2009).

3 Xawery Dunikowski (1875–1964) won the competition to design the monument to Stalin. A plaster cast of his unrealized monument can be viewed today at the Xawery Dunikowski Museum of Sculpture, a division of the National Museum in Warsaw, located in the Królikarnia Palace. For more on Dunikowski, Szapocznikow, and Polish trajectories of socialist-realist sculpture, see Agnieszka Tomaszewicz, "Sculpture in Socialist Realism—Soviet Patterns and the Polish Reality," *Arts* 11, no. 1 (2021). For more details, see Waldemar Baraniewski, "Kopernik i Stalin. Treści ideowe dekoracji Pałacu Kultury i Nauki w Warszawie," *Kronika Warszawy* 127, no. 4 (2005): 53–69.

SW But was *Monument to Polish-Soviet Friendship* for a competition, or a commission without a competition? It seems amazing to me, because she was a twenty-nine-year-old woman.

AJ There is very little information. What is interesting is that she did not win it. We can find information in the literature that it was another female Polish sculptor who won, Magdalena Więcek.[4] And we don't know why Szapocznikow's project was realized, but not Więcek's. We can suppose that it's because Szapocznikow was, at the time, the wife of Ryszard Stanisławski, who was becoming quite an important person in the cultural politics of the Polish Ministry of Culture.[5] So her position was quite strong at the time. In any case, I haven't found any documents about it. The competition for the Stalin monument is much better documented than for *Friendship*. Whatever the truth is about this particular work, she was certainly devoted to socialist ideas.

MM More so than Stanisławski, who, in their correspondence, mocked her for her devotion.[6]

AJ Yes, he mocked her a bit. But she also wanted to work. I think that's important; she wanted to have commissions. It was the easiest way to do something important in terms of sculpture at the time—to have commissions for monuments. But obviously, I would say that she was committed to the idea of socialism, but not necessarily to socialist realism in formal terms.

SW Yes, but what I think is interesting about her *Stalin* is that it's not just about socialist realism. Look at the way Stalin is turning. I know from Zofia Kulik that there was a version of Michelangelo's *Moses* in the academy, which was a plaster cast like in every art academy at the time **[FIG. 2]**. And the whole thing about Michelangelo's *Moses* is that he's turning because he's just had his attention attracted, he's about to pick up the tablets and smash them. And so the way the body turns and the attention is seized is the focus, but *Stalin* is much less grandiose than *Moses*. I don't even think that the term "socialist realism" has to be invoked in terms of making this sculpture of a great leader turning. Where did Szapocznikow learn to sculpt?

4 Magdalena Więcek (1924–2008) was a key figure in the revival of Polish sculpture after the thaw of 1956.
5 Ryszard Stanisławski (1921–2000) was a prominent Polish art historian and critic, director of the Muzeum Sztuki in Łódź from 1966 to 1990.
6 Agata Jakubowska and Katarzyna Szotkowska-Beylin, eds., *Lovely, Human, True, Heartfelt: The Letters of Alina Szapocznikow and Ryszard Stanisławski 1948–1971*, trans. Jennifer Croft (Warsaw: Museum of Modern Art, 2012), 54–55.

AJ It's hard to say. One could say "at the cemetery," because, after World War II, when she lived in Prague and then in Paris, she earned her living working at stone workshops—in Paris, in the one owned by the Lerendu, near the Père-Lachaise cemetery.

SW Did she go to the École des Beaux-Arts in Paris at all, or go through it? They've got a *Moses* too.

AJ She took some classes in Prague at the Academy of Applied Art, in Josef Wagner's studio, and some in Paris at the École Normale Supérieure, in Paul Niclausse's studio. But she never completed her formal education—which is interesting, because it should have been a problem in Poland at the time. But seemingly it wasn't.

SW That photo of her, tiny next to the unrealized, unfinished *Friendship* **[FIG. 3]**. Is that in plaster? Or is it in clay before plaster? One forgets how huge the sculpture is compared to her. This issue of scale and material reminds me that I've got two interesting things to say that are a bit off topic.

I'm speaking to you from Lisbon, I've just been to the Gérard Fromanger retrospective. This is an artist who was very important in 1968. He went to China at the height of Maoism, although he wasn't exactly a Maoist; a question is posed about his political engagement. Needless to say, the whole exhibition is *entirely formalistic*. Paintings are hung on white walls

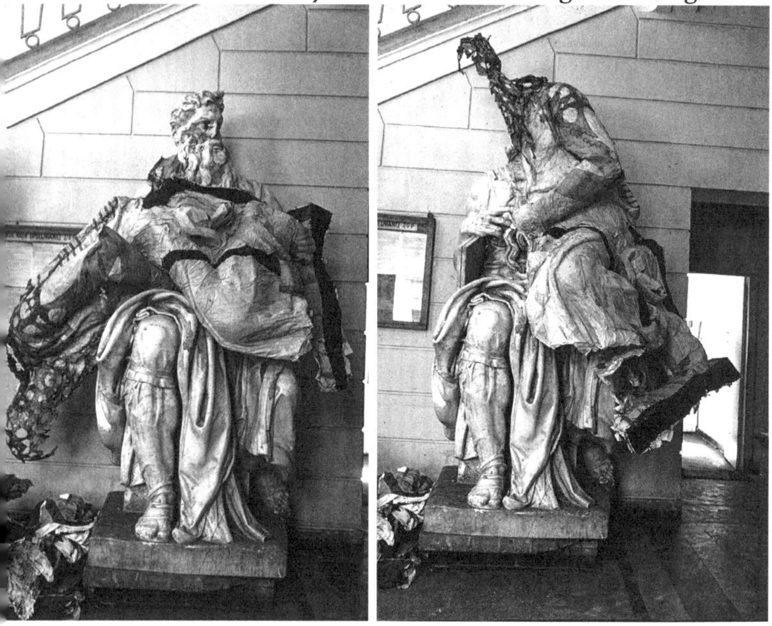

FIGS. 2.1–2.2 ZOFIA KULIK, *INSTEAD OF SCULPTURE*, 1968–1971, FRAGMENTS OF SLIDE SHOW ON THREE SCREENS. DIPLOMA PIECE AT THE SCULPTURE DEPARTMENT, ACADEMY OF FINE ARTS IN WARSAW

with absolutely no explanation about anything. The brochure is something like four paragraphs; it's either that or a very expensive catalog.

There seems to be a generational hangover about modernist white spaces. Decontextualizing everything and wiping out history. It's very much ongoing, and it means that none of the general public, no young people, are going to understand anything at all about this artist. Except that his art is all very nice and jolly.

There's a way of *not* doing this. The entire history of the white square, the white box—I mean, before Brian O'Doherty critiqued the white cube[7]—is to do with the invention of white space. It's to do with hygiene and the Bauhaus. And it's a way of expelling everything, thinking that something is neutral. I wrote down words that were in Thomas Phifer's description of the building: "progressive, optimistic, transparent and populist in spirit." How is this going to work if it's completely white?

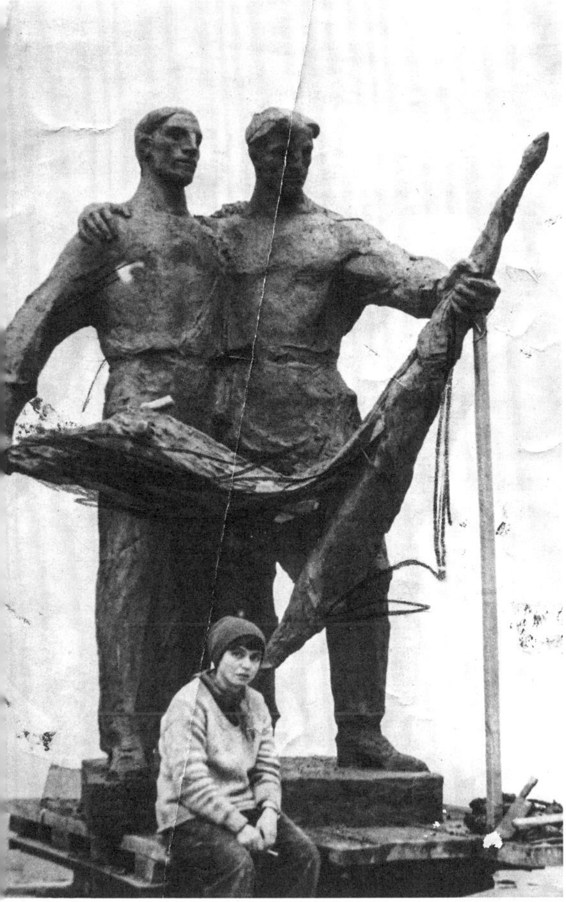

FIG. 3 ALINA SZAPOCZNIKOW DURING THE MAKING OF THE *MONUMENT TO POLISH-SOVIET FRIENDSHIP*, 1954

7 Brian O'Doherty, "Inside the White Cube: Notes on the Gallery Space, Part I," *Artforum* 14, no. 7 (March 1976): 24–30.

As for *Friendship*, you really want a beautifully done display case. It can be discreetly put somewhere. There needs to be a story. I find the narrative, especially the question about whether "amputated friendship" is possible, so valuable. These are huge questions, and they can't only be answered in the exhibition catalog—or this book.

AJ I think what you're saying is very much related to the title of the sculpture itself, *Monument to Polish-Soviet Friendship*. No one uses this title today. For most people, it's just *Friendship*. In a sense, part of the significance of the monument is that if it's not "amputated," then it's at least removed from the foreground. It's disappeared for almost thirty years.

SW Speaking of what's going on in the news at the moment, what can "Polish-Soviet Friendship" or "Polish-Post-Soviet Friendship" or "Polish-Russian Friendship" possibly mean—in terms of the present, but also in terms of history and the history of trauma? The trauma must be dealt with, but not in a way which is beholden to the traumatic and repressed hatred of a previous generation. I think that it's important for the original title to be restored.

MM This also makes me think of Piotr Piotrowski's text on the traumaphobic versus the traumaphilic institution.[8] He suggested that the National Museum of Contemporary Art (MNAC) in Bucharest hides from its past and represses it, as opposed to MSN in Warsaw, which actively engages with it and tries to work through it. So there is this psychoanalytic dimension to the program of the Museum under the current leadership. And I think that the plan to have the sculpture in the lobby is a culmination, in a way, of the active process of working through, which is at the center of the institution's mission.

AJ One more thing about the title. I think it was when the sculpture was in the DESA Auction House in 2019 that it started to be titled simply *Friendship* **[FIG. 4]**. It happened during the moment of showing the sculpture to the public again, before the Museum received it from the new owner. That was when the title changed in public perception.

8 Piotr Piotrowski, "New Museums in East-Central Europe: Between Traumaphobia and Traumaphilia," in *1968–1989: Political upheaval and artistic change*, ed. Claire Bishop and Marta Dziewańska (Warsaw: Museum of Modern Art, 2009), 148–66.

SW I think the proper title should be restored.

AJ On the other hand, we have this law in Poland, the decommunization law of 2016, which prohibits the propagation of communism and other totalitarian regimes.[9] In the context of this law, the change in the title acquires a different meaning.

SW I want to say something about concepts and laws and bureaucracy. I find it very interesting that this law is from 2016. I would like to compare this problem with some other works of art. One is Sophie Calle's project from 1996 called *The Detachment* or *Die Entfernung*. Calle went to Berlin in the 1990s, after all the post-Soviet sculpture had been whisked away, including the beautiful dove, the Picasso-inspired bronze metal dove on the side of a building.[10] At the back of Calle's book all the laws are reproduced that were passed—obviously some time before 1996—to eradicate all the old communist and Soviet names. What interests me is this strange delay, also related to trauma, from a bureaucratic point of view.

MICHAŁ MURAWSKI

" I think that the plan to have the sculpture in the lobby is a culmination, in a way, of the active process of working through "

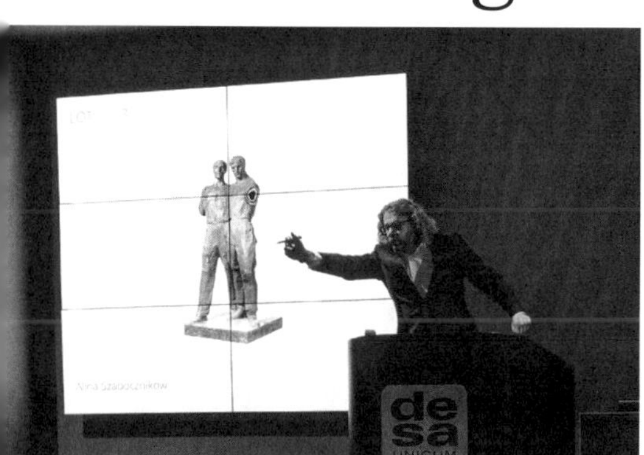

FIG. 4 ALINA SZAPOCZNIKOW'S *FRIENDSHIP* AT AUCTION AT DESA UNICUM ON MARCH 28, 2019; THE WORK WAS SOLD FOR 1.7 MILLION PLN

9 See Magda Szcześniak and Łukasz Zaremba, "Paranoid looking: on de-communization," *Journal of Visual Culture* 18, no. 2 (2019): 209–33.

10 See Clare Edwards, "Sophie Call: The Detachment / Die Entfernung" (master's thesis, The Courtauld Institute of Art, supervised by Sarah Wilson, 1998).

As far as I understand it, the chronology begins in 1989 with the Solidarity elections. Then in 1990, we have this very important article for conceptual art called "Conceptual Art 1962–1969: From the Aesthetic of Administration to the Critique of Institutions,"[11] which is about the way that conceptual projects are essentially linked to bureaucracy and institutions, such as the museum institution. And so the phenomenon of delay is extremely interesting. You know, like—"oh, whoops, we forgot to do it!" This incredible delay before the 2016 laws.

MM The temporality is strange and uneven, but this process started already in 1989, and the first wave of it happened in the early 1990s—there was the renaming of streets and the removal of a large number of monuments. Then it had a kind of second wave, arguably after Ukraine's Maidan, but it was also linked to the shift in Polish politics, which took a sharply anticommunist, iconoclastic turn with the election of the right-wing Law and Justice party in 2015.

SW There is all the bizarreness of bureaucracy and institutionalization, which leads to your other point about amputation, because it not only expresses the violence that this body has received, but also the violence of bureaucracy. When one considers the *Venus de Milo*, psychoanalytically speaking, there is the issue of restitution or repair. And so when you look at this amputated body—and we haven't even discussed it physically, how the two bodies are melded, what it's like without the banner—it instinctively provokes a desire for reparation, which is very much linked with healing.

When you think about mutilated sculpture, you think about Melanie Klein and D. W. Winnicott. There is this idea of *future* friendship and *future* hospitality and reparation, a kind of dialectical other of the violence of mutilation and trauma. It relates also to your use of the word "liminal" to refer to the way the sculpture is poised between the past, the present of perception, and the potential of the future.

AJ We should concentrate for a moment on the act of violence. Let's talk about the situation when *Friendship* was amputated. What were the conditions or

11 Benjamin H. D. Buchloh, "Conceptual Art 1962–1969: From the Aesthetic of Administration to the Critique of Institutions," *October* 55 (Winter 1990): 105–43.

circumstances of this violence? It was actually so banal; it happened just because the sculpture was too huge.

SW But it was also designated as waste before it was amputated. I've been to that place around the back of the New Tretyakov Gallery in Moscow, where they had a graveyard of undesirable sculptures. Undesirable sculptures exist that people don't mutilate, or you can have toppled and mutilated sculptures, which are actually defaced in an act of iconoclastic desire.

MM Yes, it wasn't really an iconoclastic act of amputation, but what was significant was the moment that it happened. And I think the reason they couldn't get it out was because the sculpture was installed in the Palace of Culture before they put the doors in. By the time the doors were in, it was impossible to get the sculpture out, although they could probably have taken it out through the service door at the back, but perhaps they didn't know about it or couldn't be bothered. But you can just conjure this atmosphere of chaos in which someone decided—"oh shit, the door is too small; we've got a chainsaw, let's just cut the arms off."

AJ What has happened to the arms, where are they? In 1998, when Katarzyna Bielas and Dorota Jarecka found the sculpture and wrote an article about it in *Gazeta Wyborcza*, they wrote that the arms and the banner were still in the yard of the sculpture's owner **[FIGS. 5.1–5.3]**.[12] And what happened later, we don't know.

SW Is it better without them? I think they function in very different ways formally. Maybe for us today, *without* is more eloquent in some ways than *with*.

AJ It's easier to consider this as a kind of a new sculpture. Not the one originally created by Szapocznikow, but somehow transformed into a new sculpture that can have new meanings. It's easier to call it just *Friendship* if it's without the banner and without the arms holding it.

SW Just general, abstract *Friendship*. However, general friendship is one thing. But if you then say that it can be a symbol of gay pride or of other types of philia—this could be interesting and potentially great in terms of performances or events around it, or whatever. But is it connected with its poignant essence? To make it completely new without its past is something

12 Katarzyna Bielas and Dorota Jarecka, "Była tu jakaś Przyjaźń?" *Gazeta Wyborcza*, January 31–February 1, 1998, 24–25.

that may diminish it if its past is disregarded. I would also find this comparable to the modernist act of cleansing or whitewashing, which I would disagree with. So I would like it to be as polyvalent as possible. But the richness and the kinds of tragedy and even the bureaucratic trauma should be part of the recognition of what it can symbolize if we look at it with a longer perspective.

MM But how do you do that without it being kind of didactic?

SW I don't think it's got to be didactic; I just think it's got to be *there*. Personally, I would advocate a long narrative vitrine—not something on the wall which comes over as more didactic, but something which creates intimations of possible new interpretations. Something which leaves the thing as itself, yet perfectly available for new appropriations and interpretations.

But the sculpture itself is also very strange. I mean, the way the bodies are melded in the middle—there's no space between them. They're almost like the

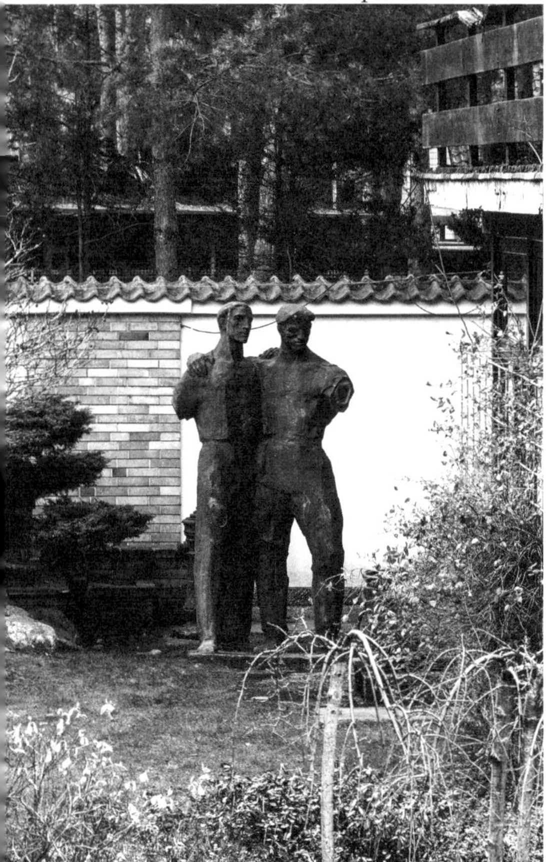

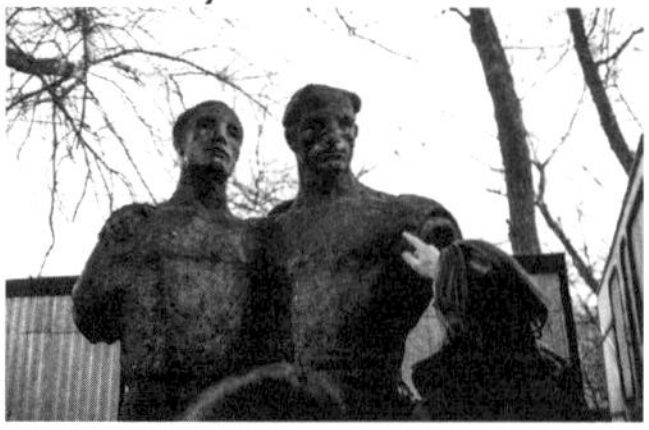

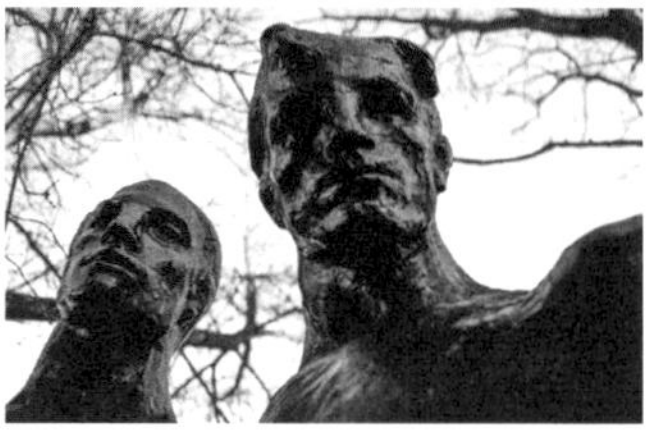

FIG. 5.1 ALINA SZAPOCZNIKOW'S *FRIENDSHIP* IN 2017
FIGS. 5.2–5.3 ALINA SZAPOCZNIKOW'S *FRIENDSHIP* PHOTOGRAPHED ON JANUARY 12, 1998 IN ZBIGNIEW BOGUSZ'S BACKYARD

kind of conjoined twin body you get in Chagall's Apollinaire painting. It's very melded into the middle. You could almost say it's slightly monstrous. It's not just straightforward friendship, is it?

AJ I wonder whether the idea of the restoration of the sculpture occurred to the Museum, because it's what institutions do: you can add the arms and the banner again.

SW And that would be a dreadful thing to do.

AJ But, you know, the center of Warsaw is like this. The Old Town is not really the original Old Town.[13] Perhaps that would be dreadful. Yet, indeed, *Friendship* without arms is more useful. It's open to many different ideas of friendship.

SW I've just had a great idea. You know how everyone loves videos and films and virtual reality because that's what they're brought up on now? You could have a kind of alcove where, rather than a didactic film, there's a hologram of the restored sculpture, like a ghost of the original.

You'd see the original and it would attract people very much. But then there would also be the alter ego of the sculpture with a different materiality. And it would be a brilliant way of doing both things at once, but without sticking the arms on. You could do a wonderful kind of ghost facsimile.

SARAH WILSON

" I would advocate a long narrative vitrine—not something on the wall which comes over as more didactic, but something which creates intimations of possible new interpretations. "

13 For background on the ideologized reconstruction of Warsaw's Old Town, see Grzegorz Piatek, *Najlepsze miasto świata: Warszawa w odbudowie 1944–1949* (Warsaw: W.A.B., 2020), 209–236; Michał Murawski, "(A)political buildings: ideology, memory and Warsaw's 'Old' Town," *Docomomo E-Proceedings* 2 (December 2009): 13–20.

MM It's interesting how *Friendship* will be displayed, because in the Palace of Culture, in the entrance hall, it was so centered—it was in the absolute center of the space, the symbolic heart of the entire building. Whereas, even though the Museum of Modern Art is quite a monumental building, and the central staircase is very impressive and grand, it's not possible to put the sculpture quite in the center. So it will be a bit off to the side, somewhat decentered. It could quite easily get lost in the flow.

SW It should be somewhere symbolic, but if you also had this other space, you could recreate the background of the old photographs as well. You could have it as a ghost body or a ghost installation.

AJ Let's talk about the Museum's idea to install the sculpture, because it's not that obvious. On the one hand, Alina Szapocznikow has always been important for MSN, starting from the 2009 exhibition *Awkward Objects*, accompanied by an international conference, through several books commissioned by the Museum, and its involvement in international exhibitions of Szapocznikow's work.[14] It's obvious that Szapocznikow is an important figure for them, but *Friendship* is a very particular artwork.

I'm thinking about the post-Soviet condition of Warsaw and the post-Soviet condition of the Museum. I think that, by displaying the work, it still places itself in this context of the post-Soviet condition. So on the one hand, it's about being open and progressive and looking to the future. But, on the other hand, it sustains the post-Soviet condition strongly—especially entering into dialog with the specific place the Museum is situated in. They enter this dialog through *Friendship*.

14 The exhibition *Awkward Objects*, curated by Joanna Mytkowska and Agata Jakubowska, May 14–July 26, 2009, at the Museum on Pańska Street, situated Alina Szapocznikow's sculptures in the context of work by Maria Bartuszová, Pauline Boty, Louise Bourgeois, Eva Hesse, and Paulina Ołowska. It was accompanied by the international conference *Alina Szapocznikow. Documents, Works, Interpretations*, held on May 15–16, 2009. Co-organized by MSN and curated by Elena Filipovic and Joanna Mytkowska, the touring exhibition *Alina Szapocznikow. Sculpture Undone 1955–1972* was presented at the Wiels Contemporary Art Centre, Brussels (September 10, 2011–August 1, 2012); Hammer Museum, Los Angeles (February 5–April 29, 2012); Wexner Center for the Arts, Columbus, Ohio (May 17–August 4, 2012); and MoMA, New York (October 7, 2012–January 28, 2013). The show was accompanied by an extensive catalog edited by Lisa Gabrielle Mark, co-published by all the above institutions and MSN. The Museum also published four books devoted to Szapocznikow: Agata Jakubowska, ed., *Alina Szapocznikow: Awkward Objects* (Warsaw: Museum of Modern Art, 2011); Jakubowska and Szotkowska-Beylin, *Lovely, Human, True, Heartfelt*; Agata Jakubowska and Katarzyna Szotkowska-Beylin, eds., *Kroją mi się piękne sprawy. Listy Aliny Szapocznikow i Ryszarda Stanisławskiego 1948–1971* (Kraków: Karakter; Warsaw: Muzeum Sztuki Nowoczesnej, 2012); and Marek Beylin, *Ferwor: życie Aliny Szapocznikow* (Kraków: Karakter; Warsaw: Muzeum Sztuki Nowoczesnej, 2015).

SW The photo you gave us of *Friendship* in the entrance hall of the Palace of Culture is from 1961 **[FIG. 6]**. And then your wonderful essay in *Awkward Objects* about her *Goldfinger* says that Szapocznikow began working on body fragments in 1962 **[FIG. 8]**.[15] So I was thinking, were she to see this mutilated monument, she would feel terrible and very upset; it's not as though she would like it. On the other hand, it's amazing that all her work after *Friendship* is about mutilation. There's a way in which the two things are strangely linked.

Speaking of words for things that are strange or awkward, I was interested to learn that the word "weird" comes from "wyrd," which is Anglo-Saxon for "fate." And there's something fatal about the whole progression into mutilation. It's very strange, you know, from a Freudian point of view, *après la lettre*, after the whole thing's become mutilated.

AJ Yes, but there is a difference in scale. The Museum has a couple of Szapocznikow's other works, but they are tiny **[FIG. 7]**. Also, *Friendship* is a very phallic sculpture. Amputated, *Friendship* is especially phallic. It would be interesting to see the relationship between *Friendship*, the amputated *Friendship*, and Szapocznikow's later works, which are very much... I wouldn't like to say "feminine," but somehow formless, or at least dissolving.

MM Just think of putting them side by side. That would be weird—and fatal.

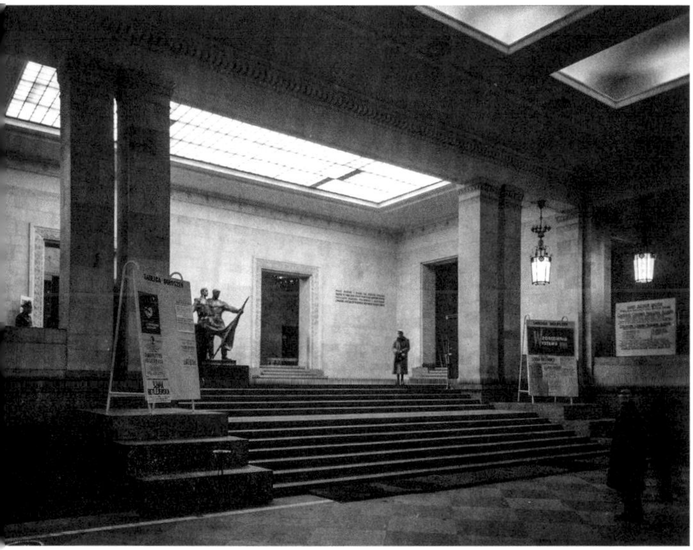

FIG. 6 ENTRANCE HALL OF THE PALACE OF CULTURE AND SCIENCE WITH ALINA SZAPOCZNIKOW'S SCULPTURE, 1961

15 Agata Jakubowska, "Alina Szapocznikow's *Leg* and *Goldfinger*: Between Reality and Illusion," in Jakubowska, *Alina Szapocznikow: Awkward Objects*, 123–32.

AJ Yes, but that was her art, after *Friendship*. I actually like this contrast, but I don't know what to do with it. Because somehow representing Szapocznikow with *Friendship*... As you said, Sarah, I agree that the mutilation of *Friendship* would not surprise her.

SW There's a very funny analogy, which offers a discouraging parallel. But I'm thinking of "Number 1 London," Apsley House, which is a very strange address, the famous house of the Duke of Wellington. And when he beat the French, a hilarious—highly serious—nude, monumental sculpture by Canova of Napoleon holding a small statue of Nike was erected. So, you obviously don't want to do that, which makes it look comic

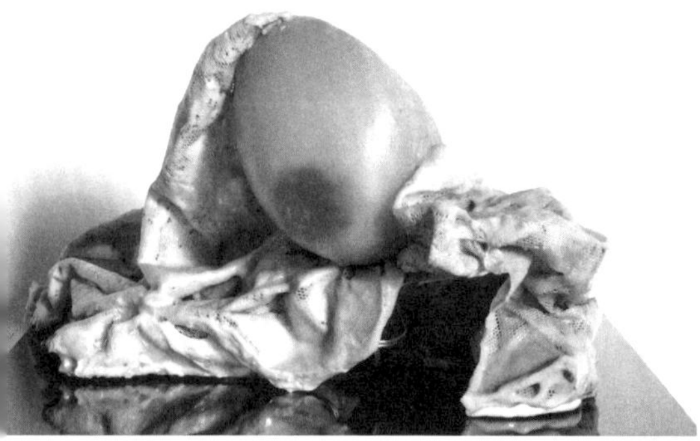

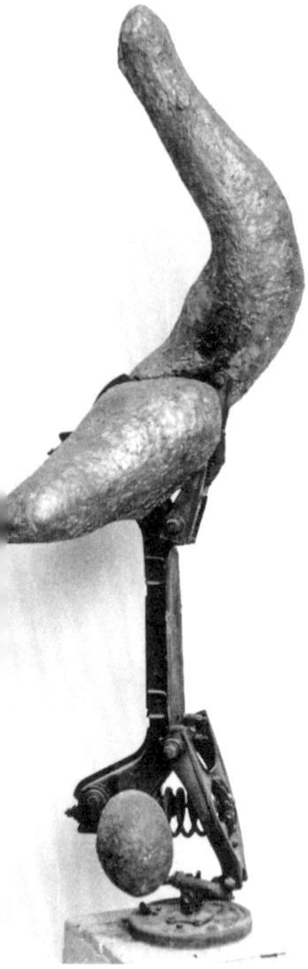

FIG. 7 ALINA SZAPOCZNIKOW, *LAMP III (FETISH IX)*, 1970, BREAST CAST, POLYESTER, PLASTIC MESH, ELECTRIC LIGHT, 10 × 45 × 25 CM
FIG. 8 ALINA SZAPOCZNIKOW, *GOLDFINGER*, 1965, GOLD-PATINATED CEMENT, CAR SPRING

in terms of the problem of proportion, makes it lose gravitas in some way. Evidently, if you're going to show it, its aura is going to require a certain amount of space.

MM To go back to the delay that you mentioned, Sarah. The new wave of iconoclasm, which later spread to Bristol and the United States and South Africa and the whole world, I think you could say that it started in Ukraine in 2013, when they took down the Lenin statue in Kyiv. First one Lenin in Kyiv, and then hundreds fell. And then the Maidan and the ensuing war happened. The new appreciation for socialist-realist sculpture also coincided with this new global iconoclastic moment, which arguably began in Ukraine in 2013–2014.

Next, the Rhodes Must Fall movement started in South Africa in 2015-and spread to the UK and the US, culminating in the Black Lives Matter movement, and the veiling and eventual removal of hundreds of statues of people associated with slavery and racism in the United States and globally over the last few years. This started with the veiling of the Robert E. Lee monument in Charlottesville in 2017, and culminated with hundreds of topplings in the wake of George Floyd's murder in 2020. So the chronology is pretty clear. There is an extended moment, starting in the mid-2010s, where these decommunization laws coincide with the wave of iconoclasm. Whatever happens to *Friendship* now, it will inevitably be written not only into the 1950s and the 1990s, but also into this long wave of iconoclasm, from Maidan to Black Lives Matter.[16]

MICHAŁ MURAWSKI

" The new wave of iconoclasm, which later spread to the whole world, I think you could say that it started in Ukraine in 2013, when they took down the Lenin statue in Kyiv. "

16 For an analytical comparison of differential dynamics of decommunizing and decolonizing iconoclasm, see Szczęśniak and Zaremba, "Paranoid looking."

SW Indeed, so if you strip all the context from it, the arms and the socialist-realist emblems and the banner, basically you're getting back to the bare body—Giorgio Agamben comes to mind here—back to something very bare and basic, which is *pre* all the added-on ideology and the appurtenances and flags. And that's why I think *Friendship* is very poignant. It is, in a way, like a Polish *Venus de Milo*. It could be something connected to the idea that person-to-person, *bare friendship* is supremely important. It could be very important as a future-orientated monument.

MM Some sort of reconciliation.

SW Yes, rather than just smashing things up or cutting them off. Of course, you're right that *Friendship* is very *man–man*, not very *woman–woman*. But it's not as though patriarchy has been abolished.

And in this context, these amputated bodies imply vulnerability and reconciliation; vulnerability means being able to be wounded. So it's the idea of patriarchy and patriarchal structures and maleness actually being vulnerable and open to change, open to the possibility of reconciliation. I think that the actual openness of the body, and the fact that everything's been taken away from it, ideologically and symbolically, is very important within the context of patriarchy.

Not to speak of the fact that it's got a female signature. It's not as though we're talking about exactly the same sculpture made by a man—it was made by a twenty-nine-year-old woman. When we discuss vulnerability, as well as reparation, the key book for performance art is *The Body in Pain* by Elaine Scarry.[17] In it, she describes how, in the past, the whole point of torture was not for the pleasure of hacking off people's limbs—it was to do with making people speak, and the idea of the question. And so here this amputated, mutilated, vulnerable male body actually asks a question.

AJ Yes, but we should not forget the conditions in which the sculpture was made. It was made by a twenty-nine-year-old woman, but it was a commission from the ruling party.

17 Elaine Scarry, *The Body in Pain: The Making and Unmaking of the World* (New York: Oxford University Press, 1985).

SW But surely it was subversive—her reply to them, in a certain way.[18]

AJ I am not so sure. I know that we like to think Szapocznikow was subversive, because it helps us to like her—but I'm not so sure. She did a commission; they liked the sculpture; they put it in the center of this building. So they did not consider it subversive in any way.

SW I agree with you; I was wrong there, but it's not over-exaggerated in the way that Arno Breker's *Kameraden* is, for example. If one were trying to discuss what you've just said, you would look at *Kameraden*—there is this completely over-the-top, overly baroque, overly virilized masculinity. Whereas *Friendship* is not over-virilized, or overly academic; it retains a certain freshness.

AJ If we compare different stages of the sculpture, we see that she moved from one representing people that are more lively to one that represents them as more static, a type of representation that she may have considered more acceptable to the party. So it was definitely not a subversive sculpture. It's more subversive now, I would say. Again, because it's amputated.

MM Of course, Szapocznikow's is not the only monument to the "friendship of the peoples," understood in the Soviet sense. In the context of Polish-Soviet relations or the Soviet Bloc, "friendship" is a word that's necessarily associated with Russian claims to "symmetrical" friendship with fraternal nations. And, in fact, there is also a somewhat comparable dispute about the monument to Russian-Ukrainian friendship in Kyiv, next to the Maidan, positioned underneath a huge metal rainbow **(SEE CHAPTER 1)**.

AJ There were also a couple of battles in Poland over monuments by Dunikowski and by Hasior that pertained to Polish-Soviet Friendship.[19] They wanted to demolish these monuments, really great works of art. Finally, what was decided was that they could be kept, but that you would need to remove the words. You need to remove the information that it has anything to do with Polish-Soviet Friendship or Soviet soldiers or such.

MM And the only way you can keep a monument is if it has human relics buried within it or underneath it.

18 For reflection on the subversiveness of Alina Szapocznikow's work, see Agata Jakubowska, *Portret wielokrotny dzieła Aliny Szapocznikow* (Poznań: Wydawnictwo Naukowe UAM, 2008), 52–72; and Beylin, *Ferwor: życie Aliny Szapocznikow*, 108–10.

19 Tomaszewicz, "Sculpture in Socialist Realism."

AJ Another thing I wanted to mention is that *Friendship* without the Polish-Soviet dimension opens up different aspects. And the act of amputation also opens up different aspects. One aspect that we have not discussed yet is the history of this part of the city. In this part of Warsaw, many buildings and half-ruined buildings, left over from the war, were destroyed to make way for the construction of the Palace.

And this was also partially a Jewish district. The border of the Jewish district, which became the Jewish Ghetto during German occupation, ran through Parade Square, which is also very important in the context of Alina Szapocznikow's history.[20] So when talking about the amputated *Friendship* in this place, the first thing that comes to mind is the Soviet and post-Soviet condition. But it's also about the Jewish history of the city, and of this part of the city in particular. And when I saw in your book, Michał, the photo of the plaque marking the place where Chmielna Street used to run on the territory of what is now Parade Square, "Here was

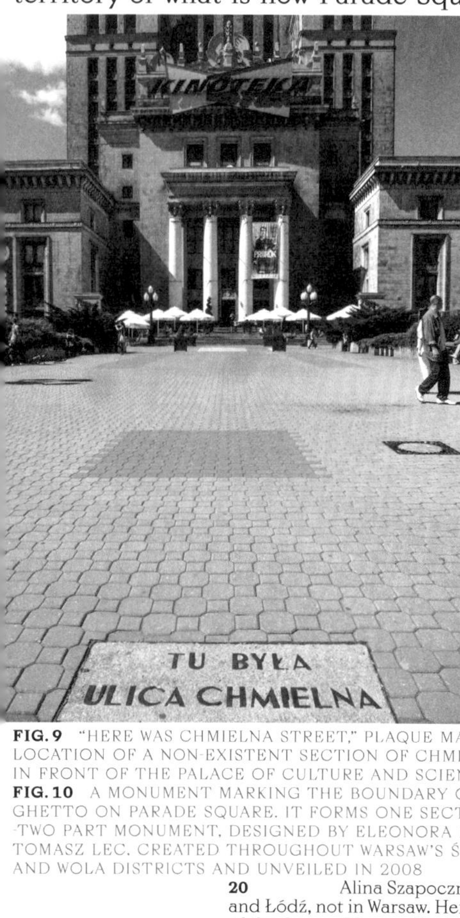

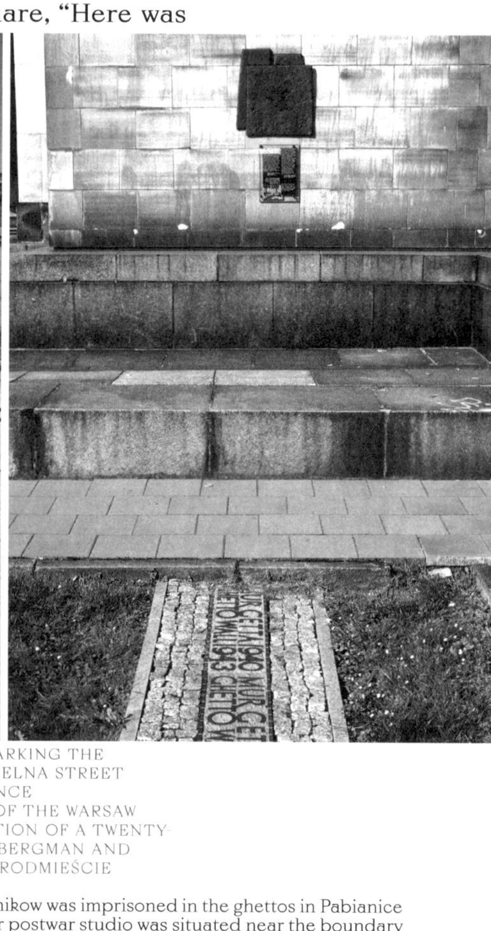

FIG. 9 "HERE WAS CHMIELNA STREET," PLAQUE MARKING THE LOCATION OF A NON-EXISTENT SECTION OF CHMIELNA STREET IN FRONT OF THE PALACE OF CULTURE AND SCIENCE
FIG. 10 A MONUMENT MARKING THE BOUNDARY OF THE WARSAW GHETTO ON PARADE SQUARE. IT FORMS ONE SECTION OF A TWENTY-TWO PART MONUMENT, DESIGNED BY ELEONORA BERGMAN AND TOMASZ LEC, CREATED THROUGHOUT WARSAW'S ŚRODMIEŚCIE AND WOLA DISTRICTS AND UNVEILED IN 2008

20 Alina Szapocznikow was imprisoned in the ghettos in Pabianice and Łódź, not in Warsaw. Her postwar studio was situated near the boundary of the former Warsaw Ghetto. For a detailed exploration of Szapocznikow's wartime trajectory, see Beylin, *Ferwor*, 11–25.

Chmielna Street" **[FIG. 9]**, I started thinking that it's an amputated street! An amputated district of the city, and an amputated city.[21]

MM Those plaques were placed there on the initiative of Józef Sigalin, then Chief Architect of Warsaw, who was Jewish and whose family were killed either by Stalin or in Treblinka. And he always under-emphasized or repressed his Jewish past, but it was on his initiative that this kind of memoir of amputation was set in the square.[22]

In the book with Alina Szapocznikow and Ryszard Stanisławski's letters that Agata edited,[23] the only reference, as far as I remember, that Szapocznikow makes to her experiences of the Holocaust and of internment is when she is justifying to Stanisławski her enthusiasm for communism, right? He insinuates that she's being infantile or childish, as a woman younger than him, in her enthusiasm for communist ideology. And she says, extremely eloquently and concisely, "no, you don't know what you're talking about, you didn't go through the camps, you didn't have this experience of suffering." And so here she deploys this experience of the most horrendous trauma that she otherwise doesn't discuss, to explain her allegiance to an ideology.

SW Yes, one imagines her body of work, with the possible exception of *Friendship* and *Stalin*, as a *reconstituted* body. I supervised two theses on her before this process of reconstitution happened.[24] Much of her work was stored in Richard Stanisławski's home for decades. During her life in Paris, both in her own right and as the wife of Roman Cieślewicz (who worked as a graphic designer for many magazines and for the Pompidou Center), she knew the whole art world, yet she was discreet about her great body of work—only her late work was revealed in her posthumous Paris show in 1973. So what happened subsequently is very interesting, and it involves this idea of rehabilitation.

21 Like several other central Warsaw streets, Chmielna starts and stops on either side of Parade Square. See Murawski, *The Palace Complex*, 85–98 for an assessment of the Parade Square designers' attitude to prewar Warsaw. Magdalena Stopa provides an illustrative (but unsentimental) history of the city that came before (or lies under) the Palace, in her *Przed wojną i pałacem* (Warsaw: Dom Spotkań z Historią, 2015).
22 Stopa, *Przed wojną i pałacem*.
23 Jakubowska and Szotkowska-Beylin, *Lovely, Human, True, Heartfelt*.
24 See two master's theses supervised by Sarah Wilson at The Courtauld Institute of Art: Amy Chmielewski, "Alina Szapocznikow's Body of Work: Sculptures 1953–1972" (2006); Dagmara Budzbon, "Alina Szapocznikow: The Ecstatic Carnival of Forms" (2008).

AJ As far as I'm concerned, what is also interesting and somehow sad is the role that the art market plays in rehabilitation. For many years, art institutions were not interested in the work. In order to restore the sculpture, the art market was necessary, the auction house played a crucial role.

Let's return for a moment to the idea of thinking about different forms of friendship, in the context of the history of the sculpture. For example, why not talk about the friendship of workers?

SW Isn't it implicitly a friendship of workers?

AJ But it's surprisingly not discussed today.

SW It's not only because people in Poland don't like discussing communism and all the scholars call it "socialism" for some reason. They're very afraid of the "c" word.

AJ Indeed, but if we are talking about the original context, or the *essence* of the work, this idea of the international solidarity of working people was there. Michał, you mentioned global situations–iconoclasm in Ukraine and Black Lives Matter–that are important now. But it's yet another aspect we can add today. If we think about the actualization of the original meanings, we could talk about the contemporary international solidarity of workers.

SW The display of *Friendship* could be a pioneering gesture in terms of accepting the sculpture in its *everything*, and that's what gives it an intermediary position, in particular at this political and geopolitical moment. Because you actually have to *work* at friendship. You know, I've got friends who don't have any friends. Either you work at friendship and have lots of friends, or you're like lots of people we know, who actually don't have many friends; men, especially, don't work at it so hard sometimes. It's interesting that friendship requires the *work* of friendship.

MM Yes, friendship and labor are intimately connected, mutually dependent.

SW "Friendship" is a word that's different from "solidarity," and "intermediary" is a word that's different from "solidarity." And obviously, I would have thought that "solidarity" still has very good vibes in Poland.

TARAS GEMBIK,
YULIA KRIVICH,
AND MICHAŁ MURAWSKI

THE "SUNFLOWER" SOLIDARITY COMMUNITY CENTER AS A FORM AND STRUCTURE OF FRIENDSHIP

The "Sunflower" Solidarity Community Center at the Museum of Modern Art in Warsaw was established as a relief center for solidarity and support in the first days after the start of the full-scale Russian invasion of Ukraine in February 2022. Currently, the Sunflower functions as an open, multilingual, and multicultural cultural center. The conversation took place on July 12, 2023.

Taras Gembik, cultural worker. Co-founder of the "Sunflower" Solidarity Community Center, the BLYZKIST collective, and the Anti-Crisis Club at the Museum of Modern Art in Warsaw. Coordinator of the Roma Community Center at the Foundation Towards Dialogue.

Yulia Krivich, visual artist, PhD candidate at the Academy of Fine Arts in Kraków, co-founder of the "Sunflower" Solidarity Community Center at the Museum of Modern Art in Warsaw. Participant in numerous international exhibitions and curator of projects in Ukraine, Poland, and internationally. Her work, in the ING Polish Art Foundation collection, among others, explores issues of identity, incorporating elements of activism and collective practices, while examining her own position as a migrant in Warsaw, where she lives and works.

MICHAŁ MURAWSKI How did it all start?

TARAS GEMBIK The theme of this book is friendship, and it seems to me that the "Sunflower" Solidarity Community Center (SDK "Słonecznik") was created precisely on the basis of friendship—mainly between us, the people who make it what it currently is: Maria Beburia, Yulia Krivich, Kaja Kusztra, Natalia Sielewicz, Bogna Stefańska, Kuba Depczyński, Sebastian Cichocki, and myself. But there were many more such people at the beginning—it seemed that half of Warsaw met at the Museum at 3 Pańska Street; it's impossible to forget. To this day, I feel enormous gratitude to each and every one who was with us then, in February 2022. All this was also made possible by the involvement of the Museum staff.

YULIA KRIVICH We are friends with each other and we're very close. We did a lot together before, and it was natural that we would work together again.

TG The day after the outbreak of the full-scale war, on February 25, 2022, we met with Yulia, Marta Romankiv, and many other friends. We knew we had to do something, we couldn't sit idly by. We immediately thought about the Museum, which we were friends with. We started painting protest banners there. It was then that the first requests from Ukraine for medical help reached us.

TARAS GEMBIK

> "To this day, I feel enormous gratitude to each and every one who was with us then, in February 2022."

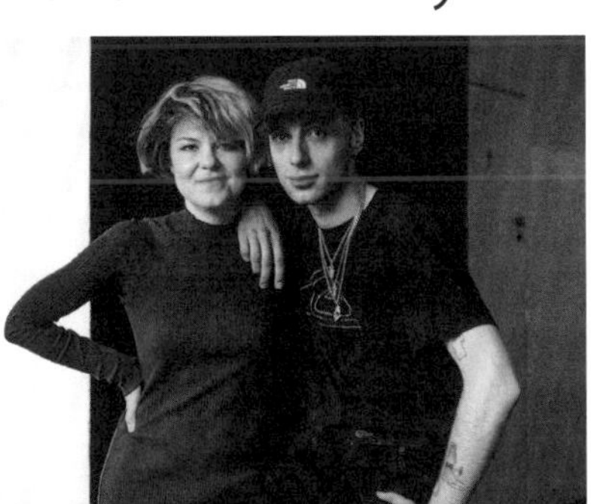

FIG. 1 YULIA KRIVICH AND TARAS GEMBIK, 2022

YK I will only add that even before the full-scale invasion, Marta and I were asked to paint a large banner. This was when Putin announced that Donbas and Luhansk were "Russian territories." Everyone expected war, but only in Donbas. So we decided to paint a huge banner, with the naive slogan "No to war." On the third day of the full-scale invasion, when we were painting it, a lot of people came to the Museum on Pańska Street and we started painting banners together for a protest in front of the Russian embassy.

TG We did the banner painting, then we started a fundraising drive for medicine together with the Małgosia Braunek "Bądź" Foundation, with which we also collected medical equipment. To this day, we continue raising funds for help and sending transports. Then, thousands of displaced people found them-

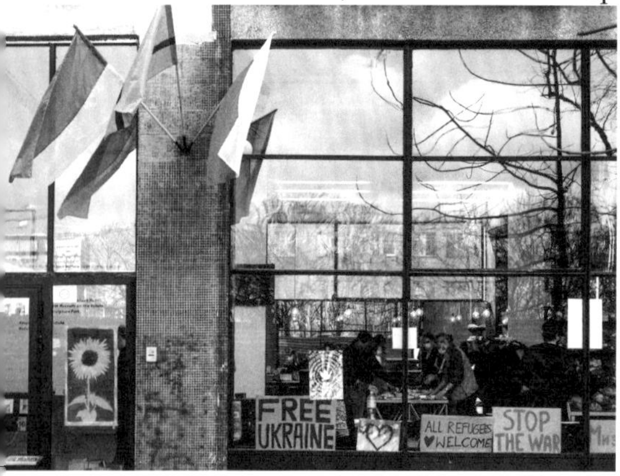

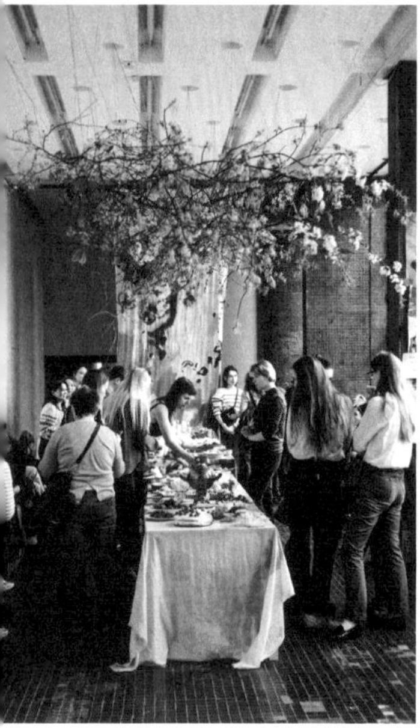

FIG. 2 ENTRANCE TO THE MUSEUM ON PAŃSKA STREET, HOSTING THE SUNFLOWER, MARCH 2022
FIG. 3 A COMMUNITY MEAL DURING EASTER CELEBRATIONS AT THE SUNFLOWER, 2022

selves on the streets of Warsaw. It turned out that the system was failing in various parts of the city, including at railway and bus stations. So we thought that we could set up a relief center in the Museum, which is located very close to the Warsaw Central railway station.

YK We can therefore say that the Sunflower arose spontaneously. It's not that we decided to do it, it just happened by itself. Everyone was shocked, no one knew what to do, everyone wanted to help. The center emerged very naturally. People started gathering there. Importantly, the space on the first floor of the Museum stood empty because post-Covid restrictions were still in place, the café was closed, etc. Nothing was happening in those two large halls, so it was a perfect moment to put them to use. Kitchen facilities were also available, where we immediately started preparing sandwiches and cooking meals.

TG A very important issue related to the beginnings of the Sunflower was that at some point the Museum lost control, like many other Warsaw institutions. Everyone was confused, and so were we. I remember the chaos. The pandemic was still officially going on in Poland, so the Museum had to follow certain restrictions, and then suddenly hundreds of people started passing through 3 Pańska Street. All previous laws and regulations ceased to apply. This was a very important moment when we took over the reins.

YK I remember moments when the entire Museum team came to us and asked: what are we doing today? As if we had become managers for a moment and taken control.

At that time, numerous institutions were attempting to provide help and transform their galleries into shelters for refugees, very noble ideas. Sometimes those ideas didn't work, because what it takes is not only infrastructure, but also special competences and long-term cooperation with people. Such initiatives—such as a shelter for BIPOC and Roma people organized by Biennale Warszawa or a fantastic shelter in Wrocław designed by Japanese architect Shigeru Ban—existed for several months.

The Sunflower emerged as a goods collection and fundraising hub, a support center for people on the move, and a collective operating at the intersection of a cultural institution and grassroots activism.

We managed to organize ourselves differently, and thus for the long run, because we were able to constantly adapt activities to the needs of people who were arriving in Poland at that time.

The Museum management gave us space and allowed us to manage it, which benefited everyone. But they did more than just give us a free hand—for example, Joanna Mytkowska and other managers tapped into their contacts to support the fundraisers we organized. Most of the team was actively involved in providing help and support.

MM Did you have the keys to the space on Pańska Street?

TG Yes, we did. That's an important thing, such keys. After a few weeks, when the situation stabilized somewhat, we decided that it was a good time to come up with a certain form, a certain structure that would enable us to continue operating sustainably. And since then we have been operating as the "Sunflower" Solidarity Community Center.

YK We organize artistic events that aim to support aid and social-impact initiatives. We host workshops, meetings, performances, and discussions about migration, Eastern Europe, and Russian colonialism. We also organize poetry nights, charity events, and film screenings. The international think tank SONIAKH, an online platform counteracting disinformation and propaganda in the face of the Russian invasion, was also established at 3 Pańska Street. At the same time, the Sunflower operates as an artistic collective, collaborating with other cultural institutions in Poland and abroad.

MM How did the Solidarity Community Center's name and visual identity come about?

YK Kaja Kusztra worked with us and created a lot of graphic designs. We organized new events every day and Kaja managed to keep pace with the demand for new posters day and night

The logo, like everything else, was created through collaboration [FIG. 4]. Photographer friends offered to set up a free studio at 3 Pańska Street for people who needed ID photos for Polish registration documents. Do you remember those long queues for photocopiers, currency exchange offices, and photo studios at that time? It was mostly mothers with children who came to us to have their photos taken, and while the mothers were waiting in line, someone had to take care of the children. So we started collaborating with the Maria Grzegorzewska University for special education, whose students conducted drawing and therapeutic workshops with those kids. One of these workshops was devoted to drawing sunflowers. Kaja added a face from a painting by Maria Prymachenko to one of the drawings. Just then, on February 28, 2022, the Historical and Local History Museum in Ivankiv was burned down to the ground as a result of Russian shelling, destroying twenty of Prymachenko's paintings.

The name "Sunflower" was invented spontaneously by Kuba Depczyński. It was inspired by a viral video about a woman in Henichesk who wanted to put sunflower seeds in a Russian soldier's pocket so that they would grow when he gets killed. We always start

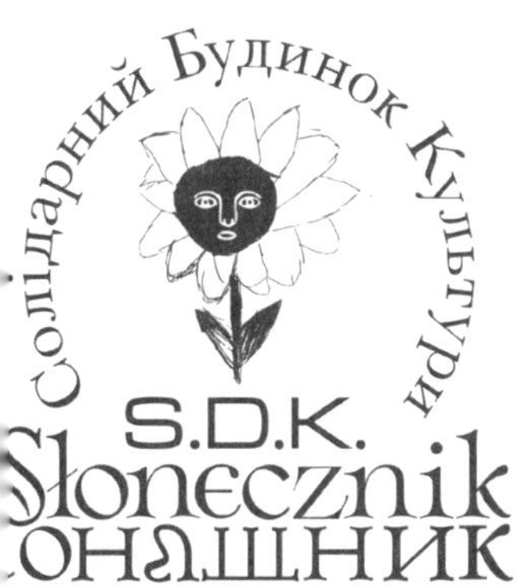

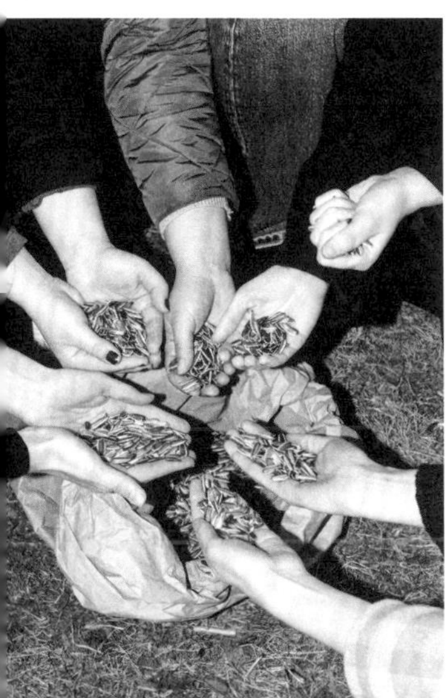

FIG. 4 THE SUNFLOWER LOGO, DESIGNED IN 2022 BY KAJA KUSZTRA AND THE "SUNFLOWER" SCC COMMUNITY
FIG. 5 SUNFLOWER SEEDS HELD BY MEMBERS OF THE SUNFLOWER TEAM AND FRIENDS: JULIANA ALIMOVA, TARAS GEMBIK, YULIA KRIVICH, KAT OLESHKO, PLANETA, MARTA ROMANKIV, NADIA SNOPEK, ASIA TSISAR

with this story when we talk about the Sunflower. We show this video because it is very powerful. It gave us a lot of strength as an expression of symbolic protest at a very difficult time—Russian troops were near Kyiv then.

It's important to emphasize that in Polish, the Sunflower is not called a "community center" but a "House of Culture" (Dom Kultury). I personally like the concept of the House of Culture very much, and I am emotionally attached to it. In Dnipro, where I am from, there is the Ilyich Palace of Culture, a beautiful building where I started attending drawing and painting classes when I was twelve, but the 2000s essentially marked the decline of its activity **[FIG. 6]**. I feel sentimental about the institution of the House of Culture, and I like the fact that it is possible to somehow use this aspect of the Soviet legacy, changing its meaning to move away from the painful or traumatic experiences of the past, and also combine it with the Museum of Modern Art in Warsaw in 2022. I really like the fact that it is not just a "center," but, in the original name, it is precisely the "Sunflower" Solidarity House of Culture.

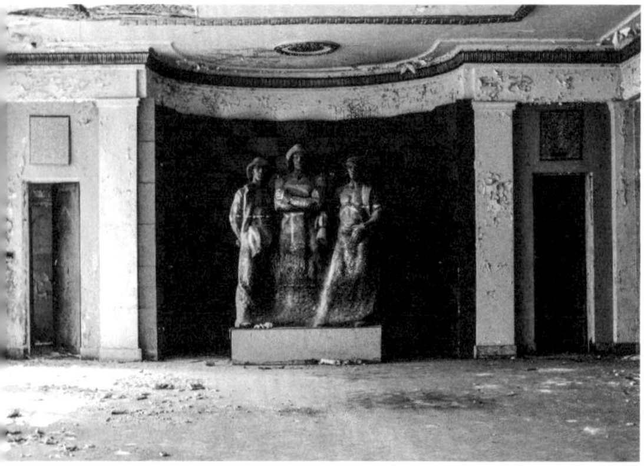

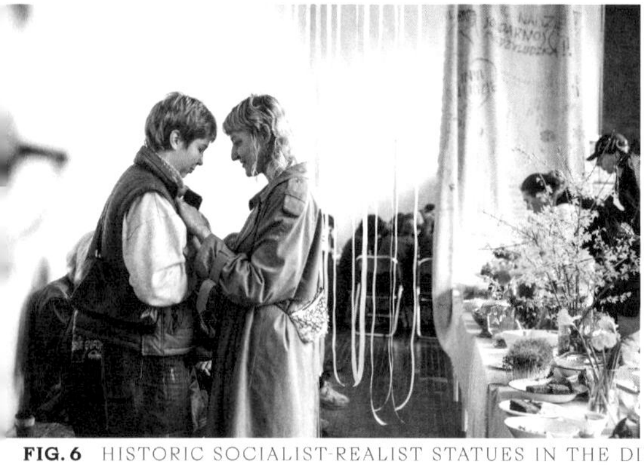

FIG. 6 HISTORIC SOCIALIST-REALIST STATUES IN THE DILAPIDATED INTERIOR OF THE ILYICH PALACE OF CULTURE IN DNIPRO, UKRAINE. PHOTO: YULIA KRIVICH, FROM *THE PALACE OF CULTURE* SERIES, 2016

FIG. 7 THE SUNFLOWER IS A SPACE OF SOLIDARITY, FRIENDSHIP AND EMPATHY. EASTER CELEBRATION IN 2023

MM But not the "Sunflower" Palace of Culture?

YK No, although in Dnipro it was the Palace of Culture, already in serious decline at the time, with ruined Lenin busts in the corridors. It only housed an art school, which I went to.

TG In my town, in Kamin-Kashyrskyi in Volhynia, there was only one House of Culture, the only institution of this kind in the town, so I also have a lot of sentiment for this place. My mother is a violinist and all the concerts took place there, as did all the artistic and cultural life in the town.

YK So the name and this whole structure appeared right in the first days. We were in a frenzy. Dissociation. I was sitting on a bench somewhere, crying, then there were people in my house, girls that my neighbor kept bringing from the border. I no longer really remember how things happened.

MM Apart from that, were you in contact with your families and friends in Volhynia and in Dnipro?

YK They called all the time.

MM During those days and later, did you gain a deeper understanding of concepts such as solidarity, friendship, empathy?

YK You know, I'm glad I live in Central and Eastern Europe and I'm among people who understand what's going on. I don't have to explain it to them. The "wave of solidarity" could be very strongly felt in Poland, and that was beautiful. Maybe a little naive, but beautiful. Regardless of their background and political views, people supported Ukraine, driving to the border to pick up refugees. But I know that at the same time on another Polish border, that with Belarus, people were dying. It's terrible, and we have to talk about it too. Nevertheless,

YULIA KRIVICH

> " The 'wave of solidarity' could be very strongly felt in Poland, and that was beautiful. Maybe a little naive, but beautiful. "

at that moment I felt very safe in Poland—not so much in physical terms, just because there was no war going on here, but in psychological terms, because I was in a safe space. This was crucial for us when creating and working at the Sunflower, which was intended precisely as such a safe space for people fleeing war, migrants, refugees—for everyone in need.

This first surge was, of course, temporary. It is natural that people cannot keep the same level of excitement for long when faced with an exceptional situation. But all there was at the beginning were people, volunteers, our friends who shuttled to the border, helped at train stations, etc. For the first time in eleven or twelve years of my life in this country I saw a different Poland, which I had not seen before. Of course, this changed and we returned to everyday life, but even with all the issues, I saw that there was potential. I felt a similar energy during the "Black Protests" for the support of womens' reproductive autonomy.[1] And it was a very powerful experience in every respect.

MM Let's return to the topic of friendship, to the new Museum building, and the idea that it will house Alina Szapocznikow's *Monument to Polish-Soviet Friendship*, a sculpture created in 1954 in praise of friendship between the two countries. Of course, this plan had already been conceived earlier, after the work was bought at auction in 2019 and deposited with the Museum. However, the outbreak of full-scale war sparked some discussion on the topic. Do you have any thoughts?

TG History is difficult. There is no denying that our legacy is not only modernism, but the aesthetics of Stalinist socialist realism. People whom I personally believe and trust very much are working on this issue, the curatorial team, the Museum management, and others.

The beautiful thing is that this sculpture is deformed, its hands are missing. It seems to me that the future in which it will be inscribed will depend on us: the public, the educators, the people who will create the Sunflower. On the other hand, we see what is happening to such monuments in Ukraine, where they

1 The Black Protests began in Poland in 2016, when the Law and Justice-led government proposed further tightening Poland's already very restrictive anti-abortion laws and instituting a near-total ban on abortion. The laws were passed and implemented in 2020 and, despite the promises of the new government elected in 2023 to reverse them, they remain in place to this day. The social movement which was formed during the protests—the All-Poland Women's Strike—remains active and, at the time of writing, the Black Protests continue.

are dismantled. However, most of the culture and art community is of the opinion that they should not be destroyed, but preserved and placed in museums, which must critically reflect on this heritage.

YK I understand that the history of Szapocznikow's sculpture is very significant, and the severed arms have a symbolic meaning. What's more, it is a link with the nearby Palace of Culture and Science, which I also consider a beautiful building and symbol, the heart of Warsaw. The point is to build something on this traumatic past.

This is all the more significant, given that the white Museum building standing next to the Palace looks quite detached from its surroundings. So, in a sense, *Friendship* doesn't only exist inside the Museum, but also embeds the building in its environment.

This is another element in the current discussion on the use of the term "post-Soviet," as Olexii Kuchanskyi wrote in their essay in *SONIAKH digest*.[2] I like this idea of building something not "beyond" but on the basis of what we already have. The point is not to destroy and reject, but to build and transform.

TG This is the context we live in, and it cannot be erased. We already know that we need to learn from history to avoid repeating it in the future, but 2022 has shown that those "never again" slogans are simply rubbish. It is up to us how we will continue to steer and manage it.

YK Nevertheless, installing this sculpture in such a central place in the building—regardless of whether it will stand with or without Nikita Kadan's work alongside it[3]—is a very strong gesture. Coming back to the term "post-Soviet," you need to be careful with it. For example, Associated Press journalists were advised not to use this terminology. It seems to me that we should exercise similar caution about totalitarian symbolism in Poland and other countries. I have nothing against using it, but this question needs to be asked because we are talking about the very center of the capital, where the Museum of Modern Art is to open—a long-awaited institution, one of the largest modern art museums in this

2 Olexii Kuchanskyi, "Exodus from the post-Soviet Condition," *SONIAKH digest*, November 24, 2022, https://soniakh.com/index.php/2022/11/24/exodus-from-the-post-soviet-condition/.

3 Nikita Kadan's sculpture *Gazelka* —a steel flag—will be displayed at the MSN collection exhibition in 2025 as a counterpoint to Szapocznikow's work.

part of Europe. And placing the *Friendship* sculpture there reintroduces a primarily post-Soviet context.

MM Piotr Piotrowski once wrote about traumaphilia vs. traumaphobia in the context of art museums' approach to history. The Museum of Modern Art did not exist yet, but Piotrowski gave the example of the National Museum of Contemporary Art (MNAC) in Bucharest, situated in the People's Palace, a monumental government building erected by Ceaușescu, which, in his opinion, was traumaphobic because, despite its location, it distanced itself from the local trauma.[4] Ten years ago, this traumaphilia seemed to be a good direction for us, but maybe now it's different, maybe we need to change our approach

YK The point isn't now to change, erase, and ruin again. I think Polish society and other postcommunist countries still need this discussion. Are we still post-Soviet in 2024? It's a bit like the cover of the first Polish issue of *Vogue* magazine: the Palace of Culture, a black Volga limousine, and beautiful girls. A kind of self-exoticization.

MM Have you already imagined the best place for the Sunflower in the new MSN building?

TARAS GEMBIK

“ What will be done to make this Museum more open, more tolerant, more empathetic, more multilingual, multicultural, etc. I hope that this building will also offer space, especially, for socially excluded, marginalized groups. ”

4 Piotr Piotrowski, “New Museums in East-Central Europe: Between Traumaphobia and Traumaphilia,” in *1968–1989: Political upheaval and artistic change*, ed. Claire Bishop and Marta Dziewańska (Warsaw: Museum of Modern Art, 2009), 148–166.

TG We joke among ourselves that it would be best if they would just give us the space at 3 Pańska Street; we would be happy to stay there—I got used to it. The new Museum now seems very sterile, white-cube style, but I am very curious how it will be arranged.

MM As the work progresses, the Museum building seems whiter and whiter to me. A bit exaggerated in this whiteness.

YK It just looks very strange next to the Palace of Culture, and I'm surprised that it's so white. Interestingly, in recent years, many museums have been wondering how to move away from the white-cube model, and here the long-awaited Museum of Modern Art is being created, which is a white cube not only on the inside, but also on the outside! A white cube squared.

TG What seems much more important to me is what will be done to make this Museum more open, more tolerant, more empathetic, more multilingual, multicultural, etc. I hope that this building will also offer space, especially, for socially-excluded, marginalized groups, that it will be multilingual, and that each and everyone will feel at home there. This is very important in a world of ongoing wars and escalating crises.

MM It is fascinating how this building will transform this institution and all these relationships we are talking about today, which have spatial, ideological, and practical dimensions—truth, friendship, and solidarity in the face of horrific events.

TG I'm concerned about this, but the Museum is still under construction and bottom-up initiatives are still possible. I'm afraid that this spirit will be lost as a result of "professionalization" and the operation of the institutional machine, which unfortunately often excludes certain people and groups.

MM Will solidarity and friendship, which are somewhat at odds with this professionalization, still be possible in the context of such a building? Will it allow these bonds to be maintained, or will the whiteness and vastness of this architecture compel a different outcome? This will be an interesting experiment.

TG At the Sunflower, today and in the future, we want to forge trans-local solidarity in spite of evil: multilevel, multidirectional solidarity. Solidarity with people and groups who, like us, want to regain freedom, culture, identity, and the right to their land.

YK Poland is a great place where many trails converge, where everyone meets: on the border of the European Union, right next to Ukraine. For example, a lot of people now come here from Central Asia: Tajikistan, Kyrgyzstan, Kazakhstan, etc. This region is not widely known in Poland and Europe. We would like the Sunflower to reach beyond the Ukrainian community, and serve to spread knowledge about art as well as artistic and activist communities in various countries.

This is our plan for the future. We understand that it's difficult to talk about solidarity with Ukraine without also talking about solidarity with other countries that were and are under Russia's thumb. Their situation is, in a sense, even worse than that of Ukraine. However, the whole of Europe and the world reacted to this war, and it would probably be different in the case of Belarus or Kazakhstan. What matters to us is Ukrainian solidarity with all countries that are trying to wrest independence from Russia, as well as with all countries and groups that are fighting a decolonial struggle.

ZYGMUNT BORAWSKI,
MARLENA HAPPACH,
DOROTA JĘDRUCH,
AND MICHAŁ MURAWSKI

WE NO LONGER HAVE TO ERASE ANYTHING

Parade Square (Plac Defilad) is a sensitive point in the history and urban planning of Warsaw. This huge socialist-realist square was built in 1955 on the site of a nineteenth-century district largely destroyed by the Nazis, part of which had been incorporated into the Warsaw Ghetto. It became the site of events and confrontations that shaped Poland's postwar history. A few snapshots: Labor Day parades on May 1; Leonid Brezhnev speaking from the Tribune of Honor, which has been preserved to this day; Władysław Gomułka announcing reforms as part of the political thaw in 1956; John Paul II celebrating mass in 1987; a gigantic marketplace and other spontaneous architecture of early capitalism emerging here after 1989; merchants clashing with police in 2009; the reprivatization scandal breaking out in 2016; Piotr Szczęsny committing self-immolation in protest against restricting democratic freedoms during the rule of the Law and Justice (PiS) party in 2017. All of this forms a mosaic of changes leading from authoritarianism to neoliberalism. Settled in 2017, the competition for the design of Central Square (Plac Centralny, part of Parade Square) was organized to integrate this space into the logic of the planned New Center of Warsaw, with an emphasis on greenery, pedestrian traffic, and zero-emission transport. Is this type of eco-therapy enough to heal old traumas? Or perhaps this can only be achieved by means of a courageous confrontation with our own history? Dorota Jędruch and Michał Murawski discuss these issues with one of the designers of the new square, Zygmunt Borawski of the A-A Collective architectural studio, and City Architect of Warsaw (from 2016 to 2024) Marlena Happach. The conversation took place on February 20, 2023 (and was updated in February 2024).

Dorota Jędruch, lecturer at the Modern Art History Department of the Institute of the History of Art, Jagiellonian University in Kraków. Co-curator of exhibitions, including: *Impossible Objects* (Polish Pavilion, 14th International Architecture Exhibition in Venice, 2014), *Home at Last: The Polish House during the Transition* (8th WARSAW UNDER CONSTRUCTION festival, 2016), *Museum Power* (National Museum in Kraków, 2021). Co-founder of the Institute of Architecture foundation. Regular contributor to the quarterly *Autoportret*.

Marlena Happach, architect, urban planner, and social activist based in Warsaw. Co-founder of the Odblokuj Association. From 2012–16, she was vice-president and then president of the Warsaw Branch of the Association of Polish Architects (OW SARP). From 2016–24, she served as City Architect of Warsaw and was the director of the Office of Architecture and Spatial Planning of the Capital City of Warsaw. Since June 2024, she is acting director of the National Heritage Institute.

A-A Collective, an international interdisciplinary practice focused on architecture, with members in Basel, Copenhagen, Milan, and Warsaw. The collective came together in Switzerland, founded by Zygmunt Borawski, Martin Marker, Furio Montoli, and Srdjan Zlokapa. They are the architects behind the winning entries in the competitions for the Warsaw Central Square (2018) and the Arch for Sønderjylland in Kolding, Denmark (2020).

Zygmunt Borawski, architect, educator, and journalist. Co-founder of international architecture studio A-A Collective, with which he won the competition for the design of the Central Square in Warsaw, Poland in 2018. He has simultaneously been leading his private practice since 2020. From 2015 to 2020, he was the editor of the Architecture and Design section of the Polish cultural magazine *Przekrój*. He taught at the Warsaw University of Technology (2021–2022) and has been a teaching assistant at the Accademia di Architettura in Mendrisio, Switzerland, since 2022.

CENTRAL SQUARE

ORGANIZER: CAPITAL CITY OF WARSAW
ARCHITECTURAL AND LANDSCAPE DESIGN: A-A COLLECTIVE (ZYGMUNT BORAWSKI, SRDJAN ZLOKAPA, FURIO MONTOLI, MARTIN MARKER)

COLLABORATION (PLANTING PLAN): MARTA TOMASIAK

CLIENT: MUNICIPAL ROADS AUTHORITY (ZDM) OF THE CITY OF WARSAW

CONTRACTOR: BALZOLA POLSKA SP. Z O.O.

DOROTA JĘDRUCH I believe that from a topographical point of view, no Parade Square exists. It is more of a theoretical construct. I am unable to delineate its boundaries, and the almost identical façades of the Palace of Culture and Science confuse my sense of direction. It happened to me many times that I circled around the Palace in search of this place. That space is often traversed by random travelers who do not even register it. If we lend this site a spatial identity, and if we endow it with an architectural image, we can allow it to be defined urbanistically. But first of all, I would like to ask about the memories and emotions that the Palace of Culture and Parade Square evoke in you.

MARLENA HAPPACH I have had a strong bond with the Palace for a long time. I'm a Varsovian by birth. Where I lived as a child, it could be seen from the windows on the horizon. It seemed to mark the center of my world. To this day, it helps me orient myself in the city wherever I am—it's my compass. And I will always have an emotional approach to it, because it is not just a point on the map, but—just like for thousands of people from Warsaw—a symbol of the place where we grew up.

DJ And the square?

MH I don't remember the May Day parades, but I remember the great market, the Merchants' Department Store (KDT) halls, then the subway and the "Frying Pan."[1] I was fascinated by the idea of emergent architecture as described by Aleksandra Wasilkowska, which explains

1 "Patelnia"—the colloquial name of the square located in front of the southern exits of the Centrum metro station.

the natural way in which the bazaar was created here in the 1990s. Although it's not entirely true, because it was planned. Henryk Drzewiecki, the city's Chief Architect at the time, together with Krzysztof Domaradzki, delineated these alleys to temporarily manage the space. As a result, it was not developed in the 1980s and 1990s – they did not want to leave it to chance. Later, competitions were held to find a way of developing the site. I remember that when I took up my position, the director of the Warsaw Rising Museum, Jan Ołdakowski, asked me what I would do in Warsaw as City Architect if I could only do one thing. Without hesitation, I answered that it would be Parade Square.

ZYGMUNT BORAWSKI Until the end of the 1990s, the Palace almost did not exist for me. My life was confined to the Mokotów area; I went to school there and rarely ventured into the city center. Only on weekends my father and I went to the Mirowskie Market Halls[2] for shopping, but even then he managed to avoid the Palace—I don't know if that was on purpose. I was more intrigued by the Marriott and Elektrim skyscrapers.

I said "almost" because I had a view of it from my attic room in Mokotów, so I saw it every morning when I got out of bed and when I went to sleep at night. At some point it also became visible at night, when a clock was installed on it in 1999, followed by red aircraft warning lights in 2010. For a long time I had no reason to visit the Palace. I was afraid of it, of its scale and

2 Hale Mirowskie—two twin market halls in the Mirów neighborhood in central Warsaw.

monumentality. Now, however, I have perhaps even too much to do with it. The Palace has become an important part of my life. I've come to like it, to appreciate its architecture and incredible interiors.

DJ So working on this project does not involve an emotional burden for you?

ZB As a resident of Warsaw, it's hard not to have an emotional attitude toward the Palace—you always have an opinion about it. Over time, I've come to appreciate it. However, I believe that its sprawling nature makes it impossible to approach it. Its proportions are very problematic—not so much in terms of height, but in terms of the way it projects itself onto the city, on the horizontal, not on the vertical axis. Paradoxically, however, this sprawl makes it the only public building that still stands its ground in the struggle against the glass corporate towers, and it courageously punctuates the urban skyline.

ZYGMUNT BORAWSKI

" As a resident of Warsaw, it's hard not to have an emotional attitude toward the Palace—you always have an opinion about it. However, I believe that its sprawling nature makes it impossible to approach it. "

DJ Your design for Central Square, encompassing a vast, separated portion of Parade Square, was selected in a competition organized in 2017. From the very beginning it was widely discussed, which was also due to the open formula of the competition, as requested by, among others, The City Is Ours (Miasto Jest Nasze) association. There were public consultations, an exhibition and a post-competition discussion, workshops for local institutions and businesses—that is for those operating on and around Parade Square—for adults and youth, and online consultations, which were extremely popular.

MH This was one of the ideas that guided me and which I talked about when running for the position of City Architect. We were looking for a possible consultation procedure in public procurement law that would work in this case. We used an

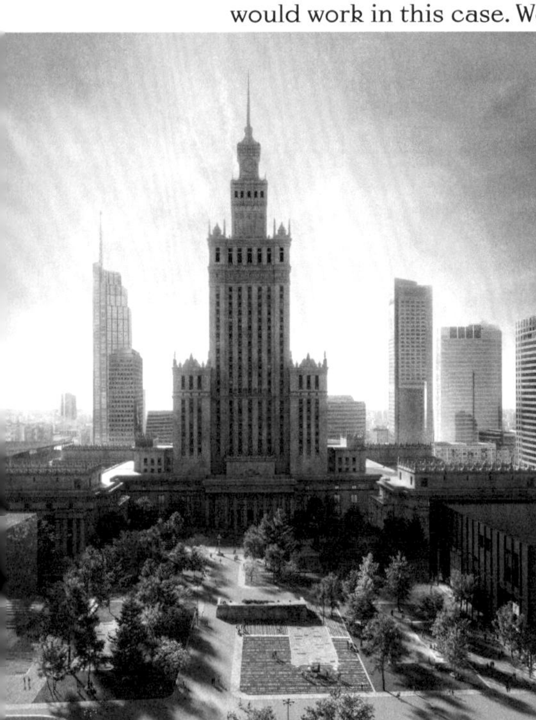

FIG. 1 VISUALIZATION OF THE DESIGN OF WARSAW'S CENTRAL SQUARE BY A-A COLLECTIVE, BIRD'S-EYE VIEW

unusual formula, which has never been repeated because it has major drawbacks. In fact, we carried out two separate procedures. First, there was a competition in which we selected five entries, followed by public consultations and the second stage of the competition, in which we selected one winner. It was risky, but I don't regret it. We were tired of talking about the square, because there had been a lot of similar consultations and discussions before. More and more designs were created on paper, but in reality nothing changed.

DJ So this was a certain model of involving the public in the competition procedure under existing law?

MH Yes, although it requires great openness on all sides, because the idea was also that the authors would modify their designs under the influence of the consultations.

DJ After the consultations and the second stage of the competition, you decided that A-A Collective's concept best met your expectations. What were the criteria and justifications for selecting the winning design?

MH The openness of the competition meant that a lot of works were submitted, of very different quality. In the assessment, we took into account many aspects, starting with prosaic technical elements such as water drainage. One of the most important issues was the underground parking garage planned at this stage. At the time, everyone assumed that it was to be a space for mass events, where the city's New Year's Eve celebrations or the Great Orchestra of Christmas Charity (WOŚP) grand finale could be organized. Trees were therefore excluded not only because of the garage, but also as an obstacle to the organization of mass gatherings. Not everyone knows that there is a significant difference in levels between the steps to the Palace's front square and Marszałkowska Street, so accessibility for people with limited mobility was an important element in the discussion.

In hindsight, I see several trends that dominated the submitted projects. One of them was an open form—a square where anything can happen. I recognize this way of thinking from the redevelopment of the square in front of the ZODIAK Warsaw Pavilion of Architecture. But even in such a small square it is difficult to organize something all the time. And Parade Square is too large to function without a leading, permanent program. The second trend was for park landscape-type designs, of which there were also very many. Such concepts are great and can be implemented in many places in the city, but here we wanted something more. There were also designs based on a clear main idea, ingenious in their approach to the site, but also open to what could happen there. And there were very few such entries. From among the shortlisted five, apart from the winning one, I also recall a design that covered part of the square with water[3] and a proposal to build a sunken basin in the center of the square.[4] In the second stage, which took place after the consultations, we paid particular attention to the quality

3 Entry No. 02: Michał Czeszejko-Sochacki, Antoni Domicz, Małgorzata Pizio-Domicz, Dawid Wiśniewski.
4 Entry No. 16: Jakub Figel, Filip Kurasz.

of public space and its ability to dynamically respond to constant changes in the city. The winning design stands precisely for this—grass, water, or stone can appear in the outlines of the formerly existing tenement houses, but the idea remains the same. It is flexible and at the same time never loses its identity.

DJ According to the report on public consultations,[5] this design was also the most commented on.

ZB And the most criticized.

DJ Perhaps not so much the most criticized, but very hotly discussed. It was the subject of as many as 831 out of the 1,670 surveys completed online. How did you create the design? How do you operate as a studio?

ZB It all started in Paris in 2017, where I went to an architecture writing workshop organized by the Architectural Association. After a few days, I was joined by Srdjan Zlokapa, with whom I studied at the Academy of Architecture in Mendrisio and we became close friends. I mentioned the Parade Square competition to him and said that I would really like to do it. I also knew that Martin Marker was working with Srdjan, so we contacted him and started thinking.

DJ So that's when you got together as a studio. You didn't work together before?

ZB We didn't. It was only then that we formed a partnership. Here, we come to who we are and why we designed the square in this and not another way. Srdjan is a Bosnian Serb who has spent his entire life in Italy because his family fled there from

5 "Jaki Plac Defilad? Przeczytaj raport z konsultacji społecznych!" Urząd m.st. Warszawy, December 13, 2017, https://architektura.um.warszawa.pl/-/jaki-plac-defilad-przeczytaj-raport-z-konsultacji-spolecznych-.

the war. Martin is 100% Danish, but he has an exceptionally un-Scandinavian passion for the Baroque.

In the second stage of the competition, we were joined by another friend from the academy, Furio Montoli, who is half-Italian, half-Japanese, but grew up in Milan. I, in turn, am half-Italian, half-Polish, I was born in Florence and I often went there for vacations and public holidays. Italy and Italian architecture have been and remain a constant point of reference for us.

DJ When I look at your website and the website of Thomas Phifer, the designer of the Museum of Modern Art and the TR Warszawa theater buildings, I can clearly see a difference: his projects are solid, decent, beautifully designed, but also cold, and yours are truly temperamental and eclectic.

ZB This eclecticism has many sources, but it comes mainly from the fact that we make all decisions democratically. It's not easy, because there are four of us, so when it is two against two, we have an impasse and arguments start, but in the end we manage. A journalist once asked us

ZYGMUNT BORAWSKI

" I showed the team the old street grid, and so we thought it would be great to refer to it somehow. We were lucky because this grid gave us many possibilities. "

where our office was, and one of us cleverly replied that it was "somewhere between easyJet and WhatsApp." Between low-cost airlines and instant messengers. And, horror of horrors, this is exactly how we designed the entire Central Square.

When we started working on the design, we knew that history would be a very important element of it—you can't escape it when designing in Warsaw. One day I showed the team the old street grid, and so we thought it would be great to refer to it somehow. We were lucky because this grid, which suddenly became the leitmotif of the design, gave us many possibilities, among other things because it diverged from the axis of the Palace of Culture. We realized that this monumental spatial arrangement can only be dismantled by sticking strictly to the historical one and not aligning the axis of Złota Street with the axis of the Palace, because that would further strengthen the symmetry of the arrangement. We were delighted that these two axes clashed with each other. A fabulous posthumous dialectic of bourgeois speculation and Soviet authoritarianism.

DJ Yes, the axiality and centrality of this arrangement are located somewhere in the center of the world, as Zbigniew Benedyktowicz wrote in his essay "Widmo środka świata" (The specter of the center of the world).[6]

ZB We do not disturb the symmetry of the existing arrangement,

6 Zbigniew Benedyktowicz, "Widmo środka świata," *Konteksty: polska sztuka ludowa, antropologia kultury, etnografia, sztuka* 45, no. 1 (1991): 16–32. Drawing on Mircea Eliade's thought on the manifestations of the sacred in the secular realm, Benedyktowicz writes: "The Palace of Culture interests me, therefore, as an element of the symbolic imagination, as a structure of long duration. That's why I want to look at the Palace of Culture in relation to the complex and symbolic cycle of the 'center,'" 18. See also Michał Murawski, *The Palace Complex: A Stalinist Skyscraper, Capitalist Warsaw, and a City Transfixed* (Bloomington: Indiana University Press, 2019), 178–242.

apart from planting a few trees behind the tribune that do not line up with the axis of the Palace. The disruption of symmetry visible from the bird's-eye view will not be so noticeable in the actual space, at street level.

DJ What period does the street grid you use come from?

ZB From the first half of the twentieth century, but it had begun to take shape in the first half of the nineteenth century. At the time, small industrial plants and workshops were

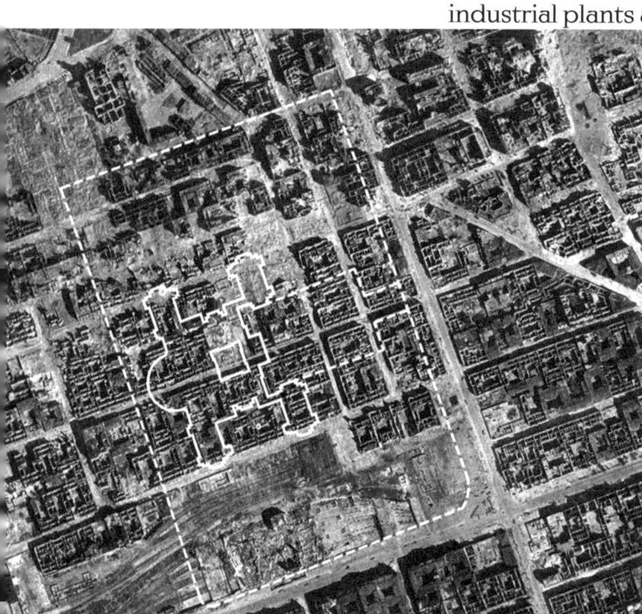

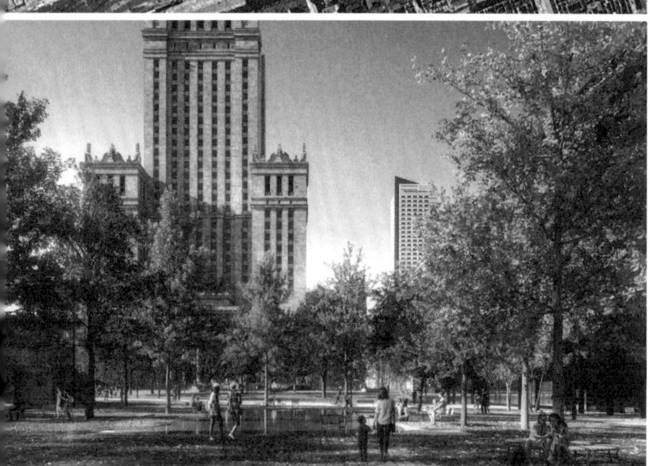

FIG. 2 AN ARCHIVAL PHOTOGRAPH OF WARSAW'S DEVASTATION AFTER WORLD WAR II IS OVERLAID WITH THE MODERN-DAY FOOTPRINT OF THE PALACE OF CULTURE
FIG. 3 VISUALIZATION OF THE DESIGN OF WARSAW'S CENTRAL SQUARE BY A-A COLLECTIVE, POND VIEW

built on Złota, Wielka, and Zielna Streets. At the turn of the twentieth century, they began to be supplanted by tenement houses, and things continued in this way right until World War II. At first, we wanted to combine all possible historical layers and precisely map the transformations of the city center. I started collecting all the maps I came across: from the nineteenth century, the turn of the century, the interwar period, and from World War II. We also started looking for various plans for the postwar reconstruction of the city, including Maciej Nowicki's design.[7] We then created a palimpsest of five, six, seven layers—existing, non-existent, and imagined—from which we could create an entire composition.

DJ Did you have any other ideas for it apart from introducing greenery?

ZB No. Greenery is a very characteristic element of Warsaw—a city with many parks and green squares. Greenery is omnipresent here and we would like it to be present at Central Square as well. From the very beginning, we dreamed of candelabra growing out of the lawns.

DJ But this greenery is postwar; the city does not owe it to nineteenth-century Warsaw.

ZB I know, but our goal was not just to recreate prewar Warsaw. One of the layers that we keep is the socialist-realist layer. But it was the greenery that allowed us to adopt a truly radical course. During the first stage of the competition, we decided to leave less than half of the

7 Maciej Nowicki (1910–1950) was a Polish architect working internationally, notably including the United States, and author of plans for the postwar reconstruction of Warsaw.

paved surface and turn the rest, 60–70 percent, into a park-square—a huge lawn where you can lie down, play ball, and organize parties. The marked inner yards of the former tenement houses were supposed to be lonely islands in a sea of greenery. At that stage, we imagined that each institution based at the square could have its own courtyard and

ZYGMUNT BORAWSKI

"From the very beginning, we wanted to retain elements of the socialist-realist composition: the candelabra, the tribune, which would slowly overgrow with vegetation in the spirit of eighteenth-century English parks."

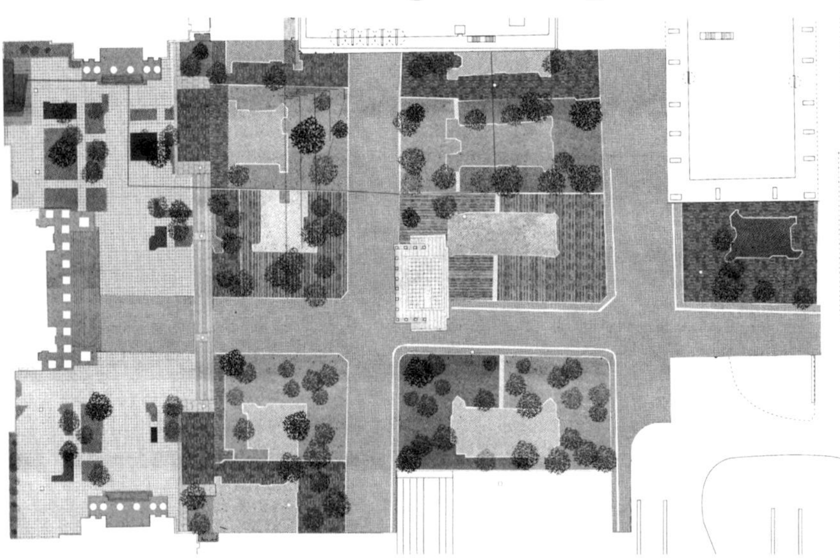

FIG 4 VISUALIZATION OF THE DESIGN OF WARSAW'S CENTRAL SQUARE BY A-A COLLECTIVE. SQUARE PAVING AND PLANT ARRANGEMENT SCHEME

organize events there. Each one was to be paved with a different type of stone. From the very beginning, we wanted to retain elements of the socialist-realist composition: the candelabra, the tribune, which would slowly overgrow with vegetation in the spirit of eighteenth-century English parks. We got a lot of flak for wanting to keep the tribune, including from the *Gazeta Wyborcza* daily newspaper. However, we wanted to superimpose all these historical layers on top of each other to create, as in Robert Venturi's work, a complex and sometimes self-contradictory composition.

DJ What was the significance of this historical layer for your partners who know the identity of this place only from theory?

ZB Srdjan and Martin were delighted with the prewar street grid and socialist-realist buildings. They knew the origins of this architecture and its political connotations. We have all read Aldo Rossi's *The Architecture of the City*, and decided that these elements are part of Warsaw's collective memory and we don't want to get rid of them. At the beginning, our obvious inspiration were Italian squares marked out in the Middle Ages and the Renaissance, which, however, were devoid of trees. Establishing parks was not necessary then, because you could quickly go beyond the walls of the much smaller cities at the time. Today, building a two-hectare, completely paved square devoid of greenery and trees in the heart of a European metropolis would not be, to put it mildly, a good idea.

DJ A square and a park are not the same. You are talking about a "park-square," a hybrid form. What other inspirations accompanied your design?

ZB For example, Place des Vosges in Paris or Place Dauphine, which I like for its characteristic triangular shape, intimate scale, and its surface made of natural minerals, on which residents play boules. We have often thought about these squares, although they are too formal, constrained by a corset of symmetry. Piazza Fontanesi in Reggio Emilia and the Beestenmarkt in Delft are also beautiful. These are large, rectangular squares with a regular grid of trees and old stone floors. However, we did not only look at squares, but also carefully studied Alvar Aalto's designs. His town halls in Seinäjoki and Säynätsalo use, among others, terrain stairs covered with overgrowing grass. Aalto was exceptionally good with landforms and beautifully integrated his buildings with the landscape.

MH I often mention the example of Seinäjoki in discussions. Without it, it's hard for me to explain that the square can be green. The prevailing belief is that a square is concrete, or the design is referred to as a hybrid, something like a park.

DJ What plant species did you include in the design? Allegedly some of them are invasive?

ZB We have fifteen species of trees, eleven shrubs, forty-one perennials, six bulb plants. We will plant, among others: three-thorned locusts, narrow-leaved ash trees, ginkgo bilobas, edible dogwoods, katsuras, Japanese magnolias, bird cherry trees, beeches, larches, and maples. Originally, we planned robinias, because the few planted back in the 1950s on the nearby Piękna Street look great. However, dendrological consultations showed that they pose a major threat to other species, so we replaced them with linden trees.

DJ The competition design was created in 2017. Since then, there have been many opportunities to discuss it, including as part of the abovementioned public consultations. Various arguments have been raised against it. For example, that it is an intellectual provocation. Were you aware that your work could be controversial?

ZB Yes and no. We expected there would be polemics, but we didn't think we would be accused of provocation. From the very beginning we approached the matter very seriously. The desire to create something radical did not come from the desire to show off, but from the belief that in the era of climate change we need to start thinking radically. In addition, Central Square required a radical design because the Palace of Culture itself is a very radical building.

ZYGMUNT BORAWSKI

> "We expected there would be polemics, but we didn't think we would be accused of provocation. From the beginning we approached the matter very seriously."

DJ I think these accusations reveal the belief that the idea will not work in reality.

ZB It will work if we take care of what gets accomplished. This applies to all common spaces. The project may seem like an intellectual provocation because our work is strongly based on research and we like the collage technique. It is very important to us that the design is functional and aesthetic, but also tells a story. We value architecture as a medium that tells a story.

DJ But will the users know this? The outlines of tenement houses and their inner yards will only be visible from a bird's-eye view. Maybe these old streets need to be signposted or explained further in some way?

ZB The streets will be signposted, but I don't think this is the essence of the idea. Street outlines are intended not only to show how things used to be, but above all to encourage reflection and the discovery of various relationships. We don't want to serve everything on a plate. This is not what our architecture is about. We want to get people interested in history and the forms it creates.

DJ There was also an opinion that, due to the overgrowth of vegetation and the absorption of elements by greenery, the project takes on a dystopian look. Someone called it "Pompeian," a work about ruins...

ZB But Pompeii is beautiful! While documenting the square, I had Piranesi's *Vedute di Roma* above my desk. I don't see anything dystopian in architecture being overgrown by nature. In many Italian parks we can find sculptures, walls, columns, and capitals bathed in greenery. There is incredible poetry in it and wonderful testimony to the passage of time.

DJ How did the design change during the second stage of the competition, after the public consultations and negotiations, and then during the implementation stage?

MH It changed not only because of the consultations. The decision to increase the number of trees is, for example, to some extent the result of the discussion about Warsaw's Five Corners Square.[8]

ZB Initially, we planned seventy trees, eleven meters high and twenty centimeters in circumference. After Marlena's intervention we now have 109 trees, fifteen meters tall and thirty centimeters in circumference. Greenery was part of the design from the very beginning, so increasing its presence was not a problem.

The biggest change between stages one and two was that the design was simplified. We returned to the original concept of preserving only two historical layers: prewar and postwar. We aimed to clearly outline the tenement houses, passageways, and inner yards. In addition, one suggestion dominated in the comments—that the stone floor surface should be increased to make the square more functional and accessible. We also had to keep more of the stone surface at the point where the square meets the Palace of Culture—in the original version the lawn went right up to the walls of the palace—and at the point where it meets the TR and MSN buildings.

8 Plac Pięciu Rogów is an urban square in the center of Warsaw, revitalized between March 2021 and July 2022.

DJ The surface is a very important element of the design. How did you choose the materials? How much of the original Parade Square paving have you preserved?

ZB At the beginning, we planned to use the entire old paving surface. However, the need to provide people with limited mobility with access to the main communication routes forced us to give up the traditional, split-granite pavement. Instead, we decided to design strings of new split-face cobbles. We used colorful large-format stones to mark the outlines of old tenement houses. We were looking for stone that would be easily available on the Polish market so as not to increase costs unnecessarily. We found several types of colorful granite from the Baltic Sea area. We didn't want to import marble from Italy or Portugal. However, we used the most common Strzegom granite on communication routes.

DJ So you do not introduce a division into prewar and postwar Warsaw, since, for example, the cubes filling the outlines of the prewar inner yards are materials recovered from the socialist-realist square.

ZB We want to reuse as many materials as possible. The entire surface of the upper level of the square, where it meets the Palace of Culture, will be thoroughly cleaned. All old stone slabs with damaged corners will be repaired. In addition, the stone that flanked the Tribune of Honor will be cleaned and reused in the former inner yards, as will the square's original paving stones. So we mix a lot, laying a socialist-realist floor on the prewar outlines.

DJ What do you think about Thomas Phifer's design for MSN and TR Warszawa, and how did you relate to it?

ZB I treated it primarily as a frame, in accordance with the terms of the competition. In the design, the Museum is treated as a background, whereas the actual point of reference, a kind of "wallpaper" for us, was the Palace.

DJ Perhaps the Museum is supposed to create a kind of frame to fill?

ZB Yes, and fortunately this building is like that. We didn't think about the Museum as something that is supposed to outshout the Palace of Culture. That's why we positioned ourselves facing away from the Eastern Wall,[9] away from the Museum and toward the Palace.

DJ The Palace gives this place a very strong symbolic context. Especially now, in the era of the revival of Russia's imperial ambitions, the political nature of the place may take on new meanings. I wonder sometimes if we, in Poland, did not in fact come to appreciate the Palace on the wave of postmodernism, as a kind of quote that could be put in inverted commas. Maybe now it's time to foreground the history behind it once again?

MH The surroundings of the Palace have been constantly taking on new meanings since Russia's invasion of Ukraine in February 2022. Paradoxically, it was in this place that we felt a sense of community with the Ukrainians attacked by Russia. For me, this front square, these bars,

9 "Ściana Wschodnia"—architectural and urban complex in Warsaw erected in the years 1962–1969 according to the design of Zbigniew Karpiński and Jan Klewin on the Eastern side of Marszałkowska Street.

this park, this urban sports square, this terrace, create a place that brought us together.

MICHAŁ MURAWSKI I will also add that similar discussions took place in relation to another theme of this book, i.e. Alina Szapocznikow's sculpture *Friendship*, which will be placed in the MSN lobby. We wondered whether this was the right decision after the Russian full-scale invasion of Ukraine.

ZB I would really like this sculpture to be placed in the square.

DJ Why? Isn't its ambivalent meaning a problem?

ZB Because its whole story sounds like a joke and is paradoxical, and also very Polish. There is a sculpture competition, someone wins, but a different design is implemented. Later, the sculpture stands in the hall of the Palace for almost forty years, where no one pays attention to it. In 1992, the director of the Palace orders it to be scrapped, but it cannot be done because the work is too large, so someone cuts off the banner and the hands holding it and takes the sculpture to their own garden,

MARLENA HAPPACH

“ We no longer have to erase anything from the history of the city. We don't have to force the Palace into a new environment and pretend that it is something it is not. ”

where it stands for thirty years until it is finally sold at auction for over a million zlotys. In the meantime, various institutions are looking for it and demanding it, but for years there has been a legal mess and no one wants to agree to anything. Finally, after many adventures, stripped of dignity and mutilated, the sculpture ends up in the Museum. For me, this is a story about Parade Square as such. I believe that the sculpture fits this square like no other, because, like the square itself, it is a calque of our history.

I also want to emphasize that one of the ideas for the functioning of the square is to take advantage of the proximity of MSN, for example by making use of outdoor sculptures, which relate to the program of the Museum.

MM Some of the remains of Parade Square can also be used, such as the candelabra or the tribune. Sculptures from the Museum's collection can be displayed in front of its building as part of temporary exhibitions.

MH I think the approach to the Palace is changing. I can actually see this in the context of your design, in which everyone notices the outlines of old tenement houses. However, it's not just about the Palace, but about subsequent layers of meaning and history, including the tribune as an element of the socialist-realist setting of the square. We no longer have to erase anything from the history of the city. We don't have to force the Palace into a new environment and pretend that it is something it is not. We can keep the memory, but we can also use the Palace and the square for various purposes, including completely new ones.

DJ In a sense, also appropriating them to create new ways of understanding and new functions.

MH Using existing elements in the design is extremely important to me. Are we dealing with appropriation here? Or is it about taking responsibility? The most frequent approach is just to clean everything up and do something completely different there.

DJ What are the results of archaeological research carried out in the square? Do they say anything new about its history?

ZB The archaeological discoveries were extremely exciting for us. We knew that we might come across something during construction, but no one expected that on the section between the tribune and the Palace we would discover a fully paved and preserved Złota Street with tram tracks and cast-iron wells. We did a geodesic mapping, and it turned out that our drawing coincides perfectly with the historical street outline.

DJ We are dealing with a place burdened with a difficult history and marked by violence. This is not only about the war, the context of the creation of the Palace and its aggressive form, but also later events, such as the Battle of KDT,[10] reprivatization, and most recently the self-immolation of Piotr Szczęsny.[11] How can we deal with this history?

MH The act of self-immolation took place while we were deciding the competition. There were even

10 SEE CHAPTER 2.
11 SEE CHAPTER 1.

calls to stop the procedure and cancel the whole thing. I spent a lot of time thinking about it. I went to the site where this tragedy happened, right next to the tribune, where candles had been laid and where a spontaneous memorial had taken form. A commemorative plaque has since been installed, but back then cars were parked there. This was not any kind of spectacular place. Given what happened, the question was: should we leave this parking lot, this makeshift thing, or do the opposite? We chose the latter, although

ZYGMUNT BORAWSKI

> “ No one expected that on the section between the tribune and the Palace we would discover a fully paved and preserved Złota Street with tram tracks and cast-iron wells. ”

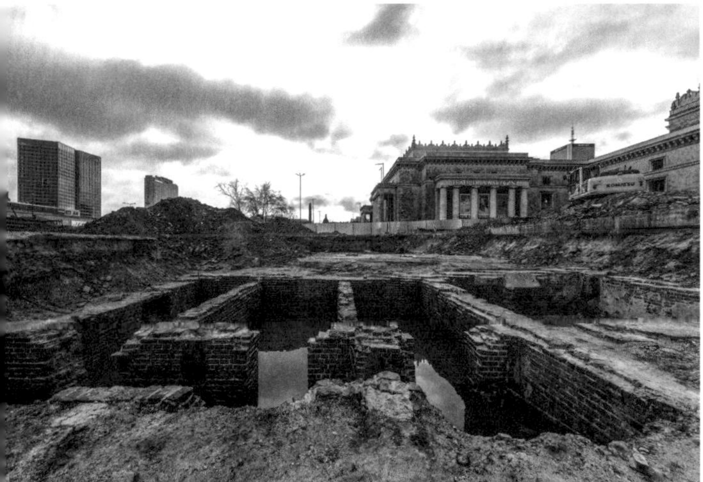

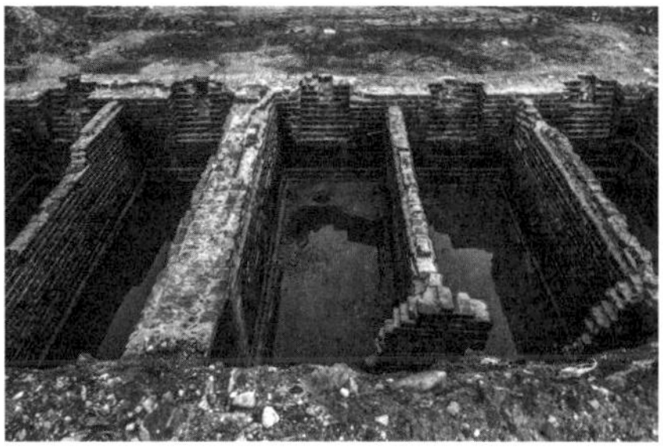

FIGS. 5.1–5.2 REMNANTS OF PREWAR BUILDINGS UNEARTHED IN 2024 DURING ARCHAEOLOGICAL EXCAVATIONS ON PARADE SQUARE ON THE SITE OF THE FUTURE CENTRAL SQUARE

not unanimously. Today I think it was the right decision. I think that our message—that creating high-quality, open, and accessible public space is an element of building a democratic world for all of us—remains valid.

DJ Yes, Piotr Szczęsny's demands were about democracy. This is especially important in this site, on which both totalitarianism and aggressive neoliberalism have left their mark. Is the square supposed to change history, or can it familiarize us with it and commemorate it? How do you imagine its symbolic impact?

ZB It should make us reflect and I guess familiarize us with history. It seems to me that the approach of younger generations to socialist realism and its legacy has changed significantly. I am aware of all the negative connotations that this architecture has. It was intended to overwhelm individuals, but the oppressive system also played quite a role in the way its walls and proportions felt. Nowadays, when we can separate socialist realism from its authoritarian roots, it turns out to be a really good piece of architecture. Socialist-realist buildings in Poland are more graceful and subtle than those in Moscow or Berlin. Last year I walked around Stockholm with my father in search of the best prewar buildings in the style of Nordic classicism. We couldn't help but feel that some of them could have easily been erected in postwar Warsaw.

DJ How do you imagine the neighborhood of Central Square and the MSN building functionally? Marlena, in an interview published in the book *Who Will Reclaim Plac Defilad?*

WARSAW UNDER CONSTRUCTION 9, you voice the hope that the MSN building will fill the square with activities, and that this is, to some extent, the responsibility of the institutions that operate in the area.[12]

MH I believe in this more and more. I was worried about the functional program of the square when the MSN and TR Warszawa complex itself was still being discussed and there was no talk at all about what should be built on the square. However, these buildings primarily affect each other in the passage connecting them—this is where we'll probably see most events and installations. But I hope that the whole square will have a life of its own. I am inspired by actions such as the *Plac Defilad Project*, organized by Teatr Studio, in which various forms of activities were arranged in this space. It turned out that it was possible.

ZB I don't know of any other capital city where you can enter four theaters from one square.

MH Although I think that since we have so many cultural institutions here, commercial functions should be located on the opposite side.

MM And why not housing? If life is needed there, let people live there. Let it be social housing.

MH Good question, I was also wondering whether a residential function would make sense there. Functions should be mixed in the city. There is no other square in Warsaw without direct inhabitants, and the organization of mass events interferes with the residential function.

12 "Szukanie konsensusu. Z Marleną Happach, dyrektorką Biura Architektury i Planowania Przestrzennego miasta stołecznego Warszawy, rozmawia Tomasz Fudala," in *Kto odzyska Plac Defilad, WARSZAWA W BUDOWIE 9* (Warsaw: Muzeum Sztuki Nowoczesnej w Warszawie, 2017), 169.

Ownership issues are still not resolved. And expropriation is only possible for public purposes. So I wonder if this wouldn't be the most expensive social housing in the world.

DJ The Museum of Modern Art, which dedicated the ninth edition of the WARSAW UNDER CONSTRUCTION festival to Parade Square, has also declared that it wants the area to become a place of political practice. The square is, of course, heavily marked by politics, but how can it also become a site for the practice of democracy?

ZB How to create political space? Difficult question. If people feel that the space belongs to them, they will gather there to express their dissatisfaction and argue for a better tomorrow. My partners and I believe that the multithreaded nature of the square and the diversity of its spaces make it possible for as many people as possible to feel at ease there. In *The Human Condition*, Hannah Arendt writes about the "space of appearance," that is, the sphere in which individuals gather as equals to engage in political action and discourse, and to participate in dialog, debate, and shared decision-making. I know it sounds very lofty, but I would really like the square to work like that. However, space itself will not be enough if we do not work to revive the public sphere, and this can't be done without the square's hosts: MSN, TR Warszawa, Teatr Studio, Teatr Dramatyczny, the Palace of Culture, etc.

DJ It seems that in a modern panoptic city, it is very difficult to create a space that will encourage gathering and protesting. Often, such seemingly "political" places are subject to extra surveillance, and it is better to meet in a more spontaneously chosen location. Is video monitoring envisaged at the square?

ZB We have monitoring because the City Guard requires it, otherwise we wouldn't get a building permit. But the cameras are only on the side of Marszałkowska Street. On the other hand, there are power sockets located throughout the square, so it will be possible to organize an alternative concert or happening.

DJ Protests also require access to infrastructure.

ZB In addition to the infrastructure and power supply, there is also the Tribune of Honor, which can serve as an excellent stage for DJs, but above all as an ideal place for speeches and protest gatherings. Our design was the only one that assumed the preservation of the tribune at the competition stage. Disenchanting history also involves turning elements of oppression into elements of resistance.

DJ Around the square we have a group of people and institutions who call themselves and whom you call in your municipal literature "local hosts."

MH At the consultation stage this was only a seed, but then a group of local hosts actually emerged.

DJ On the occasion of the WARSAW UNDER CONSTRUCTION festival in 2017, Artur Jerzy Filip proposed certain models of co-management of the square by intersectoral groups: residents, local NGOs, experts, politicians, and businesses, recalling existing Western examples.[13] Is the possibility of ensuring these hosts' participation in the process of deciding about the square being taken into account today?

MH It's quite complicated. We must remember that these are not completely independent units, but municipal cultural institutions funded from the city budget, and the Palace of Culture is also managed by a municipal company. Theaters use the space in the Palace, so cooperation in this field is still ongoing, but I think it should also extend to the external space.

DJ I just wonder whether such ad hoc and activist activities will lose their momentum over time. Maybe it's worth tailoring a separate curatorial program for this place?

MARLENA HAPPACH

“Warsaw's problem is still that there are many good, pleasant, fantastic places that, however, do not yet form a network, or that this network is severely interrupted. In the New Center of Warsaw project, we strive to connect them.”

13 Artur Jerzy Filip, “W czyich rękach? Lokalni gospodarze i postulat hybrydowego współzarządzania Placem Defilad,” in *Kto odzyska Plac Defilad*, 142–59.

MH I think that from the perspective of the entire New Center of Warsaw, it is important not only to create a program financed from the city budget, but above all to build relationships and establish cooperation. A good director will turn even the worst space into a nice venue, but this will end once the director is gone. And the point is for the space to fuel itself. This means that its users must also participate in the process.

DJ You have already mentioned the New Center of Warsaw project, which includes the redevelopment of Parade Square. How will this square change Warsaw in the future and how does it fit into a broader program?

MH I don't know to what extent it is a matter of the future and to what extent it is really a return to the historical art of city building. A square is a space that must be seen within the entire network of streets that lead to it, a constellation of other squares and parklets with functions that complement the network. In my opinion, Warsaw's problem is still that there are many good, pleasant, fantastic places that, however, do not yet form a network, or that this network is severely interrupted. In the New Center of Warsaw project, we strive to connect them.

DJ How was the current idea for this part of Warsaw influenced by the masterplan of Michał Borowski, the city's Chief Architect in 2003–2006, which envisaged a cultural function in front of the Palace, contained in buildings which correspond in height to that of the Palace's side wings?

MH It's difficult to give a clear answer to this question. Some elements are its continuation, for example the particular symmetry of the future square and the dimensions of these buildings. In my opinion, that plan arose from a certain fascination with La Défense and the vision of a part of the city operated entirely from underground. A lot of provisions were also introduced there for Euro 2012. However, no one was talking about reprivatization at the time, and it is a huge problem. The long time between the competition and the commencement of implementation was also caused by problems with land ownership.

DJ Some Warsaw residents probably miss this nineteenth-century urban fabric, but this past interferes with the implementation of public investments.

MH This is true, although it seems to me that there is no single tendency, only different strong factions. The "octane lobby," convinced of the need for many parking spaces, is very influential. In addition, there is a sentiment for the nineteenth-century city and tenement houses, which it would be best to simply recreate. There is also a third tendency, also very strong, to arrange a large park here, leaving only greenery. A beautiful idea, but not entirely possible.

MM Why?

ZB Because with such dense underground infrastructure and such legal problems as we have now with the ownership of property, it is impossible to create a park there.

MH Or it would be the most expensive park in the world. Some people draw this park and these buildings without even thinking about the fact that there is a metro tunnel on one side and a railway line on the other. In addition, there is a changing approach to heritage. The pavilions of the Śródmieście railway station, along with the entire urban layout, have already been listed as historical landmarks.

DJ So the current modifications are mainly about facilitating traffic flows?

MH They are about creating space for pedestrians. This is the purpose of new above-ground street crossings and improved traffic routes informed by a pedestrian logic. And also about rainwater recovery. Mechanisms of cooperation with businesses and institutions located nearby are also important. Central Square is one of the keystones of the entire New Center of Warsaw project. We are very keen to ensure that this particular development is not isolated from others, but connected with them. We also hope that one day our landscape protection resolution will come into effect, which will allow for the calming of visual information in these spaces.

DJ The landscape protection resolution, which introduces legal regulations concerning visual order, such as large-format advertising, may also potentially trigger the process of gentrification. For example, it could mean restricting the small-scale trade that was practiced around the Palace. I wonder if we will not miss this kind of space, which is an important social phenomenon and a place accessible to different classes and small initiatives, for example those belonging to migrants.

In defense of the famous kebab stand near the square, several hundred people gathered here recently (and 25,000 declared their participation in the protest on Facebook). Is there a place in Warsaw for such functions? So, at the conclusion of this conversation, I will say that if today we think about the history of Parade Square as a certain heritage, it is also worth appreciating the story of this huge marketplace, which makes us realize how important it is for the city to balance functions and to leave some freedom to its residents. I hope that Central Square will become such a free, open place.

THE BUILDING OF THE MUSEUM OF MODERN ART IN WARSAW 2005–2024

This timeline recapitulates the key moments of the MSN team's efforts to secure a new exhibition space and the construction process of the building at Parade Square. It was drawn up by Tomasz Fudala, based on data collected by Marta Ejsmont, Mikołaj Mundzik, Marcel Andino Velez, Paweł Czarnecki, and Michał Ziętek. A vital source is Jacqueline Irene Horodyńska's master's thesis, "Does the Museum Have a Future? Museum of Modern Art in Warsaw—Concepts, Designs, Implementations," written under the supervision of Dr. Hab. Waldemar Baraniewski and defended at the Faculty of Visual Culture Management of the Academy of Fine Arts in Warsaw in 2021. The first design of the Museum building by Christian Kerez and the conflict surrounding its implementation were described in the book *Christian Kerez: Conflicts Politics Construction Privacy Obsession* (Berlin: Hatje Cantz, 2009). Information about the second, implemented project can be found on the Thomas Phifer and Partners website: www.thomasphifer.com/.

Tomasz Fudala, art and architecture historian working at the Museum of Modern Art in Warsaw. Curator of the Oskar and Zofia Hansen House in Szumin (2018–) and the WARSAW UNDER CONSTRUCTION festival (2009–). He has also curated exhibitions, seminars, and public programs on modern and contemporary architecture. His articles have been published in *Domus*, *Artforum*, *Odra*, *Obieg*, *Czas Kultury*, and *Autoportret*. Awarded the Jerzy Stajuda Prize for Art Criticism (2017) and the SARP "Bene Merentibus" Medal in recognition of his contribution to the development of Polish architecture and the Association of Polish Architects.

1980S

ANDA ROTTENBERG, CURATOR AND ART CRITIC, ADVOCATES THE CREATION OF A MUSEUM OF CONTEMPORARY ART IN POLAND in the 1980s, seeing the American postmodernist Frank Gehry as its ideal architect. Even though the star expresses interest in the project, the city of Warsaw fails to commit itself regarding the establishment of a new institution (no location or construction budget are assigned). In 1986, Rottenberg sets up the Egit Foundation, one of the first independent art foundations in Poland, whose activities are pursued further from 1997 onwards by the Institute for the Promotion of Art (IPS–Instytut Promocji Sztuki). These organizations strive for the creation of the new institution, gather supporters around the idea, and receive the first works for the collection. An honorary committee for the construction of the museum is formed. Letters of support are signed by, among others: Aleksander Kwaśniewski, Jerzy Buzek, Leszek Balcerowicz, and Bronisław Geremek. The mayors of Warsaw consider several locations, including: Three Crosses Square (prior to the development of its eastern frontage), the Dom Braci Jabłkowskich department store, the intersection of Dobra and Karowa Streets, and the end of the King Stanisław Axis. In 1993, Rottenberg takes over as the director of the Zachęta–National Gallery of Art, and the museum project fails to find the appreciation of subsequent administrations. Economic difficulties and the enormity of social issues unleashed by the country's transformation prevail.

1992

A COMPETITION IS HELD FOR A MASTERPLAN for Parade Square (Plac Defilad) and the immediate surroundings of the Palace of Culture and Science (PKiN), in which 700 international architecture firms take part. The competition jury is chaired by Rob Krier, a Luxembourg architect associated with the conservative vein of postmodernism. The competition is won by famous Warsaw architects Bartłomiej Biełyszew, Andrzej Skopiński, and Andrzej Fabierkiewicz, who propose a corso surrounding the palace and a crown of skyscrapers. Two contradictory ideas are present in many designs: development of Parade Square with classic city blocks in the spirit of New Urbanism, or symbolic domination of the Palace of Culture and Science by buildings competing with it. There are also postmodern proposals to rebuild PKiN or demolish it and replace it with something new.

2005
MARCH 16

Michał Borowski, Chief Architect of the City of Warsaw from 2003 to 2006, revives the long-dormant idea of the museum, which he sees as part of a new vision of the city center. Borowski tackles excessive road traffic on the city's main street (Marszałkowska) and the paucity of cultural functions. His office publishes visualizations of the possible transformation of Parade Square into a smaller and more accessible public space with a museum and a musical theater.

AN AGREEMENT ON THE CONSTRUCTION OF THE MUSEUM IS SIGNED by Minister of Culture Waldemar Dąbrowski, and Deputy Mayor Andrzej Urbański, representing Mayor of Warsaw Lech Kaczyński, in a ceremony on the edge of Świętokrzyski Park, at the intersection of Świętokrzyska and Marszałkowska Streets. Politicians and culture professionals meet under an enlarged print of Piotr Uklański's *Untitled (Pope John Paul II)* from 2004, which shows a group of over three thousand Brazilian soldiers, photographed from the air, arranged in the profile of the Pope. Although the work is a critique of the colonial policy of the Church in Latin America, after the Pope's death, it was exhibited in public space and became a site of his cult.

Soon thereafter, the government and municipal authorities sign an agreement to co-manage the museum: the city will finance and oversee the construction of the building, and the ministry will finance and supervise the museum's organization and program.

2005
APRIL 29

THE MUSEUM OF MODERN ART IN WARSAW IS ESTABLISHED AS A NATIONAL CULTURAL INSTITUTION, co-run by the Capital City of Warsaw and the Ministry of Culture. The Minister of Culture formally establishes the Museum by Order No. 6 and by entering it in the register of cultural institutions and granting it a statute.

2005

JULY 11

Warsaw City Council passes a resolution on a joint cultural institution called the Museum of Modern Art in Warsaw, and the transfer of A PLOT OF LAND for the construction of its building.

2005

JULY 13

THE PROJECT DIRECTOR IS APPOINTED. Minister Dąbrowski entrusts the leadership of the Museum to art historian and manager Tadeusz Zielniewicz. Curator Anda Rottenberg soon joins the team as deputy director for programing, while the PR team is headed by actor and director Krzysztof Materna. The Museum's first headquarters is located in the Wedding Palace building, a wing of the Royal Castle in Warsaw. In 2006, the Museum moves its offices to the former shopping pavilion at 4a Bielańska Street, and in 2007–to 3 Pańska Street, where it operates until the new building is completed.

2005

JULY 23

Museum Director Tadeusz Zielniewicz appoints the BUILDING COUNCIL, comprising: Adam Szymczyk (director of the Kunsthalle Basel) as chairman, Krzysztof Jaraczewski (architect), Janusz Kubicki (coordinator of the New Center of Warsaw urban project, representing the City of Warsaw), Bohdan Paczowski (architect), and Zbigniew Włodarski (architect, Office of the Chief Architect of the City of Warsaw). The second advisory body is the MUSEUM PROGRAM COUNCIL, whose members include: Anda Rottenberg (critic, curator) as chairwoman, Mirosław Bałka (artist), Magdalena Kardasz (curator, Zachęta–National Gallery of Art), Piotr Krajewski (director of the WRO Media Art Biennale in Wrocław), Dorota Monkiewicz (curator, National Museum in Warsaw, president of the Polish Section of AICA), Prof. Piotr Piotrowski (director of the Institute of Art History at Adam Mickiewicz University), Prof. Maria Poprzęcka (director of the Institute of Art History at the University of Warsaw, president of the Association of Art Historians), Maria Anna Potocka (director of the Bunkier Sztuki State Art Gallery, Kraków), Jarosław Suchan (director, Muzeum Sztuki in Łódź), Monika Szewczyk (director, Arsenał Gallery, Białystok), Aneta Szyłak (director, Wyspa Art Institute/Wyspa Progress Foundation, Gdańsk), Adam Szymczyk (director of the Kunsthalle Basel), Milada Ślizińska (curator, CCA Ujazdowski Castle, Warsaw), and Leon Tarasewicz (artist).

2005
AUGUST 28

The Museum Program Council draws up and adopts the "PRELIMINARY CONCEPT OF THE WARSAW MUSEUM OF MODERN ART," containing guidelines for the future building. The exhibition zone is planned for approx. 10,500 m² gross, exhibition rooms are to be from 100 to 1,500 m², and specialized rooms for media presentations are also proposed. The hall and forum are planned for approx. 5,200 m², while the back-of-house area (offices, museum and technical facilities) is estimated at approx. 9,300 m². The building is also planned to house a media and book library, and a documentation center, alongside a café, a restaurant, a museum shop, and a bookstore. The Council estimates that the entire building should be approx. 35,000 m² gross, of which approx. 10,000 m² is to be occupied by shops and services. Later, such a large commercial section will be questioned by EU funding advisors as impossible to finance under EU law. As for the program, the Museum Program Council describes the new institution, among other things, as "a space for art without borders; collecting, presenting, and documenting art; intercultural dialogue; openness and readiness for change; integration of art and city life; with a positive impact on the surroundings of the Palace of Culture and Science."

2005
SEPTEMBER 12

THE MUSEUM COUNCIL is appointed, comprising: Magdalena Abakanowicz, Michał Borowski, Prof. Krzysztof Michalski, Prof. Adam Myjak, Krzysztof Obłój, Prof. Maria Poprzęcka, Prof. Andrzej Rottermund, and Danuta Wawrzynkiewicz. On the same day, the Council adopts the "Preliminary Concept of the Warsaw Museum of Modern Art."

2005
OCTOBER 2

DUTIES OF THE MUSEUM. IN MEMORY OF RYSZARD STANISŁAWSKI, the symposium at Hamburger Bahnhof-Nationalgalerie der Gegenwart is curated by Anda Rottenberg. This international meeting around the idea of a new museum in Warsaw concerns the tasks of a public art museum. In three panels, invited institution directors and art curators discuss global processes affecting museums (David Elliott, Kasper Koenig, Jean-Hubert Martin, Andrzej Przywara); collections in the process of change and collecting contemporary art (Prof. Piotr Piotrowski, Chris Dercon, Britta Schmitz); the creation of exhibitions (László Beke, Jürgen Harten, Alanna Heiss, Hans Ulrich Obrist). Conference participants record video statements about their expectations and forecasts regarding the Museum being created in Warsaw.

2005
NOVEMBER 19–DECEMBER 4

Commissioned by the municipal Consultation and Social Dialog Center, the CBOS PUBLIC OPINION RESEARCH AGENCY POLLS VARSOVIANS about the planned Museum. 77 percent of respondents support the idea of a new city square, cultural facilities, and tourist attractions in the vicinity of the Palace of Culture and Science. 48 percent have already heard about the planned MSN building. 44 percent believe that the building should be "quiet and integrated into the surroundings," while 33 percent are in favor of a building with a unique appearance.

2005
DECEMBER 15

THE FIRST ARCHITECTURAL COMPETITION FOR THE MUSEUM BUILDING AT PARADE SQUARE IS ANNOUNCED. The event is accompanied by the symbolic gesture of turning off the lights of the Palace of Culture and Science, using a special button, by public officials present at the ceremony, marking a new beginning for one of the biggest city squares in Europe. The Museum building is to be an element of the New Center of Warsaw as a joint initiative of the ministry and the city. The initial vision of the city center's development is rendered by the Office of the Chief Architect Michał Borowski in the form of a watercolor visualization, in which Parade Square is reduced to a rectangle in front of the main entrance to the palace and enclosed by the planned music theater from the south and the museum building from the north. The concept replicates a solution from the competition for the surroundings of PKiN in 1992, where the development of the square with city blocks was first proposed. The planned frontages form an "L" shape, which is later specified in the local masterplan for the palace's surroundings. Some two hundred architectural practices participate in the first competition, including David Chipperfield, Zaha Hadid, and Richard Meier.

2006
MARCH 9

WARSAW CITY COUNCIL ADOPTS THE LOCAL MASTERPLAN for the surroundings of the Palace of Culture and Science. The plan allows for a building height of 26 m in the area where the Museum is planned. On November 2, 2005, the Museum of Modern Art submits several remarks concerning the plan in development ("preserve the entire park and abandon the buildings on its eastern and western sides; allow the arrangement of existing greenery for the Museum's needs; change the status of provisions regarding the building line, arrangement of functions, and building height from mandatory to permissible; adopt the competition provisions as provisions of the plan"), but these are ignored.

2006
MAY 13–14

An informational meeting and presentation of the "Preliminary Concept of the Warsaw Museum of Modern Art" is held for Polish museum professionals at the House of Creative Work in Radziejowice. Sociologist Dr. Paweł Kuczyński presents the results of the survey *Public Opinion of Warsaw Residents about the Museum*. According to the schedule presented at the meeting, the Museum is to be built from 2007 to 2009 and opened in 2010.

2006
MAY 20

As part of the Long Night of Museums, sculptor MIROSŁAW BAŁKA STAGES THE HAPPENING *THE MUSEUM OF MODERN ART ATTRACTS*, which refers to the architectural competition for the new Museum. A mysterious opening appears in a construction container standing on the corner of Marszałkowska and Świętokrzyska Streets, which sucks in air and intrigues viewers. The installation is accompanied by Anda Rottenberg's essay about the *genius loci* of Parade Square, titled "Wind on the Square."

2006
JUNE 26

THE FIRST ARCHITECTURAL COMPETITION FOR THE MUSEUM BUILDING IS CANCELED. Due to the excess of formal requirements and their non-compliance with international regulations, as many as 140 bidders are eliminated from the competition by its secretariat. This situation gains a wide resonance among both Polish and foreign architects–Eduardo Souto de Moura, Will Alsop, Zaha Hadid, and others–which leads to the invalidation of the competition procedure. It is to be relaunched at a later date, on terms that take into account the architects' proposals.

2006
JULY 27

Acting Mayor of Warsaw, Kazimierz Marcinkiewicz, announces THE SECOND COMPETITION FOR THE MUSEUM BUILDING in the originally indicated location at Parade Square. The deadline for submitting entries is set for February 2, 2007, and the jury is to announce the competition results on February 18. The competition jury comprises: artist Paweł Althamer, Swiss architect Christine Binswanger (Herzog & de Meuron), Chief Architect of the City of Warsaw Michał Borowski (as chairman), architect Jacek Lenart (representing SARP–Association of Polish Architects, competition coordinator), architect Daniel Libeskind, Luxembourg-based Polish architect Bohdan Paczowski, art historian Prof. Maria Poprzęcka, curator and chairwoman of the Museum Program Council Anda Rottenberg, Director of the Royal Castle in Warsaw Prof. Andrzej Rottermund, Director of the Tate Gallery Sir Nicholas Serota, Director of the Design Museum in London Deyan Sudjic, Director of the Kunsthalle Basel Adam Szymczyk, and Museum Director Tadeusz Zielniewicz. By the deadline, 178 architectural firms submit bids, of which 109 are admitted to the competition.

2006
JULY

Director Tadeusz Zielniewicz describes the name Museum of Modern Art in Warsaw as provisional in a press interview for *Obieg* magazine. Based on the research commissioned by the institution, in the future it will be necessary to develop a shorter brand name, as with foreign institutions.

2006

On the eve of the competition results for the architectural concept of the building, ZUZANNA JANIN, traveling throughout Poland with her *studio_telewiZyJne* fictitious TV project, asks contemporary artists to comment on the concept of an "ideal museum." She creates the FILM *JUST BEFORE. THE IDEAL MUSEUM*, which portrays the artistic community, inscribing their voices in the discourse accompanying the museum's creation. Along with recording artists' statements, Janin films their studios. In this way, she expands the portrait of each creator to include the space where "everything begins." However impossible, the question of the "ideal museum" becomes topical and meaningful in the context of the creation of the new Museum of Modern Art. The articulation of ideas, proposals, or visions of an ideal museum acquires particular significance at this time and can indicate areas of cooperation between artists, architects, and curators. Today, the film is available online in the Museum's Filmoteka Muzeum film archive.

2007
FEBRUARY 16–18

Following deliberations, the jury finally announces the competition results. By a vote of 7:6, THE FIRST PRIZE IS AWARDED TO CHRISTIAN KEREZ, an architect running a small office in Zurich, who proposes a raw, cuboid shape consistent with the provisions of the local masterplan and competition requirements, following a conceptual construction principle in which the building is a system of columns and beams, supporting an undulating "tablecloth" roof suspended above. The project receives 92 points, the prize is PLN 160,000.

The second prize goes to Szaroszyk & Rycerski Architekci Sp. z o.o. and Buro Happold Polska Sp. z o.o.,

Warsaw (85 points, PLN 120,000), and the third prize to Atelier WW Architekten SIA, Zurich, Switzerland (79 points, PLN 100,000).

Special distinction is awarded to the studios Arkkitehtitoimisto ALA Oy, Helsinki, Finland, and GRUPA 5, Warsaw (58 points, PLN 80,000).

The jury awards an honorary mention, without financial gratification, to Planning & Consulting Anna Socha, Kraków, and Pro.Tec.O.Soc.Coop. a.r.l. Renato Rizzi, Venice, Italy.

Ten equal distinctions of PLN 65,000 each are awarded to the following bidders:

1. STEFFEN LEMMERZAHL, ARCHITEKT ETH/SIA, SWITZERLAND, PROPLANING AG, SWITZERLAND

2. K. INGARDEN, J. EWY-ARCHITEKCI, POLAND, KENGO KUMA AND ASSOCIATES, JAPAN

3. JUN AOKI & ASSOCIATES, JAPAN, ARTUR JASIŃSKI I WSPOLNICY BIURO ARCHITEKTONICZNE SP. Z O.O., POLAND

4. DÖMGES ARCHITEKTEN AG, GERMANY

5. AUGUSTIN SEBASTIAN RIVERA, SPAIN, JORGE QUESADA ORDEIG, SPAIN

6. TECTONIQUES – ALAIN VARGAS, FRANCE, MICHAŁ LESZCZYŃSKI, POLAND

7. PROF. STEFAN WESTRYCH, PROF. KRZYSZTOF DYGA, POLAND, PROF. MANFREDI NICOLETTI, LUCA NICOLETTI, FABRIZIO PAGLIANO TAJANI, PROF. LAURA BERTONI, ITALY

8. CAMILO REBELO ARQUITECTO UNIPERSONAL LDA. G.O.P. – GABINETE DE ORGANIZACAO E PROJECTOS LDA., PORTUGAL

9. SNØHETTA AS, NORWAY

10. ADAM TYLISZCZAK, BARTŁOMIEJ MARTENS, POLAND

CHRISTIAN KEREZ, MUSEUM OF MODERN ART IN WARSAW, 2009 VERSION, MODEL

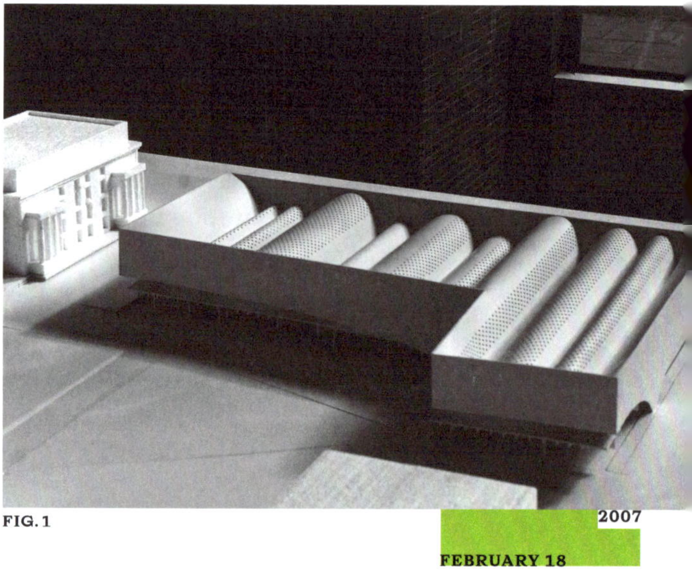

FIG. 1

2007

FEBRUARY 18

The competition results are CEREMONIALLY ANNOUNCED in the atrium of the Focus office building in Warsaw, with the participation of Mayor of Warsaw Hanna Gronkiewicz-Waltz. A small-scale model of Christian Kerez's victorious design serves as the centerpiece. The model disappoints some of the guests due to its lack of details: Kerez's concept eliminates redundant architectural elements, contrasting the building with the

Palace of Culture and Science, and relies on minimalistic means. The architect believes that the building should not overshadow the artworks presented in it.

2007
FEBRUARY 21

Some of the jury members express critical opinions about Kerez's project. As a sign of opposition to the competition results, Tadeusz Zielniewicz submits his resignation from the position of Museum Director, but this is not immediately accepted. There is HEATED DEBATE IN THE MEDIA AND INTERESTED CIRCLES about the Swiss architect's concept, criticized for its box-like nature and compared in memes to a warehouse-style supermarket. The Museum Director publicly supports the design by Arkkitehtitoimisto ALA Oy, GRUPA 5, and Jarosław Kozakiewicz, which, in the opinion of the press, discredits the idea of a democratic competition. The Museum's Program Council aligns with Zielniewicz's position.

CHRISTIAN KEREZ, MUSEUM OF MODERN ART IN WARSAW, 2009 VERSION, RENDERING

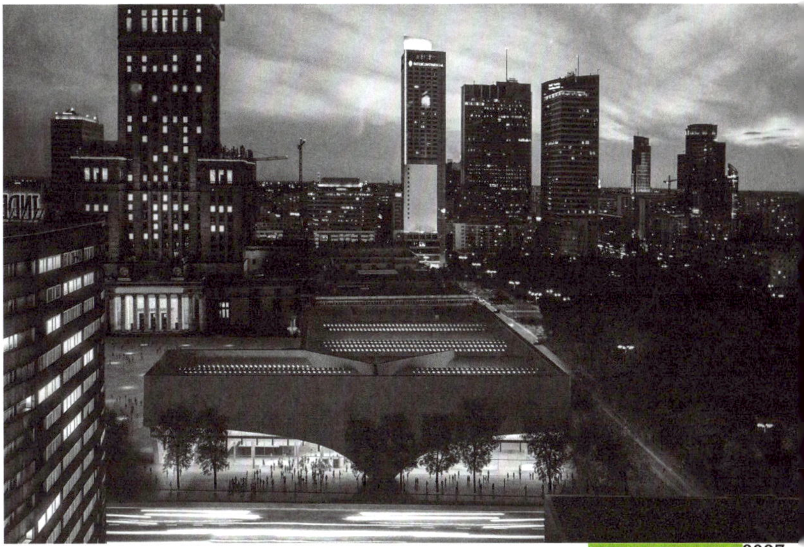

FIG. 2

2007
FEBRUARY 24

THE POST-COMPETITION EXHIBITION opens in the SARP Pavilion in Warsaw; the Polish architects' community expresses interest in Kerez's project, conveying support and solidarity. The Museum Program Council issues a statement that the winning design does not comply with the program guidelines for the building, suggesting that the city should withdraw from its implementation: "The Program Council of the Museum of

Modern Art in Warsaw acknowledges, fully understands, and supports the position of Director Tadeusz Zielniewicz, aimed at abandoning the implementation of the design that won first prize in the architectural competition. The Program Council had developed and published detailed program guidelines and the resulting functional solutions for the building, which were accepted by the Museum Council and the Minister of Culture and National Heritage. Christian Kerez's design negates these assumptions and, as a consequence, will not allow for the implementation of the Museum's social and strategic mission. The Council requests that the Minister of Culture and National Heritage enter into negotiation with the Mayor of Warsaw in order to withdraw from the implementation of this project and mediate on the adoption of a different architectural concept–one that will gain social acceptance. This will enable the Museum management to continue the mission they have started." This position is adopted by the majority of Program Council members, with Adam Szymczyk voting against it.

2007
FEBRUARY 25

SARP appeals to the recently elected Mayor of Warsaw, Hanna Gronkiewicz-Waltz, and the new Minister of Culture, Michał Kazimierz Ujazdowski, to respect the decisions of the competition jury.

2007
FEBRUARY 26

Christian Kerez is interviewed by Karol Kobos for the *DZIENNIK* newspaper. In the interview, titled "Architects Praise the Design," the Swiss architect says that he is used to disputes, because in his country public buildings are also selected in widely discussed architectural competitions: "I'm not surprised that the building planned in the very center of Warsaw triggers intense emotions. It's healthy that people want to relate to it in some way. It would be worse if they weren't interested. However, the behavior of Director Tadeusz Zielniewicz is completely unprecedented. After all, the jury's verdict was democratic, so I don't really understand why he wants to leave."

CHRISTIAN KEREZ, MUSEUM OF MODERN ART IN WARSAW, 2009 VERSION, RENDERING

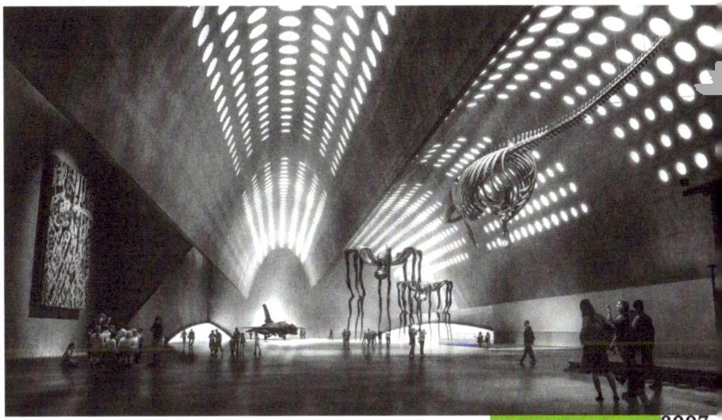

FIG. 3

2007
MARCH 2

In Hall B of the Warsaw Rising Museum, Christian Kerez delivers THE LECTURE *THE MUSEUM OF MODERN ART IN WARSAW AND OTHER PROJECTS*, organized in cooperation with the Twórców Architektury Foundation. He presents his views on architecture, as well as his way of working on designs and their implementation. In addition to the winning and hotly discussed MSN project, Kerez presents other designs. After the lecture, which is attended by approximately 400 people, the architect answers questions from the audience.

2007
MARCH 7

Several Museum team members, as well as Deputy Director for Programing and Chairwoman of the Program Council Anda Rottenberg, RESIGN FROM THEIR POSITIONS in reaction to the actions of Director Tadeusz Zielniewicz. The conflict among the team and within the Program Council is a clear manifestation of the conflict in the entire artistic community: the clash of different visions of the Museum, but also methods of making decisions of momentous importance for society. Procedures, transparency, negotiation of positions, and mediation competences struggle to get accepted into the post-transformation society.

2007
MARCH 12

After meeting with the architect and consultations with the Minister of Culture and SARP, Mayor of Warsaw Hanna Gronkiewicz-Waltz announces that she will respect the jury's decision.

2007
MARCH 19–20

The Program Council and the Council of the Museum of Modern Art in Warsaw dissolve themselves, and the Minister of Culture accepts THE RESIGNATION OF MUSEUM DIRECTOR TADEUSZ ZIELNIEWICZ.

2007
JUNE 6

During the inauguration of the exhibition in the Polish Pavilion at the International Art Exhibition in Venice, Minister of Culture Kazimierz Michał Ujazdowski announces the APPOINTMENT OF ART HISTORIAN JOANNA MYTKOWSKA, co-founder of the Foksal Gallery Foundation in Warsaw, then employed as an art curator at the Centre Pompidou in Paris, AS THE DIRECTOR OF THE MUSEUM OF MODERN ART IN WARSAW.

2007–2024
NOVEMBER 23

The Museum rents 1,000 m² on the first floor and second floor of an apartment block at 3 Pańska Street, at the back of the "Emilia" Furniture Store. The Museum team, consisting of several people, launches program activities there. The spaces on Pańska Street are Emilia's former "auxiliary outlet" (the store's pavilion is separated from the block by a pedestrian passage; the buildings are connected by two second-floor skyways and an underground tunnel). Unused and partially vandalized, the interiors regain their splendor. The MUSEUM ON PAŃSKA STREET, with a large-scale mosaic by Kazimierz Gąsiorowski in the former café space on the second floor, hosts many exhibitions (by Alina Szapocznikow, among other artists), academic conferences, debates, and film screenings. In 2012, the Museum inaugurates its program in the EMILIA building itself, which ceases to be a furniture store and is sold into private hands (2012–2016). In 2017, after the demolition of Emilia by a developer planning to erect a skyscraper in this location, the Museum moves its exhibition program to a temporary pavilion on the bank of the Vistula River.

2008
APRIL 12

Mayor of the Capital City of Warsaw Hanna Gronkiewicz-Waltz and architect Christian Kerez, the winner of the competition, sign the CONTRACT FOR THE DESIGN OF THE MUSEUM BUILDING at the Museum's headquarters on Pańska Street, in the presence of Minister of Culture Bogdan Zdrojewski. Kerez is to complete the design within twelve months and present the construction documentation within the next year. Construction works are scheduled to start in spring 2011.

CHRISTIAN KEREZ, MUSEUM OF MODERN ART IN WARSAW, 2009 VERSION, MODEL

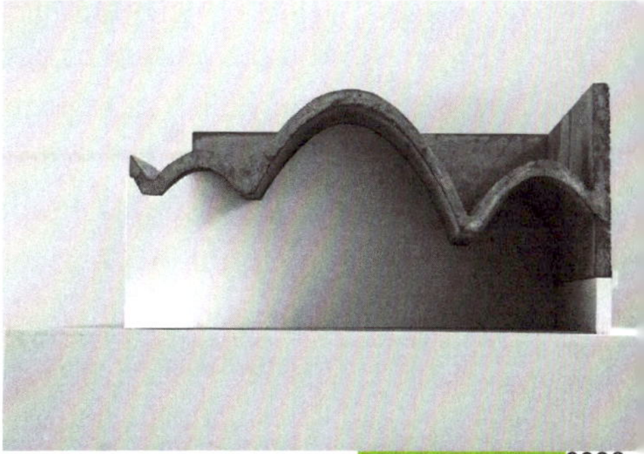

FIG. 4

2008
JULY 15–SEPTEMBER 14

The exhibition *CHRISTIAN KEREZ. NEW PROJECTS OF THE MUSEUM OF MODERN ART IN WARSAW* is held at the Museum, with graphic design by Ludovic Balland. The exhibition presents models in various sizes, visualizations, and blueprints from the studio, which the architect and several members of his team assemble on large tables set up in the Museum on Pańska Street. The show documents the course of design work and serves as a summary of the first stage of the competition concept's development. Kerez distinguishes three motifs in his design: the building as a landscape; reversal of the tension between the interior and exterior of the planned museum; its integration with the center of Warsaw and conveying the dynamic character of this space. Kerez presents a modified concept of the building, the program of which–at the request of the city hall, expressed after concluding the contract–is expanded to include a theater function. The battle to build the permanent seat will be one of the Museum's most important missions during its initial years.

CHRISTIAN KEREZ, MUSEUM OF MODERN ART IN WARSAW, 2009 VERSION, RENDERING

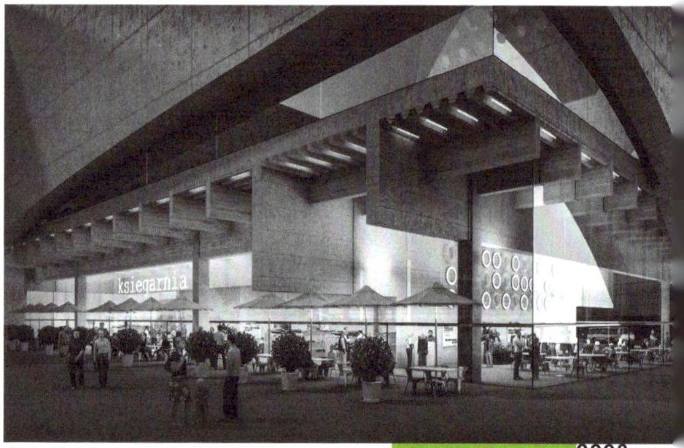

FIG. 5

2008
DECEMBER 4

THE CONFERENCE *NEW MUSEUM* organized by the Museum raises the question of ambitions and hopes related to the development of new buildings for art, from a global and Polish perspective. Is it possible to define the relationship between architecture and the profile and image of a museum? Placing MSN in the context of other museum, architectural, and conceptual projects is a prominent goal of the institution's educational program, hence leading architectural studios, museum directors, and curators are invited to share their experiences. Conference participants include: Anselm Franke (Extra City, Antwerp), Massimiliano Gioni (New Museum, New York), Mike Guyer (architect, Gigon Guyer Architekten), Christian Kerez (architect, ETH/SIA), Jarosław Lubiak (Muzeum Sztuki in Łódź), and Joanna Mytkowska (MSN).

2008
DECEMBER 5

The museum begins its PROGRAM ACTIVITIES ON THE FUTURE SITE OF THE BUILDING. The first event, *Henryk Stażewski. Nine Rays of Light in the Sky*, is a reconstruction of a monumental light composition shown on May 9, 1970, in Wrocław as part of the Wrocław '70 art symposium. The following years witness the presentations of Daniel Knorr's performance *Awake Asleep* (May 29–June 14, 2009), Daniela Brahm's special project on the Tribune of Honor at Parade Square as part of the first edition of the WARSAW UNDER CONSTRUCTION festival (October 3–November 22, 2009), as well as Ryan Gander's public project *Really Shiny Things That Don't Mean Anything* at Parade Square (October 28, 2011–March 30, 2012).

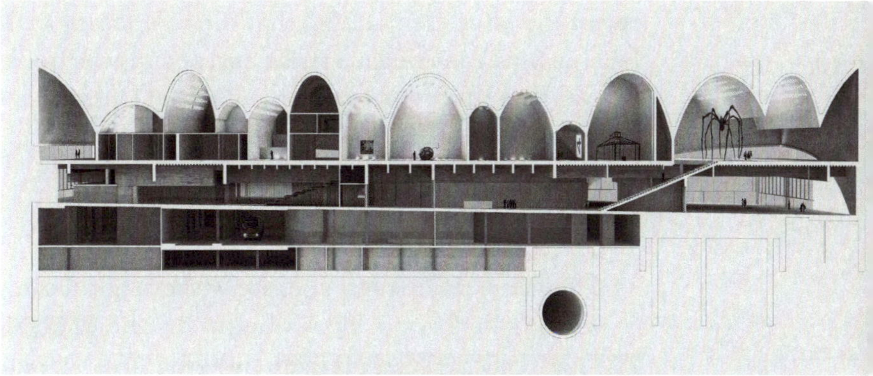

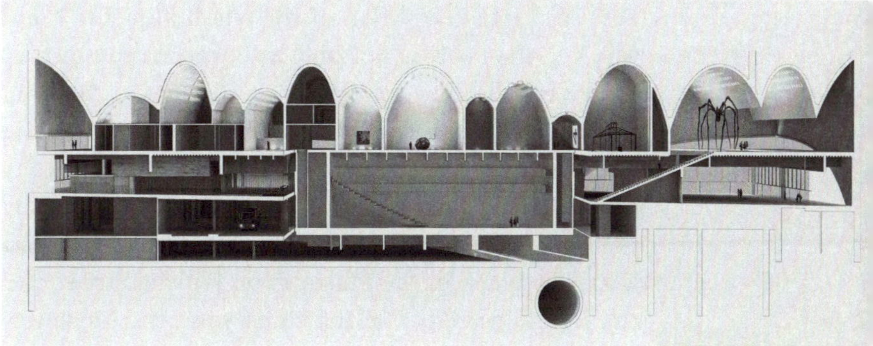

FIGS. 6.1–6.2

2008
DECEMBER

The city negotiates with Christian Kerez for A THEATER FUNCTION TO BE ADDED to his design, as the Museum building should also house the TR Warszawa theater, which is at risk of losing its current space.

2009
JULY 21

"THE BATTLE OF KDT" takes place as vendors from KDT (Kupieckie Domy Towarowe–Merchants' Department Store) clash with police officers and security guards trying to evict them. The construction of KDT, a temporary market hall at Parade Square, was permitted in 2001 by Mayor of Warsaw Paweł Piskorski. It marks an intermediate stage in the square's evolution, between the unregulated trade of the transformation years and the new development of this site planned by the city hall. In 2008, Hanna Gronkiewicz-Waltz had decided not to extend the contract with KDT vendors, the reasons being the planned construction of a link for the second metro line, the construction of MSN, as well as the ramshackle structure of the hall itself, likely to pose a construction hazard in the future. The city hall proposes to build a new market hall at the corner of

Złota and Marszałkowska Streets, but the vendors reject the offer. Demanding that the temporary KDT hall remains, they begin a strike and occupy the building, which leads to riots and a blockade of Marszałkowska Street.

2009

The Museum decides to operate without a building, in various locations. Works begin on the WARSAW UNDER CONSTRUCTION FESTIVAL, subtitled "City Design Festival." In the opinion of the small Museum team, who see themselves not only as curators, but also as activists, it is vital to institute a change in thinking about architecture, pay greater attention to public space, and introduce new architectural policies in a city that is struggling with numerous issues caused by political transformation. The first edition of the festival takes place in the Museum on Pańska Street and the Emilia pavilion. In the same year, the Museum—on the initiative of artists Paweł Althamer and Monika Sosnowska, and in cooperation with the Targówek District Office—begins to establish the BRÓDNO SCULPTURE PARK, which is an important non-museum project of the new institution.

2010
SUMMER

THE CONCEPT OF A BUILDING HOUSING BOTH MSN AND TR WARSZAWA is presented. At the same time, a conflict escalates between Kerez and the municipal development agency, the Capital City Development Authority (SZRM), which is to oversee the project. The SZRM imposes fines on Kerez for delays in design work.

2010
NOVEMBER 9

A NEW LOCAL SPATIAL DEVELOPMENT PLAN IS ADOPTED for the area surrounding the Palace of Culture and Science and Parade Square. The concept created by the Municipal Spatial Planning and Development Strategy Studio features low buildings with a height of 24–26 m on the southern and eastern sides of PKiN. The development in this area is to match the height of the existing, opposite frontages of Jerusalem Avenue and Marszałkowska Street. Kerez is forced to modify his design. The local plan envisions dense development around the Palace. It allows for the construction of three tall buildings off Emilii Plater Street. Two of them—at the south-west corner of PKiN—will be higher than the Palace itself, with a planned height of 233–245 m (the Palace itself measures 231 m with the spire, and less than 168 m without it). The Waban company files a claim to one of the plots under the planned TR theater; the case continues until the claimant is expropriated by the city; further court proceedings last until 2023. In turn, plots at Emilii Plater Street under the prewar address 70 Chmielna Street, are laid claim to by businessman Maciej Marcinkowski, who in the same way bought the rights to a plot at Castle Square (Plac Zamkowy) in the Old Town and built an office building there.

2010–2012

TENSION BETWEEN KEREZ AND THE CITY FLARES. The SZRM imposes further penalties on the architect for delays in providing design documentation. Kerez explains that city hall officials constantly demand changing the building's height, the size of the theater hall, and supplying technical studies, which are not his responsibility. He comments on the cooperation with the SZRM as follows: "They had no idea about me or my work, they didn't follow the design process, they didn't even look at the plans. ... The problem is deeper, structural. The officials I met are incapable of making decisions. Every decision has overwhelmed them. When in 2010 they did not want to accept the building permit design and sent me a list of things to improve, I tried to convince Mayor Wojciechowicz to appoint a steering committee with independent experts that would make decisions and resolve conflicts. Wojciechowicz established a committee, but with Paweł Barański [SZRM director]. It was like a joke."

The dispute also involves unresolved claims to plots of land that cannot be transferred to the Museum, which in turn makes it impossible to obtain a building permit. The non-transparency of the process and the lack of willingness to engage in a dialog with the architect and the Museum as the building's user become further reasons for the failure of this collaboration. After this experience, traumatic for everyone involved, the Museum team gradually concludes that it is necessary to conduct the construction project independently, which will allow for taking into account the institution's functional needs and ensuring the quality of architecture.

2012
MAY 9

Acting on behalf of the City of Warsaw, the SZRM notifies Christian Kerez—and public opinion—that, due to the architect's non-compliance, THE CITY IS WITHDRAWING FROM THE CONTRACT for the design of the Museum building. At the same time, it announces that on April 30 it filed a lawsuit against Kerez with the District Court for seven million zlotys in contractual penalties for delay in delivering design documentation. The architect denies all allegations and presents facts that incriminate the Warsaw administration, pointing out, for example, that coordination of the project with tunneling for the second metro line would delay the construction of the Museum by two years.

2012
SEPTEMBER

Architect Mikołaj Mundzik begins cooperation with the Museum to ADAPT THE FORMER "EMILIA" FURNITURE STORE for its temporary headquarters. The renovation of Emilia falls through; the building is sold by its owner, the municipal Capital City Internal Trade Company (SPHW), to a private real estate developer, Griffin Real Estate. The Museum rents Emilia as its temporary headquarters from 2012 to 2016, and shows many important and popular exhibitions there. The Long Night of Museums on May 14, 2016, marks the end of this period; in the following months the modernist pavilion is demolished by the developer to make room for a high-rise building. The city plans to reconstruct Emilia later in front of PKiN off Świętokrzyska Street.

Mikołaj Mundzik, in cooperation with architect Tomasz Galik, will start working on reviving the process of designing a new building for MSN, in which the Museum would act as the client.

After an almost two-year break in preparations for the construction of the new Museum building, which, by the city hall's decision, is to be combined into one functional and architectural complex with the new headquarters of the TR Warszawa theater, THE PROCEDURE FOR SELECTING THE ARCHITECT OF THE ENTIRE PROJECT IS ONCE AGAIN ANNOUNCED.

The Museum, in its new role as the client, announces a public procurement notice for the preparation of multidisciplinary design documentation for the Museum and TR Warszawa buildings. Andy Klemmer of the Paratus Group, involved in the expansion of the Solomon R. Guggenheim Museum in New York, among other projects, advises MSN in carrying out the entire process. The Museum decides to proceed in two stages.

As a result of organizational changes, the responsibility for selecting the architect and then for implementing the project is transferred from the City of Warsaw to the Museum until a building permit is obtained, and only then will the project be divided between the two institutions. In this process, the Museum is to cooperate closely with the management of TR Warszawa and the Warsaw authorities; a committee is established comprising leading Polish architects and urban planners, as well as municipal and ministerial officials, to select the designer. This provokes dissatisfaction in SARP, whose members would prefer yet another architectural competition for the Museum's design.

Out of thirty-five applications submitted in the "negotiated procedure with prior notice," fifteen are selected and admitted to the second stage: C.F. Miller A/S and Niras A/S (Denmark), Van Berkei en Bos UNStudio (Netherlands), BLOND&ROUX Architects (France), Thomas Phifer and Partners (USA), Inżbud Tomasz Trepka (Poland), WXCA (Poland), PAS PROJEKT ARCGI STUDIO (Poland), JSK Architekci and nsMoonStudio (Poland), PROCHEM S.A. (Poland), Studio A4 (Poland and Spain), Biuro Architekt Kaczmarczyk (Poland), Henning Larsen Architects A/S (Denmark), Fiszer Atelier (Poland), Foster+Partners (Great Britain), and Schmidt Hammer Lassen Architects (Denmark). In the next stage, the Museum presents functional guidelines for the MSN and TR Warszawa buildings to the architects.

THOMAS PHIFER AND PARTNERS, MSN AND TR WARSZAWA THEATER, 2015. EARLY CONCEPT PHASE RENDERING WITH THE MUSEUM'S WHITE FABRIC FAÇADE

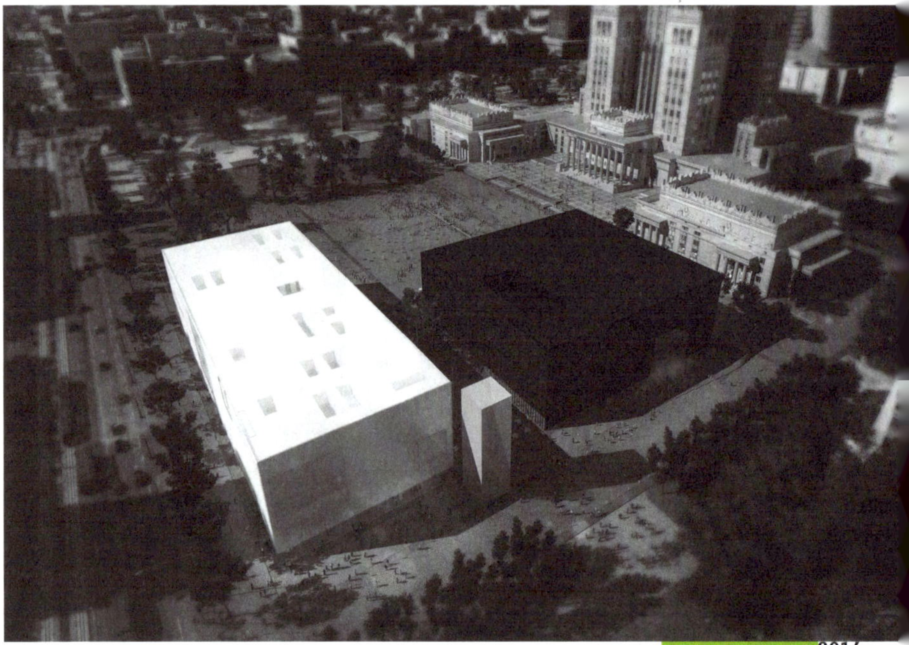

FIG. 7

2014

JULY 31

Announcement of the results of the procedure for selecting a new architect of the headquarters of the Museum and TR Warszawa. The evaluation committee comprises: Joanna Mytkowska (MSN director), Wojciech Gorczyca (director, TR Warszawa), Grzegorz Piątek (architecture critic), Marek Mikos (director, Office of Architecture and Spatial Planning of the Capital City of Warsaw), Wojciech Kwiatkowski (director, Financial Department of the Ministry of Culture and National Heritage), Ewa P. Porębska (editor-in-chief, *Architektura-Murator* magazine), Mirosław Bałka (artist), Krzysztof Nowakowski (president of the Board of the Society of Friends of the Museum and member of the Museum Council), Magdalena Staniszkis (SARP competition judge), Maciej Miłobędzki (SARP competition judge), Jerzy Grochulski (architect, coordinator of the SARP Expert Team), and Tomasz Janowski (director, Culture Department of the Capital City of Warsaw).

Among the twelve bids submitted by Polish and foreign firms, THE COMMITTEE SELECTS THE CONCEPT PRESENTED BY THOMAS PHIFER AND PARTNERS FROM NEW YORK. Two simple volumes, situated at right angles to each other—the white one belonging to the Museum, the black one to the theater—are separated by a passage along the north-south axis.

2014

DECEMBER 5

THE CONTRACT FOR THE DESIGN OF THE MUSEUM AND TR WARSZAWA BUILDINGS IS SIGNED with architect Thomas Phifer. The project's cost is estimated at PLN 522,076,250.

2015

JANUARY 28

THE MUSEUM INVESTMENT DEPARTMENT begins regular work, replacing the previous building team, and occupies an office on the ninth floor of the Palace of Culture and Science, overlooking the Museum site. Its tasks include supervising the design and construction of the new MSN headquarters; in 2017 it will also oversee THE INSTALLATION OF A TEMPORARY WOODEN PAVILION ON THE BANK OF THE VISTULA RIVER, rented from the Thyssen-Bornemisza Art Contemporary Foundation in Vienna, whose president, Francesca von Habsburg, decides to lease the structure to the Museum free of charge. The Museum will use the pavilion until the building at Parade Square is completed.

2015

MARCH 22

In a letter to Hanna Gronkiewicz-Waltz, urban activist Jan Śpiewak, representing The City Is Ours (Miasto Jest Nasze) Association, opposes the working concepts for the revitalization of Parade Square drawn up by Thomas Phifer's office and published by MSN. An OPEN LETTER TO THE CITY HALL CALLS FOR PUBLIC CONSULTATION on how to develop the eastern part of the Palace of Culture and Science area, with an emphasis on Parade Square. Activists criticize the local spatial development plan for the area around the Palace of Culture and the form of the square: "We have serious doubts as to whether an empty square of this size will be filled with people every day as shown in the visualizations. ... The square lacks a diverse range of functions and is overly dominated by public uses. ... The absence of greenery and street furniture is also striking. We do not believe that such a huge open space can be friendly, either psychologically (its scale is too overwhelming) or physically (the absence of shade during the summer months will be extremely detrimental)."

The letter, along with one thousand signatures and powerful media resonance, persuades the city hall to redefine its strategy for Parade Square.

2015
SEPTEMBER 19

SATURDAY ON THE SQUARE. At the construction site of the future buildings of both institutions, the Museum and TR Warszawa jointly organize a spatial presentation of the designs of their headquarters by Thomas Phifer and Partners. The multi-hour event includes showing Warsaw residents around the floor plans of both buildings drawn on the surface of Parade Square, taking a group photo of participants standing on the outline of the buildings, and an evening debate with the participation of residents, the architect, and invited guests.

2016
MAY 6–14

FAREWELL EMILIA. At midnight on Saturday, May 14—at the culmination of the Long Night of Museums—MSN's four-year tenure in the former "Emilia" Furniture Store comes to an end. The celebration program features concerts, performances, as well as a conference on modernist architecture and the premiere of the book *Emilia. Meble, muzeum, modernizm* (Emilia: Furniture, museum, modernism).

2017
MARCH 25

With the opening of the exhibition *The Beguiling Siren is Thy Crest*, the Museum INAUGURATES OPERATIONS IN ITS NEW TEMPORARY HEADQUARTERS—the exhibition pavilion at 22 Wybrzeże Kościuszkowskie, above the Wisłostrada tunnel, next to the Copernicus Science Centre. The 1,000 m² facility, consisting of a 600 m² exhibition hall, a bookstore, a café, and auxiliary rooms, was designed in 2008 by the Austrian architect Adolf Krischanitz for the Temporäre Kunsthalle Berlin, on the site formerly occupied by the DDR-era Palace of the Republic. The Museum on the Vistula is visited by approximately 100,000 people annually. By July 2024, thirty exhibitions will have been held there, after which the structure transforms into the Pavilion of Dance and Other Performing Arts.

2017
JUNE

The Office of Architecture and Spatial Planning announces A COMPETITION FOR THE DESIGN OF THE CENTRAL SQUARE (Plac Centralny), located between the main entrance to the Palace of Culture and Science and Marszałkowska Street.

THOMAS PHIFER AND PARTNERS, MSN AND TR WARSZAWA THEATER, 2016, MODELS

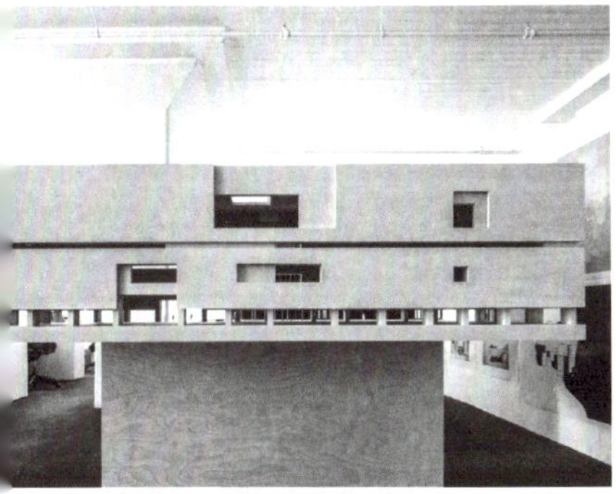

FIG. 8.1

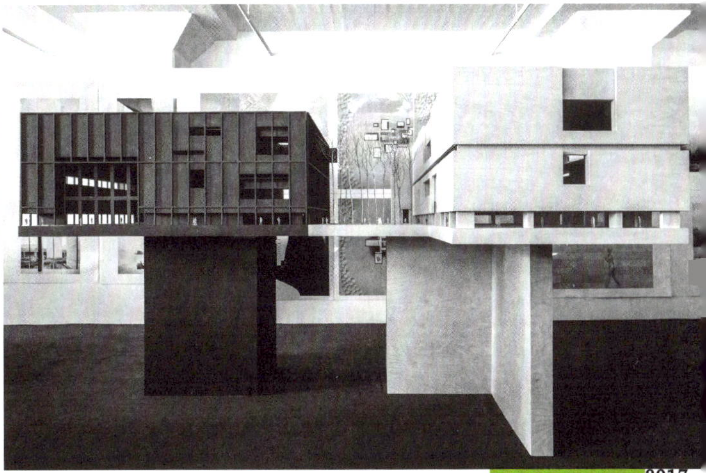

FIG. 8.2

2017
OCTOBER

The competition, which includes public consultations, is won by the A-A Collective studio, consisting of Zygmunt Borawski, Martin Marker, Furio Montoli, and Srdjan Zlokapa. Their concept of redeveloping Parade Square along the axis of Złota Street provides a space for daily meetings and cultural events in front of the Palace of Culture and Science. A more intimate square will be carved out of the huge area, boosting the attractiveness of the very center of the city. The concept draws on the pre-1939 street grid, relating to the outlines of former tenement houses. The surface of the square is to be paved with several types of stone, and the main compositional change is the departure from the symmetrical composition and axiality of the PKiN entrance and the introduction of an abundance of greenery. The square will feature lawns, over one hundred trees, forty species of flowering bulbs and perennials, and eleven species of shrubs. Honey locust trees are to be planted in the immediate vicinity of the Museum, in the forum between the MSN and TR buildings. The square will be equipped with four seven-meter-deep retention tanks, and the collected rainwater will be used to water the greenery.

WARSAW UNDER CONSTRUCTION 9. *PLAC DEFILAD. A STEP FORWARD* The ninth edition of the Festival was curated by Tomasz Fudala and Szymon Maliborski, in collaboration with Galeria Studio, with exhibition design by BudCud and Tomasz Świetlik. Staged by MSN and the Museum of Warsaw in collaboration with the Office of Architecture and Spatial Planning, the exhibition focuses on the future of Parade Square. Eight steel *Baugespann*-type poles are erected on the square, as proposed by the Kraków architectural studio BudCud (Mateusz Adamczyk, Agata Woźniczka). For the first time in Poland, the façades of the TR Warszawa and MSN buildings and the southern frontage of the future Central Square are visualized on a real scale. The *Baugespann* is a mandatory planning tool in Switzerland, used in the process of issuing building permits: the client is obliged to build a temporary, openwork structure corresponding to the planned new building or alteration so that the project can be carefully considered and its actual impact on the surrounding space understood. The poles in Warsaw feature flags designed by artist Sławek "Zbiok" Czajkowski.

The BudCud architectural duo also designs *Square Stand*, featuring models of the height of the future Museum's arcade and the interior of its lobby level from the side of Marszałkowska Street. Numerous guided tours take place in the square, and the actual sizes of other European squares are drawn on the floor with colored lines on a 1:1 scale, to show the scale of the future development (*Squares within a Square*).

The installation accompanies the main exhibition of WUC9, *Plac Defilad. A Step Forward*, which looks at the centrally located Warsaw public space through the eyes of activists, urban planners, and architects. The exhibition recapitulates several decades of planning and heated discussions, but also moments when the spontaneity of urban life, free trade, the rise of car culture, and spatial management failures prevailed over subsequent unrealized concepts. The reigning attitude of taking matters into one's own hands without regard for the welfare of the community, and general leniency toward wild reprivatization, delayed the creation of the democratic space of a city square.

STAGED AT GALERIA STUDIO, THE EXHIBITION FEATURED THE FOLLOWING ARTISTS:

ADAM ADACH,
AKADEMIA RUCHU,
KAZIMIERZ BENDKOWSKI,
DANIELA BRAHM,
DANIEL BRAILLY,
MICHAŁ BUCZEK,
PIOTR BUJAK,
ZUZANNA CZEBATUL,
MACIEJ CHODZIŃSKI,
PIOTR CHUCHLA,
JACEK DAMIĘCKI,
RAFAŁ DOMINIK,
KAROLINA FILIP,
YONA FRIEDMAN,
MICHAŁ FRYDRYCH,
ALFRED FUNKIEWICZ,
JÓZEF GAŁĄZKA,
JAN GOOTS,
OSKAR HANSEN,
KICKSPIN,
GRZEGORZ LASZUK,
DOMINIK LEJMAN,
JAN LUBICZ PRZYŁUSKI,
MICHAŁ MIODUSZEWSKI,
TOMASZ PARTYKA,
JERZY PIASECKI,
MARJORIS PIRELA,
JULIA POPŁAWSKA,
CEZARY PONIATOWSKI,
ANTONI PROKOP,
IGOR PRZYBYLSKI,
MARIOLA PRZYJEMSKA,
KRZYSZTOF PYDA,
GRAŻYNA RUTKOWSKA,
MYKOLA RYDNIJ,
TOMASZ SACIŁOWSKI,
ANNA SIEKIERSKA,
JAN SMAGA,
JERZY SOŁTAN,
STACH SZUMSKI,
SZUMOWINY,
KAROLINA WOJCIECHOWSKA,
PATRYCJA WOJTAS,
WOJCIECH ZAMECZNIK,
AND ZUZANNA ZIÓŁKOWSKA/HERCBERG.

2017
NOVEMBER 29

PIOTR PAWEŁ SZCZĘSNY, an "ordinary man," as he calls himself in the manifesto he leaves behind, commits self-immolation at Parade Square. He protests against the policies of Law and Justice and politically inspired discrimination, racism, and homophobia in Polish public life.

2017
DECEMBER

THE CONSTRUCTION DOCUMENTATION OF THE MSN BUILDING IS APPROVED. The Museum has a total area of 19,788 m², of which 4,500 m² is exhibition space. The New York architectural firm Thomas Phifer and Partners is responsible for the design, in cooperation with its partner in Poland, APA Wojciechowski Sp. z o.o., while engineering support is provided by the Polish office of Buro Happold Polska Sp. z o.o. The consortium of ECM Group Polska Sp. z o.o. and Portico Project Management Sp. z o.o. acts as the contract engineer, while legal assistance for MSN within the scope of the project is provided by the law firm Wierzbicki Adwokaci i Radcowie Prawni.

MUSEUM BUILDING–GENERAL INFORMATION:

EXHIBITION AREA: 4,574 M²
PROGRAMING AREA: 10,348 M²
TOTAL AREA: 19,788 M²
NUMBER OF BELOW-GROUND FLOORS: 2
NUMBER OF ABOVE-GROUND FLOORS: 4
BUILDING HEIGHT: 24.95 M
BUILDING DIMENSIONS IN PLAN: APPROX. 104 × 40 M

2018
JANUARY 31

THE BUILDING PERMIT for the Museum is issued. On the same day, the Cyprus-registered Waban company, which claims to have the rights to a prewar plot on the site, tries to block the process, but fails to prevent the building permit from becoming valid. Litigation with Waban lasts until 2023.

THOMAS PHIFER AND PARTNERS, MUSEUM OF MODERN ART, 2018, RENDERING

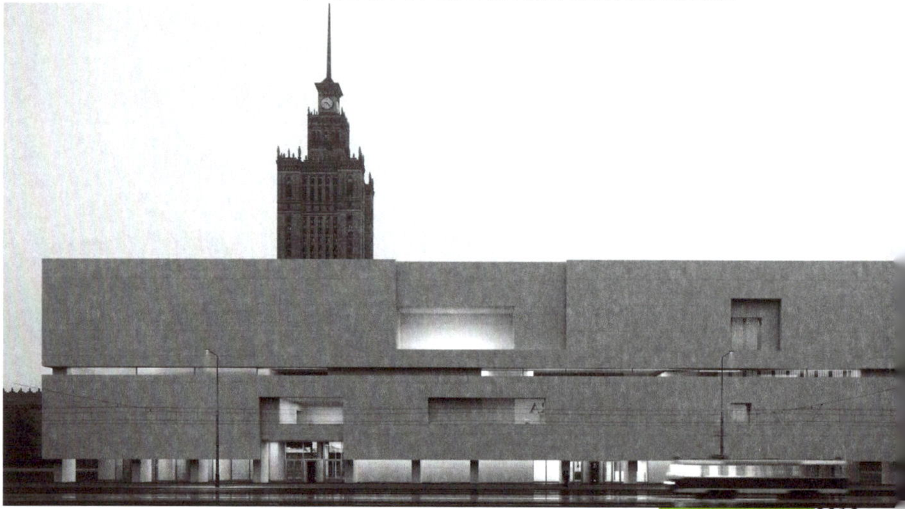

FIG. 9

2018

MARCH 22

A CONTRACT AWARD PROCEDURE FOR THE CONSTRUCTION of the Museum building (limited tender) is initiated. Five applications are received on time, and four contractors are qualified for the second stage and invited to submit offers. Since no offer is received by the deadline, the procedure is canceled on September 10, 2018.

During the first procedure for the construction of the new MSN headquarters and verification of applications for admission to submit offers, the ordering party decides to exclude one of the contractors. This is due to formal issues and the fact that the contractor has tried to mislead the ordering party as to the scope of previously realized projects. The tender committee carefully analyzes the buildings specified in the list of accomplished works, often carrying out on-site visits to verify the accuracy of contractors' statements. The excluded contractor appeals against the Museum's decision to the National Appeals Chamber, but the latter agrees with the client's position and argumentation as to the validity of the contractor's exclusion.

The challenge faced by the potential contractor exceeds the technical capabilities of the largest Polish companies. The main problem turns out to be the overly complicated design documentation for the architectural concrete of the façade. After numerous consultations with potential contractors, the design and specification of architectural concrete are modified.

A technical dialog is conducted with potential contractors before initiating another procedure.

The collected information helps optimize the design documentation regarding the architectural concrete façade and other requirements.

2018
OCTOBER 17

THE SECOND CONTRACT AWARD PROCEDURE FOR THE CONSTRUCTION of the new MSN headquarters is initiated through an open tender. The terms of participation in the procedure and the criteria for evaluating offers remain basically unchanged from the first procedure. However, to evaluate the offers, the Museum has to appoint a team of independent experts, consisting of architects, engineers, and specialists in respective fields, to assess the studies submitted by the contractors under non-price criteria, which concern, among others:

a) project safety in the context of building over the metro tunnel (procedural and corrective steps)

b) architectural concrete (evenness of texture, color)

c) integrating the RPZ Pałac power substation.

By the deadline of December 12, 2018, three offers are received, but each of them significantly exceeds the budget assumed by the ordering party, i.e. PLN 250,000,000 gross. A team of independent experts assesses that the bid from Warbud S.A., amounting to PLN 416,970,000, is the most advantageous. In order to be able to resolve the procedure, the Museum requests an extra investment subsidy of PLN 180,000,000.

2019
JANUARY 31

Warsaw City Council awards the requested funds, enabling the resolution of the procedure and the signing, on February 28, 2019, of THE BUILDING CONTRACT.

2019
FEBRUARY 28

The contract is signed with THE GENERAL CONTRACTOR, WARBUD S.A. Buro Happold Engineering is responsible for the structure of the building. The client is the Museum of Modern Art in Warsaw. ECM Group Polska S.A. and Portico Project Management are the contract engineers.

2019
JUNE 3

The construction works commence: the site is fenced; earthworks and excavations begin.

2019

The City had previously decided to expropriate for public purposes the area where the TR THEATER is to be raised—it acquires the plot only in 2019. For this reason, the construction of the Museum began prior to that of the theater. The first stage of TR, the underground part, is scheduled to start at the beginning of 2025.

2019
DECEMBER

PILING PROCEEDS on both sides of the tunnels of the M1 metro line and the auxiliary tunnel of the M2 line. The building stands on 131 concrete piles, and part of it "rests" on the Centrum metro station. During construction, the metro does not stop even for a minute, although work—constantly monitored with laser sensors—takes place just above its tunnels.

2020
FEBRUARY 20–MAY 22

TRANSFER BEAMS are installed. They are placed on piles, and only then is the emerging building suspended on them.

2020
MARCH 19

The building's FOUNDATION SLAB is laid. The construction of the new Museum coincides with the COVID-19 pandemic which begins in Poland in March 2020, utterly destabilizing living and working conditions. Subsequent lockdowns render it difficult for the general contractor to meet the schedule. Broken supply chains of various materials needed on the construction site take extremely long to rebuild, which deeply affects the pace of works.

2020
NOVEMBER

LEVEL ZERO—the new Museum rises from the ground on the surface of Parade Square.

2021
DECEMBER 19

CONSTRUCTION BEGINS OF CENTRAL SQUARE, planned in the middle of Parade Square. The project provides for over one hundred new trees, thousands of shrubs, lawns, and a shallow pond.

2022
MARCH

In the weeks following the full-scale invasion of Ukraine by Russia, Warsaw becomes a major hub for hundreds of thousands of Ukrainians fleeing the war. In response, the "SUNFLOWER" SOLIDARITY COMMUNITY CENTER (Solidarny Dom Kultury "Słonecznik") is established at the Museum on Pańska Street by a team of Ukrainian and Polish artists, activists and curators. The activities of the Sunflower are coordinated by Taras Gembik and Yulia Krivich. The Sunflower organizes humanitarian and cultural events, and functions under the auspices of the Museum. The invasion also affects the construction of the new building: many workers decide to leave and return to Ukraine in order to join the army.

2022
MAY

As part of the NEW CENTER OF WARSAW project, aboveground pedestrian crossings are introduced on Marszałkowska Street and Roman Dmowski Roundabout, which will facilitate access to the MSN building. The project includes renovation of key public spaces in the city center, with new greenery, lighting, benches, and bicycle paths.

2022
AUGUST

The building frame is completed.

2023
JULY

The building's ARCHITECTURAL-CONCRETE FAÇADE is implemented in five stages. First, the contractor presents samples of all the components of the concrete mixture and formwork, and the pouring of the façade is preceded by tests of the quality and the impact of individual materials on the color of the concrete. Trial casts of individual elements are also made: columns, walls, and ceiling. The suspended ceiling is erected.

2023
AUGUST 2

Deputy Mayor of Warsaw Michał Olszewski announces an archaeological discovery at the Central Square construction site. Excavations two meters below Parade Square have exposed tram tracks and walls of former tenement houses, well-preserved granite curbs, and basalt pavement.

2023
AUGUST

ROOF SKYLIGHTS illuminating the two upper, monumental galleries of the Museum are installed. According to architect Thomas Phifer's concept, the four galleries differ from each other in the presence or absence of natural lighting (top or side), as well as in the size and height of the halls.

2023
SEPTEMBER

The GLASS FAÇADE structure is erected.

2024
APRIL 16

DZ-2 external doors are installed on the lobby-level façade, closing the building.

2024
OCTOBER 25

Opening date of the Museum.

2025
FEBRUARY

Opening date for the INAUGURAL EXHIBITION, occupying the entirety of the completed building.

JOANNA MYTKOWSKA,
THOMAS PHIFER,
DEYAN SUDJIC,
AND MICHAŁ MURAWSKI

WHAT A CONTAINER CAN DO

The conversation took place on April 10, 2024 in Warsaw.

Joanna Mytkowska, art historian, curator of numerous exhibitions, including the Polish Pavilion at the Venice Biennale in 2005 (Artur Żmijewski's *Repetition*). Co-founder of the Foksal Gallery Foundation, she also worked at the Centre Pompidou in Paris. Since 2007, she has been the director of the Museum of Modern Art in Warsaw. In 2018, she was awarded the Igor Zabel Award for Culture and Theory.

Since founding Thomas Phifer and Partners in 1997, Thomas Phifer has completed the Museum of Modern Art in Warsaw expansions of the Glenstone Museum in Potomac, Maryland, the Corning Museum of Glass in Corning, New York, and the North Carolina Museum of Art in Raleigh, North Carolina, as well as the United States Courthouse in Salt Lake City, Utah, the Brochstein Pavilion in Houston, Texas, and houses across the United States. Projects under construction include the TR Warszawa theater in Warsaw. Thomas Phifer and Partners has received more than thirty honor awards from the American Institute of Architects. Mr. Phifer is the recipient of the Rome Prize in Architecture from the American Academy in Rome, the Medal of Honor and President's Award from the New York Chapter of the AIA, the Arts and Letters Award in Architecture, and the National Design Award in Architectural Design from the Cooper Hewitt Smithsonian Design Museum. In 2022, he was elected as a lifetime member of the American Academy of Arts and Letters.

Deyan Sudjic studied architecture in Edinburgh, edited *Domus* in Milan, was the director of the Venice Architecture Biennale in 2002, and as director of the Design Museum in London between 2006–2020, led the museum's move from a dockland warehouse to its new home in Kensington. As a journalist he writes for the *Financial Times* and *The Guardian*, and is editor of the newly established magazine, *Anima*. Critic and writer on subjects ranging from architecture and urbanism, to design and fashion. His books have been published in fifteen languages. Curator of exhibitions in museums and institutions worldwide.

DEYAN SUDJIC No matter how much experience you have looking at drawings or models, it's only when you see something taking physical shape that you really understand its scale and the quality of light, which are so important here. It's interesting to look at how a building shapes an institution, and an institution shapes a building. I guess the painful early history of this project has inoculated it against some of the possible difficulties. I think the client side has approached this in a very realistic way, without losing the sense of purpose and excitement. I found it an uplifting experience to see what a container can do to shape what will happen inside it. It's still an adolescent building, in the sense that it's got to be tested, trained, and put to work, but you can see those spaces have so much potential.

JOANNA MYTKOWSKA Today's conversation brings me back to the early days of the project. We didn't have experience. It started with a rather bombastic idea, based not on an institution's experience, but on analyzing the city plan. That's why such a big shape and so many square meters were proposed. The failures suffered in the course of the project led us to the idea that the building should be much smaller, more focused, and proceed separately from the TR Warszawa theater building. This taught us to think about the surroundings: the theater has its needs; the square has its needs. We were lucky to have so much time, this was probably the greatest advantage of a complex and not always pleasant situation.

DS During that time, you had the chance to experiment and try curatorial ideas, which is very important. Too many projects begin with a committee and an architectural idea, but without that sense of leadership continuity that takes it from the stage of planning to that of working, functioning, living.

JM Absolutely. The late urbanist Michał Borowski,[1] who was very supportive of the Museum project, invented an empty shell, not the concept of the institution. But that's not why the process failed. Its failure resulted from ownership claims to land on Parade Square, which no one was fully aware of when we started. The city didn't respond properly to that situation or take responsibility for it.

There was also no reflection on how a museum in a relatively small country with no tradition of contemporary art museums can fill a building of that size. This building is in a location that demands a very solid community behind it, and the delay actually helped develop that community. This public was built not only by us, but all institutions. There was also a process in society in which we fitted precisely, and grew together with.

DS "Museum" is a loaded word. You seem to use the acronym MSN more than the word "museum" itself.

JM Yes—which is now on the façade.

MICHAŁ MURAWSKI So you're not going to be MoMA Warsaw or something?

JM No. At the start, I thought we wanted to be Tate Modern, but

1 Michał Borowski (1950–2020), Chief Architect of the City of Warsaw (2003–2006), initiator of many key projects for the city, including the development plan for Parade Square (Plac Defilad). MSN is being built according to his local plan.

I was thirty-five and had no idea what it meant for Warsaw. The Tate was a new institution then, enjoying enormous success. We thought that's what we should follow. But years later, we decided to go with the name created by the inhabitants of Warsaw. We never called it that ourselves. We call it "the museum," but they started to call it MSN, which became a nice brand with much more resonance.

DS 400,000 visitors a year that you plan in the new building is quite a lot.

JM The National Museum in Warsaw has twice that, and that was the basis for our calculation of expected yearly visits. This is the deal with the city. The minimum they expect is 400,000, and the capacity of the building is 800,000 per year. In the beginning, there will of course be interest in the building. We'll start with the exhibition of our collection, and other shows that will be relevant for general public. One of them tells the iconographic history of women's art from the sixteenth century until today, concluding with a focus on women's protests, which were particularly powerful in Poland lately. There's an idea for the first three years, to give us some experience. Till now we've been an experimental institution. Our monographic shows attracted a bigger public, but the maximum we reached is 50,000 visitors.

DS The Louvre is planning on 7,500,000 people a year; just imagine that experience and the destruction that comes with it. I think what's special here in the Museum in Warsaw is the chance to have authenticity.

Especially in the UK, culture is seen as a way to create jobs and inject life into run-down cities. This is the malevolent aftershock of Bilbao. And you can't use culture as an alibi for social engineering. But you have many audiences, many ways of speaking to people. And yet the building itself has a unity. It's got the same tone throughout. It's a great frame. I suppose it will make everything look beautiful, which can sometimes be difficult. It will also make Alina Szapocznikow's *Friendship* sculpture look beautiful, perhaps inappropriately.

JM Somehow I don't really see things in terms of the contemplation of beauty and I doubt our audience will either. Warsaw's artistic milieu is extremely active, activism-based, and they are already very critical. Also, the lobby level, which is very dynamic and where we want to have space for debate, will certainly influence exhibitions as well. Our survey of the history of women's protests will probably be perceived as not enough, and we might be accused of turning something authentic into a canon. I'm sure there will be a lot of changes, discussions, and tension, because this building is very special. It's very exposed in this location, in this amazing architectural setting. No other museum building in Poland can be such a stage for artists. We have new buildings of course, in Kraków, or the POLIN Museum of the History of Polish Jews in Warsaw, but you can't compare. To say I see it as a potential challenge is euphemistic.

DS It's interesting how it reflects the tension too. You were talking about how the earlier project could not overcome the tensions of land ownership. The structure of this building reflects what's underneath in terms of the subway tunnels. Most of the public will not understand that, but it's extraordinary how buildings cannot help but express the forces that created them.

THOMAS PHIFER The Museum's structural pillars are not on a regular grid. There's a Soviet-era subway right underneath us.[2] I'm not sure the geotechnical investigators had any accurate drawings of the subway, so they had to excavate. The structural engineers had to decide where exactly to put the load-bearing columns and these enormous beams that cross the tunnels. So, in a sense, that archeology, that rhythm is represented when standing over this subway,

DEYAN SUDJIC

" The structure of this building reflects what's underneath. Most of the public will not understand that, but it's extraordinary how buildings cannot help but express the forces that created them. "

2 The first line of the Warsaw metro opened in 1995, but construction began in 1983. According to legend, Stalin offered Polish President Bolesław Bierut a choice between the metro and the Palace. Bierut chose the metro, but Stalin gave him the Palace anyway. In actuality, preliminary construction of a metro system began in 1953, but was halted after several years.

this relic. It is a relic of a similar kind to the Palace of Culture, which has determined this grid. And hence then the idea is that all of the structure is exposed, that we represent the rhythm of this archeology in the rhythm of the new architecture. It just grows out of the ground.

JM There is one space in the cellar where we can step onto the roof of the station.

MM The other subterranean issue that had a bearing on the construction of the Museum, and that sabotaged the Kerez project, was property reprivatization, as you have already mentioned. I gather that ownership of all the plots under the Museum was regulated already by 2013. So, I don't know whether that was a source of anxiety or not when you started working on this building, Tom?

TP Well, it wasn't so long ago that there was a little piece of property that was in the way of construction of the theater, even after the Museum issue was solved. And that piece of property was just twice the size of this room.

JM We had to actively fight for this and, in fact, we have temporary ownership of that piece of land. Because the Museum and the TR Warszawa theater started together, and officially this investment is run by the Museum, we are obliged to start building by January 2027. Otherwise, it goes back to the former owner. It was given to us for a cultural public purpose according to existing procedure. With time, we've learned to work with these complex and shifting procedures that require deep knowledge.

DS This is the product of pre-communist ownership?

JM Yes—the descendants.

MM In theory, because the claims were bought up by gangsters, effectively, in the 1990s, who later claimed they have the legal rights to be the descendants, but in fact they are speculators.

JM So, the company we were fighting with is registered on Cyprus with Russian capital. But Mikołaj Mundzik, head of our construction department, was smart enough to maneuver, and we managed thanks to that. So when Tom started, the land for the Museum was free from claims. However, we'd been discussing that very important issue for years.

MM So it's pretty uniquely shifting ground.

JM It's a typical post-communist situation of the nationalization of land. But in other circumstances you have to fight with developers. I don't know which is more brutal.

MM Okay, so by the time you came, Thomas, that was more or less clear.

TP Well it was clear, except for this small parcel on the footprint of the theater. I think it's curious how the context of the Museum is going to be affected by the construction of the theater. When there's another building there and this white building is not standing alone in the shadow of the Palace, the Museum won't seem quite as precious. The buildings were consciously designed as cousins.

JM The ownership claims were the only reason they were not built together. We had to split the process because we couldn't wait. Now I see it was a good decision, if we'd waited we would have overlapped with the populist government and construction would never have happened. That's why the theater will be built only now.

DS Some of the problems about the first competition weren't only to do with land ownership. There was also a subterranean, or not so subterranean concern that this should be a Polish architect. Is that no longer an issue?

JM During the first and the second competitions, the process was still run by the municipal authorities. Maybe the thought that it should be a Polish architect was present on that official level. When we worked on the competition we were interested in experimenting with a different quality, a different way of thinking about the Museum. Also, we have to remember that we don't have the experience in Poland of building many museums. For us, it was natural to aim for the best possible quality. Tom, what is your impression? You've met several people here.

TP Yeah, they've all been generous and welcoming. I've had nothing but an amazing experience here, particularly with the artists. Joanna

THOMAS PHIFER

" Speaking to local artists influenced how we developed the internal expression of the galleries and public spaces. "

has been pretty diligent at having dinners with artists and critiques by artists. It's been hugely helpful.

MM So, did these conversations have some impact on the design?

TP Yes, speaking to local artists influenced how we developed the internal expression of the galleries and public spaces.

JM Maybe we should collect these different phases. In the early stage, Tom was thinking about a façade made of fabric. That was our first experiment with the building, but it seemed impossible for technological reasons. Still, there are traces of experimenting with a double layer on the façade.

DS So the fabric version would be like dressing the building.

MM Like Christo?

TP Yeah, it was like a Christo. It was white. But we wanted a building here that would be strong and have a sense of permanence and solidity. Then soon, we began to investigate the white concrete and having this double layer, which added to the sense of the thickness and presence in the city.

DS Had you used it before?

TP We've done a lot of concrete buildings, but not white ones. The contractor and the person who coordinated this did an extraordinary job.

DS So it looks like panels.

TP Yeah, those are the form panels.

DS It evokes masonry...

TP It has a certain honesty to it. It shows how these panels were organized for the concrete. But there's a story here that we have to tell in some detail. There are tiny expansion joints because the façade moves along these steel plates. It was extraordinary to watch the engineering of this façade come together. It's quite an achievement. Although fabric was not pursued, the sense of abstraction with the fabric led us in the direction of the concrete. The other foundational material in the project is light. And this light is held in this white concrete volume. This is a place to encounter art, and it's a place for people to encounter each other. So they become more present in this white volume that is the container for light—we wanted this volume to be about light.

JM But there were many phases of the interior. The early design of the galleries was very different.

TP Very different. At one time—I don't know exactly what phase this was—but we, first of all, had an all-glass building with all of the art pushed into the middle. So you'd walk around the edges and then go into the middle to see the works. At this point, though, can you tell us, Joanna, why we have rooms rather than flexible spaces? That was a big decision.

JM Yes, it was a big discussion; we'll see whether it was the right decision. I love what we have, but when we started, it was common for museums and contemporary art galleries to have a huge generic space to build on. Our experience was that this requires lots of money and extra work from the exhibition architect, which is nice, but instead of art you can end up focusing more on exhibition design. The pavilion by the Vistula River designed by Adolf Krischanitz, which we are using now, is like that—one huge space, so we know what that means. We thought rooms were more effective for artists, they're confronted with architecture instead of designing the space together with their works. It's also more stable in terms of collections, one refers to architecture that is not changing all the time. This may be something very local, since our point of reference is Muzeum Sztuki in Łódź, situated in the same bourgeois palace since the 1930s, with its collection, which we grew up with, always in the same rooms. And that's infrastructure for art, for building canons. We don't believe in canons as a way of working with contemporary art, but we thought that it would be better, so we have rooms.

TP There are no two rooms that are the same size.

JM But there was also a phase when the galleries on two floors con-

THOMAS PHIFER

" The foundational material in the project is light. And this light is held in this white concrete volume. This is a place to encounter art, and it's a place for people to encounter each other. So they become more present in this white volume that is the container for light. "

sisted of equal rooms—every room was a square. But we could not work with this.

TP But it didn't start this way, as being a house of rooms. It started off being more flexible. We had huge rooms where partitions would get added later as the exhibition required.

JM With curatorial experience, I thought how we could construct a thematic show in equal boxes. It would look a bit like an art fair. But, with Eastern European art, I feel that the specificity is in the materiality. You cannot put it in very generic spaces, it is too sensitive. So that's why we thought rooms, somewhat more "domestic" spaces, would be better for us.

MM It's interesting that you say that it became more domestic over the course of the design process, but also it became whiter or more of a white cube, right?

JM Yes, but the context is important, white means something else here. The original idea behind the white Museum was perhaps to calm the cityscape down, the chaos that surrounds it. This is what Oskar Hansen meant by "architecture of the background." That was, I guess, the initial point, that the Museum would somehow erase part of the city or become invisible. In most weather conditions we see the building under construction from our offices on Pańska Street. But if it's foggy, we can barely see it, as if it's disappeared.

TP The first conceptual rendering was made along the boulevard. We took a white strip of paper and put it in perspective not as a building, but as a mirage or an abstraction, a white abstraction that could coexist with the Palace and the commercial buildings along Marszałkowska Street. Then we went through the process of trying to discover a material. One thing we didn't want to do was have a cladding system with some kind of thin layer of stone.

MM Like the Palace?

TP Yes, or with a thin glass skin. At the same time, we were looking at the foundations, at the archaeology and the rhythm of structure. The Museum began to take shape as a concrete building through and through. I mean, that façade is thick and load-bearing. The columns and the beams are massive and heavy. So inside and out, it became a building that had some integrity about its materiality.

DS It's something of a paradox with the dematerialization in the weather. But you're right, it has got that sense of mass and depth, and you feel the thresholds. I wasn't aware of the lift so much, but the depth of it, you really see it's a solid, massive building, and yet one which talks quietly.

TP Then we went to the theater, which is all darkened steel that's load-bearing. Its columns are poured cast steel and plates, and you see all of the thicknesses. So that building is a steel building. It has its own integrity, its own geometry. It was all about a search for those two materials that finally gave us a sense of integrity. So, there was a very slow evolution. I'd never had any experience with Warsaw before, and it took me quite some time to understand what to build here. The Museum and the theater are two buildings that are cousins, and they need to understand how to speak to one another, how to speak to the Palace, to the broader context of the city. They must have that sense of permanence and weight that these institutions need to stand the test of time.

JM I should mention that the process of selecting the architect was very special. After two unsuccessful competitions, another failure was out of the question. Of course, with Christian Kerez, that was not the architect's fault, but the City of Warsaw's, which we always clearly state. Anyway, this time the competition was not for the concept—we were not expecting renderings. We wanted it to be based on dialog: we were looking for someone we could collaborate with, who would listen to us, to our needs, to the function of the building.

Andrew Klemmer from Paratus Group advised us before the selection process. He more or less taught us how to work with the functional program of the building. He advocated for a different process to select the architect because we needed a solid collaboration rather than a drawing of a concept that

THOMAS PHIFER

" It took a long time to work through alternatives, to understand the organization of the Museum, to understand Warsaw a little bit better. "

might not be realizable. That's why, for Tom, the concept phase started after the selection.

TP To compliment your committee, you were patient, because it took a long time to work through alternatives, to understand the organization of the Museum, to understand Warsaw a little bit better.

DS Were you cautious about coming to Warsaw to do this project?

TP The whole process was curious because in the very beginning, I received this letter, and it just said: "Will you please fill this form out and send it back to us?" So I did that. Then several months later, I got another note that said: "Well, can you send us some work that you've done?" More months went by, and then: "Would you like to come to Warsaw to meet us?" I'd never been to Warsaw. I had only planned to stay for a couple of days, but I ended up staying for a week and went around everywhere.

It's amazing what's happening here, because sometimes when you make a work of architecture, there has already been a cultural renaissance twenty years before that, and you're making a building that responds to something that happened a long time ago. Here, it feels like this building is happening at a critical moment in the city and the country. Looking at it from the outside as an observer, I hear all of the discussions about what's going on in the world, in the art world, and the debates right now about what that building means, I am thrilled to be involved with this frothy creative process. The same thing with the theater—both buildings are rising at a pivotal time.

MM If the theater is not built, would it be the end of the world?

TP I think it would be the end of the world. The theater is going to be built, it will really help both buildings.

MM It's worth emphasizing that the Museum is the first building to be built at all on the square around the Palace.

TP Which makes it a remarkable sight that it's being built there at all.

MM People thought that it would be impossible for anything to be built there. When I was doing my research back in 2010, people were telling me that nothing will ever be built here because there is a curse.

JM They also kept saying this to us.

THE MUSEUM AND THE SQUARE 2020–2023

Marta Ejsmont, photographer affiliated with the Museum of Modern Art in Warsaw. Since 2019, she has been documenting the construction of the new Museum building and the urban transformation of the New Center of Warsaw. The relationship between people and architecture is a central theme in her photography. Her photo album *MSN. Budowa Muzeum / Building the Museum* was published in 2024.

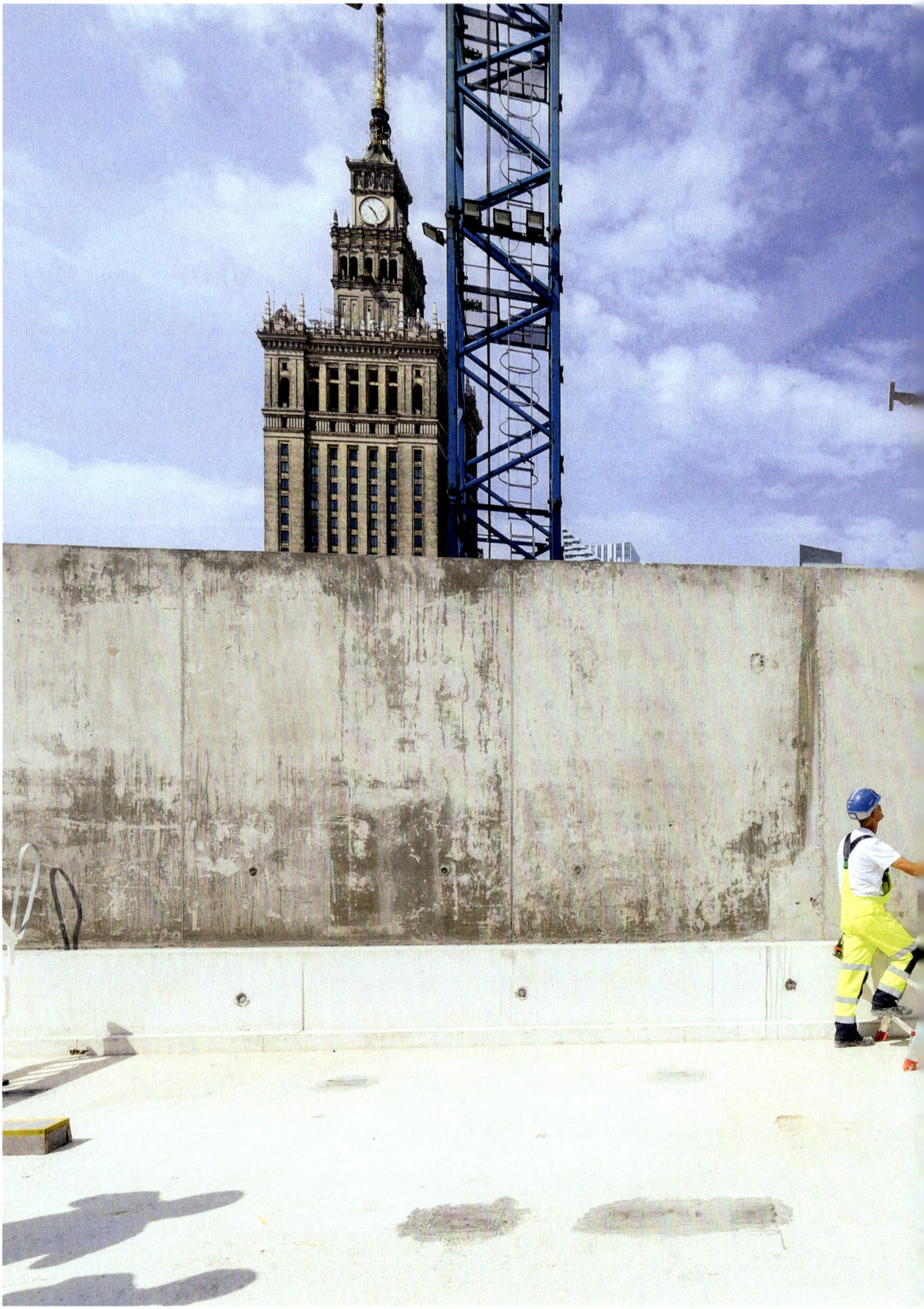

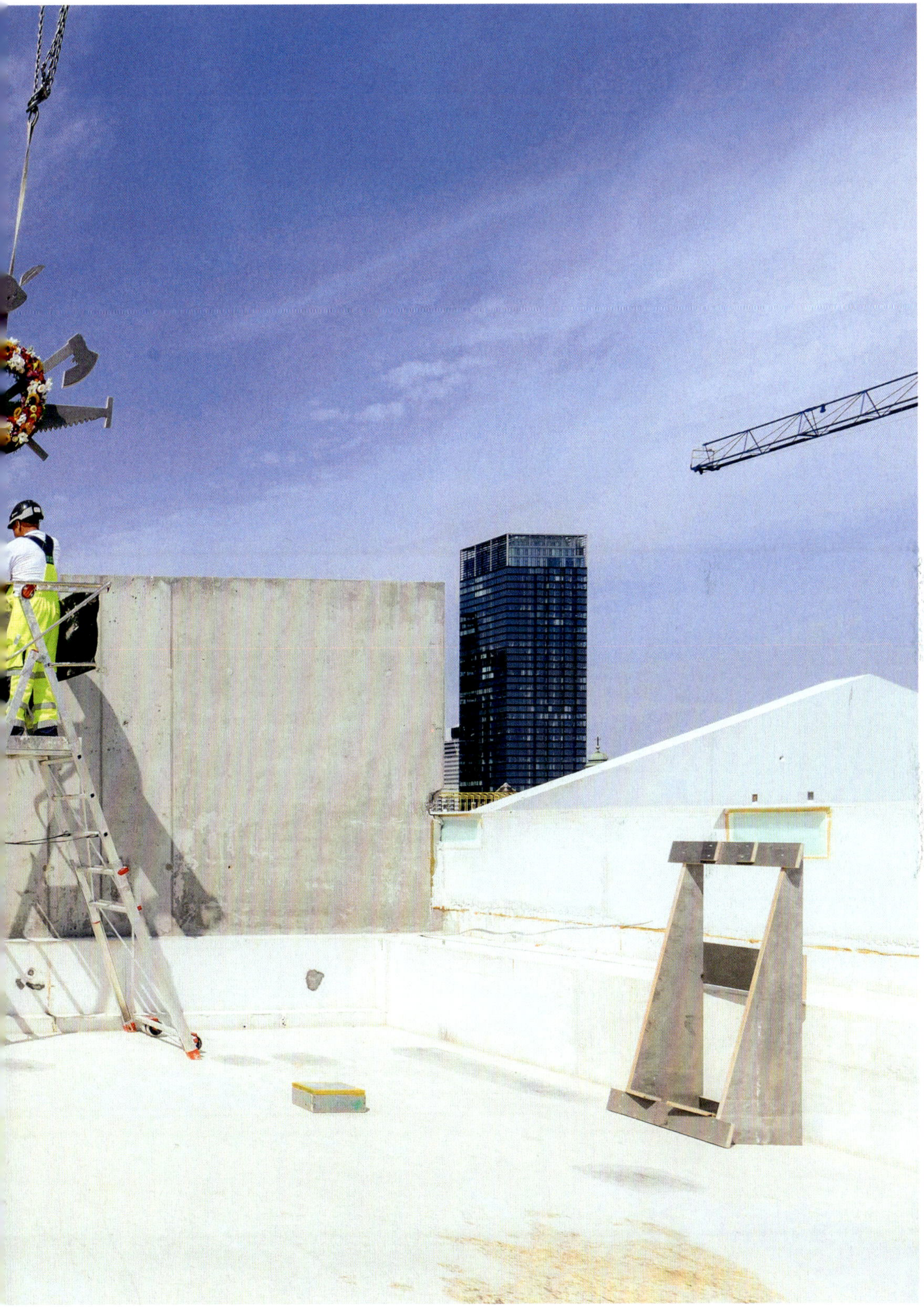

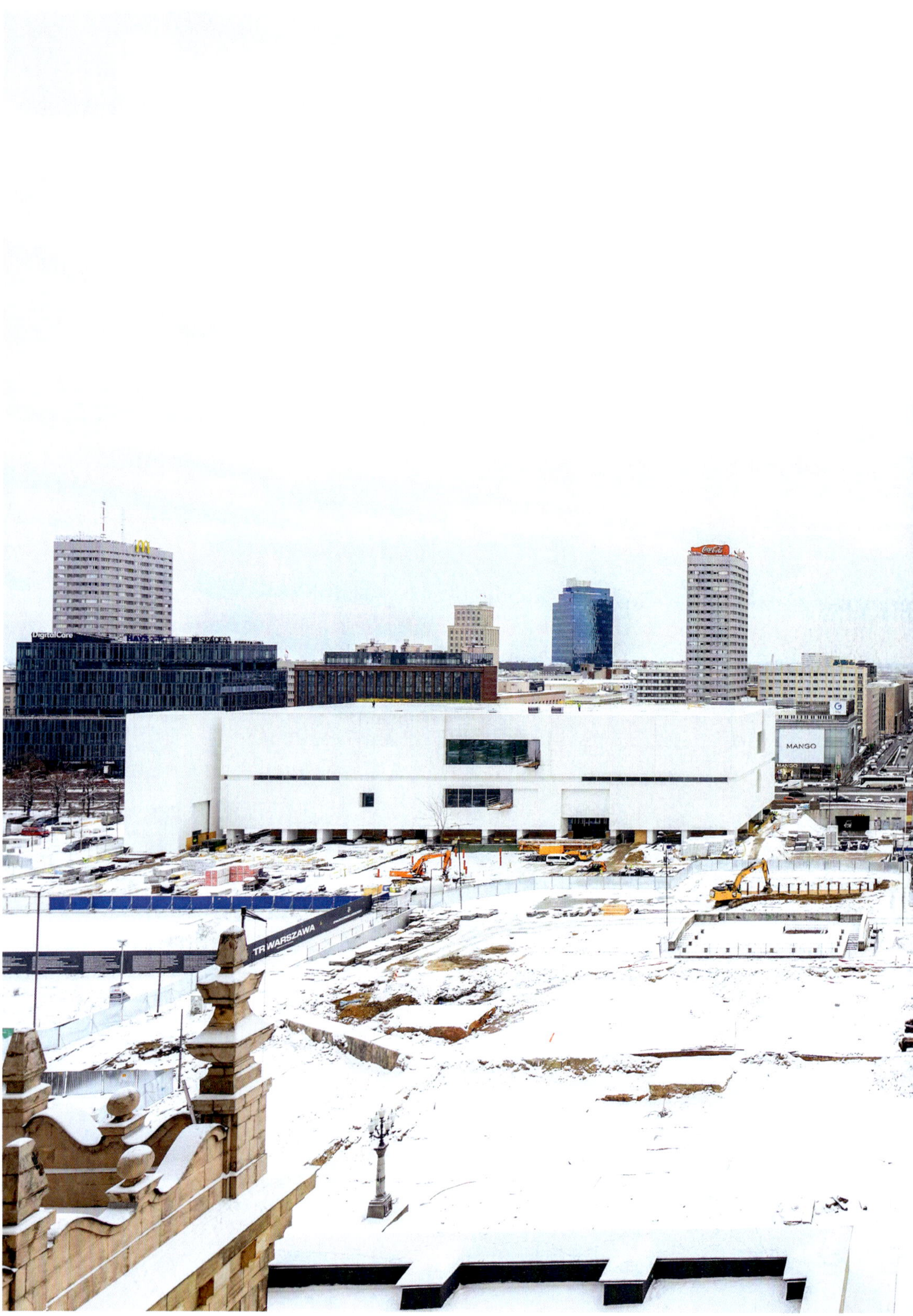
DigitalCare
HAYS
MANGO
TR WARSZAWA

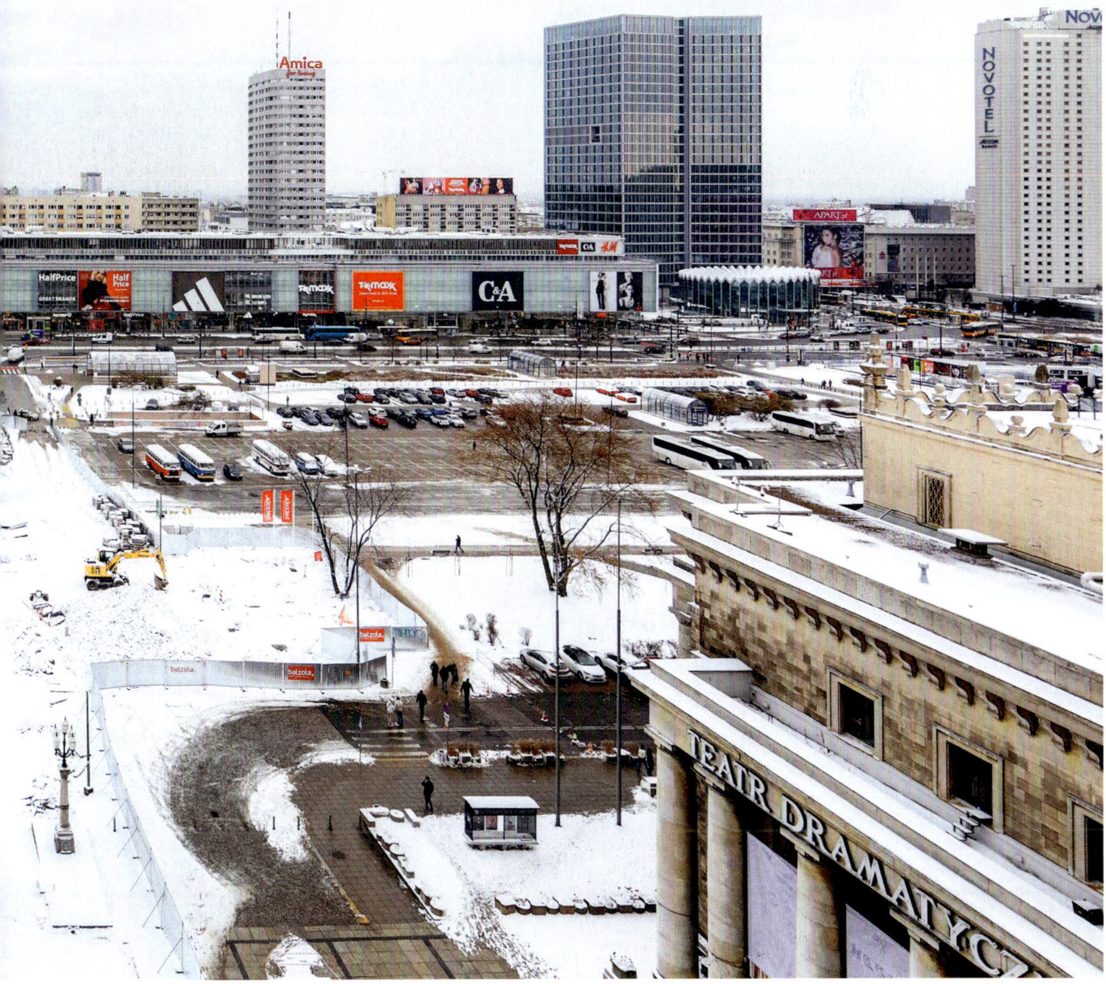
Amica
NOVOTEL
C&A
HalfPrice
TEATR DRAMATYCZ

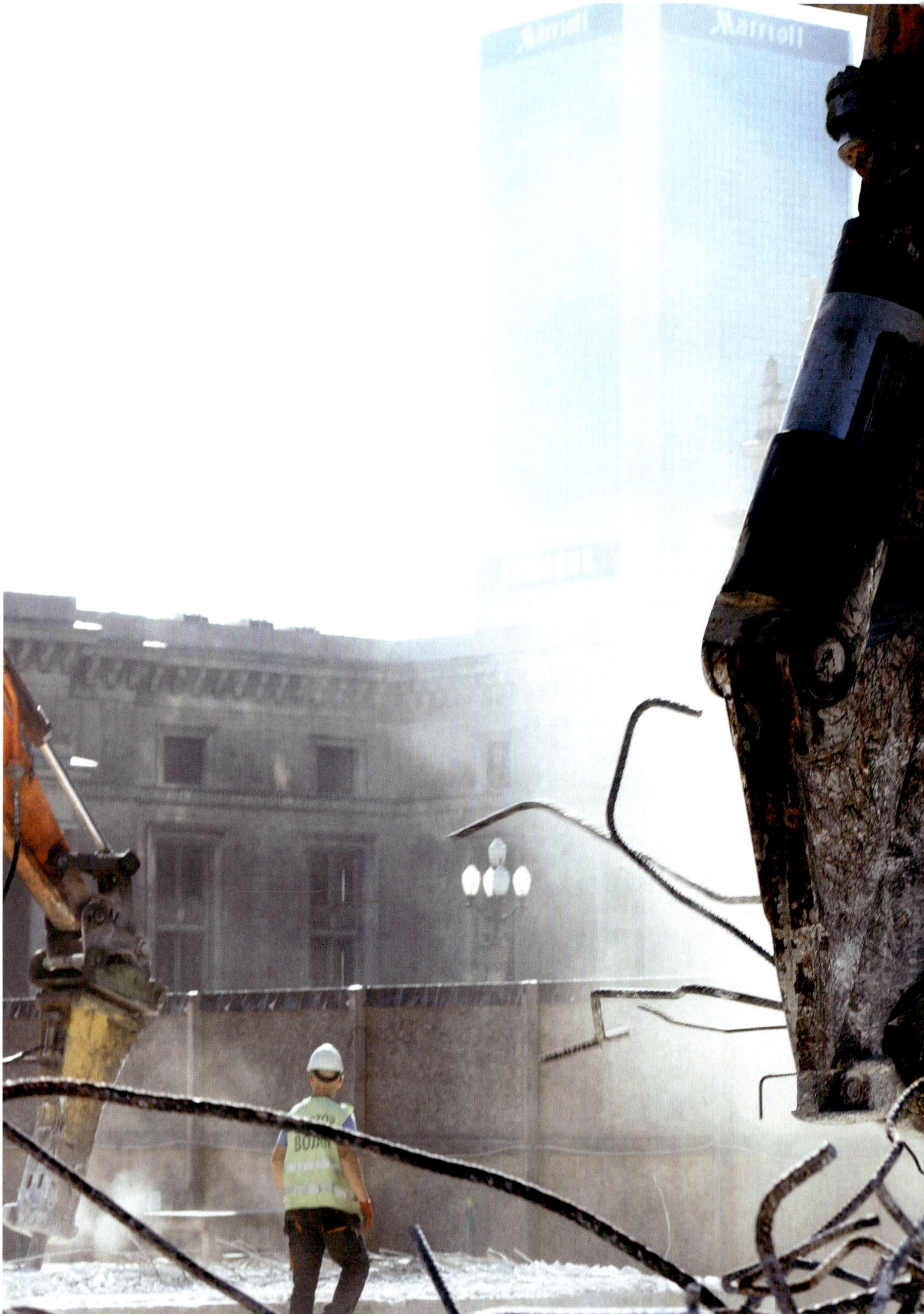
Marriott
Marriott

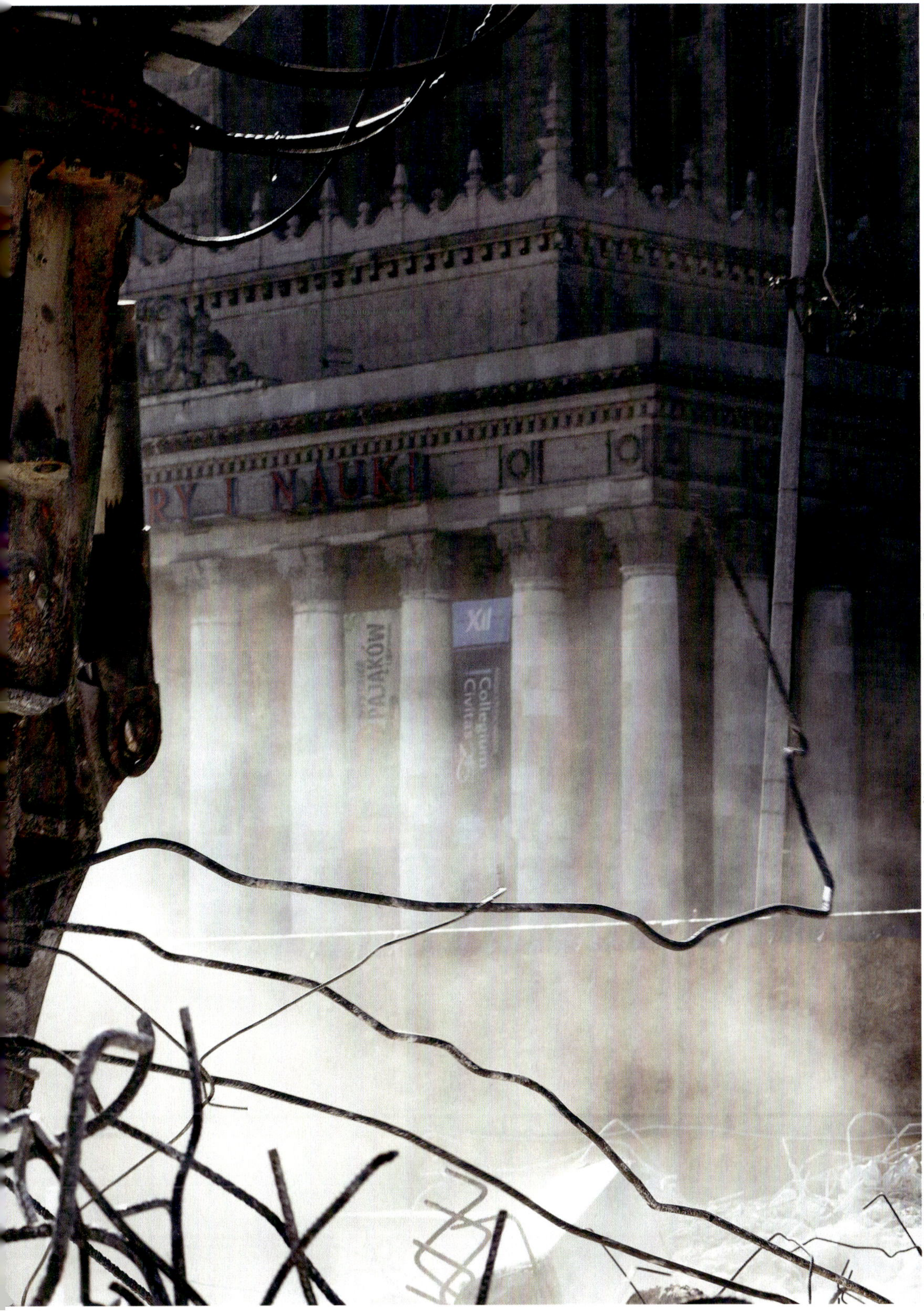
RY I NAUKI
PAJĄKÓW
Collegium Civitas

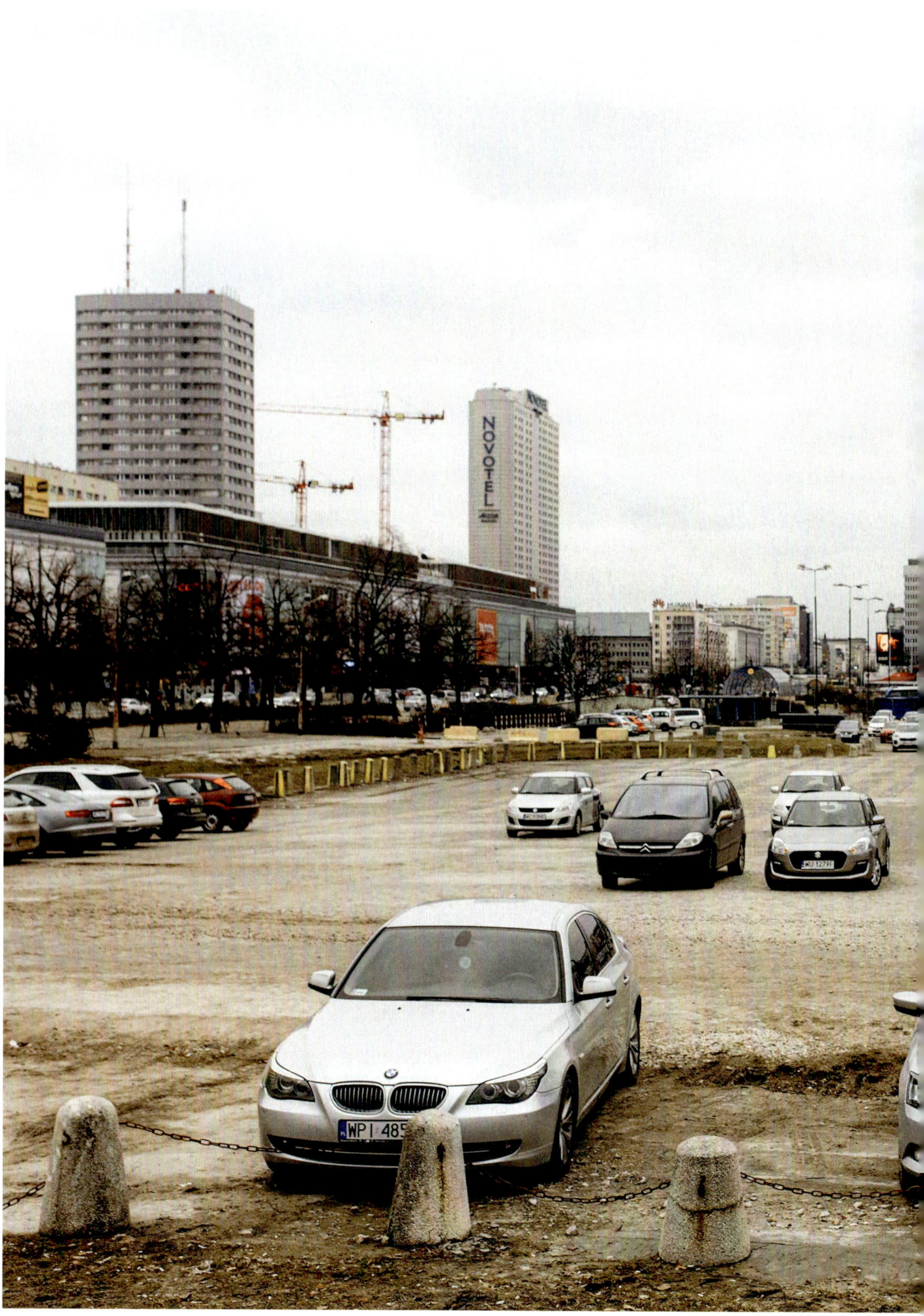
NOVOTEL

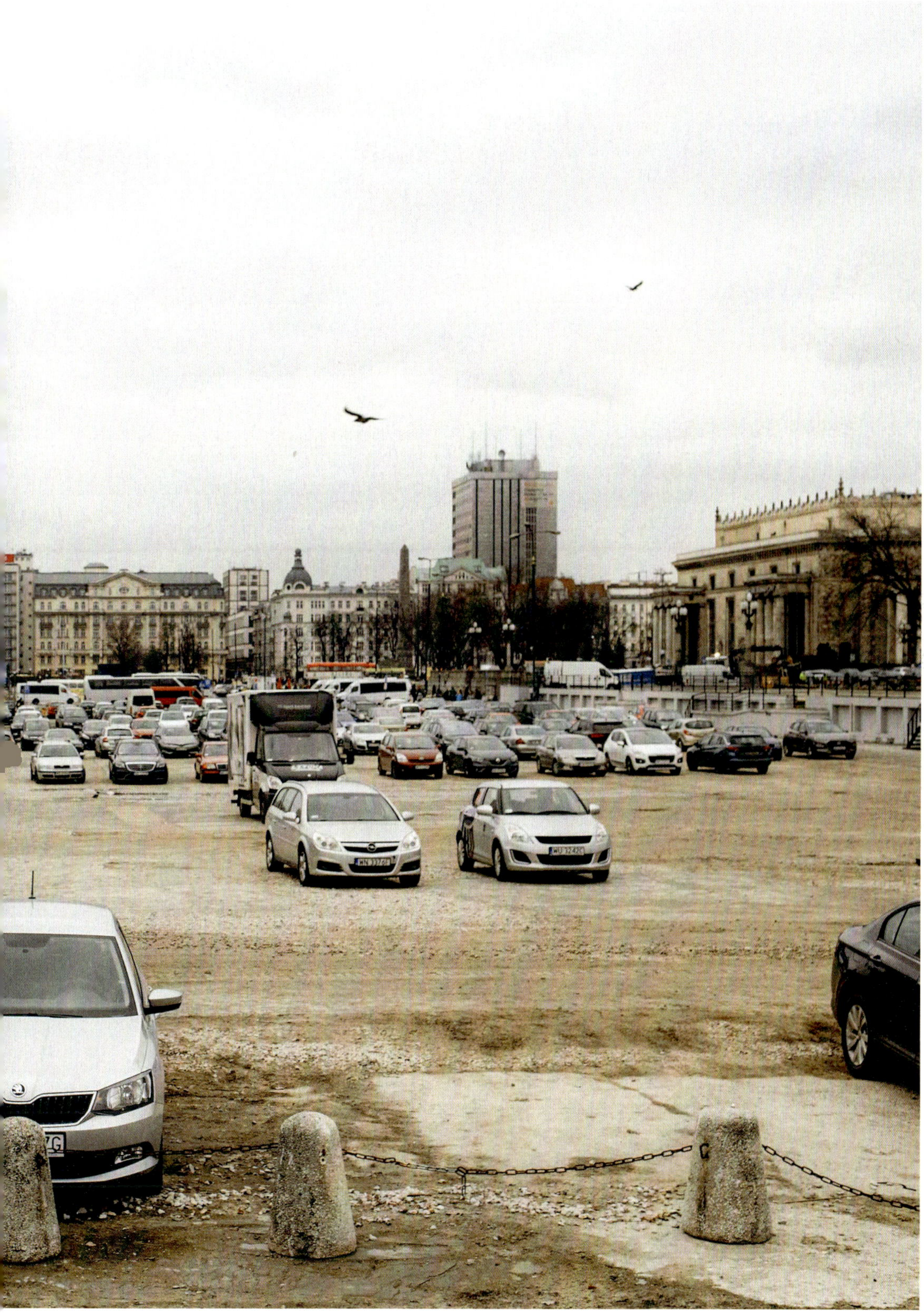

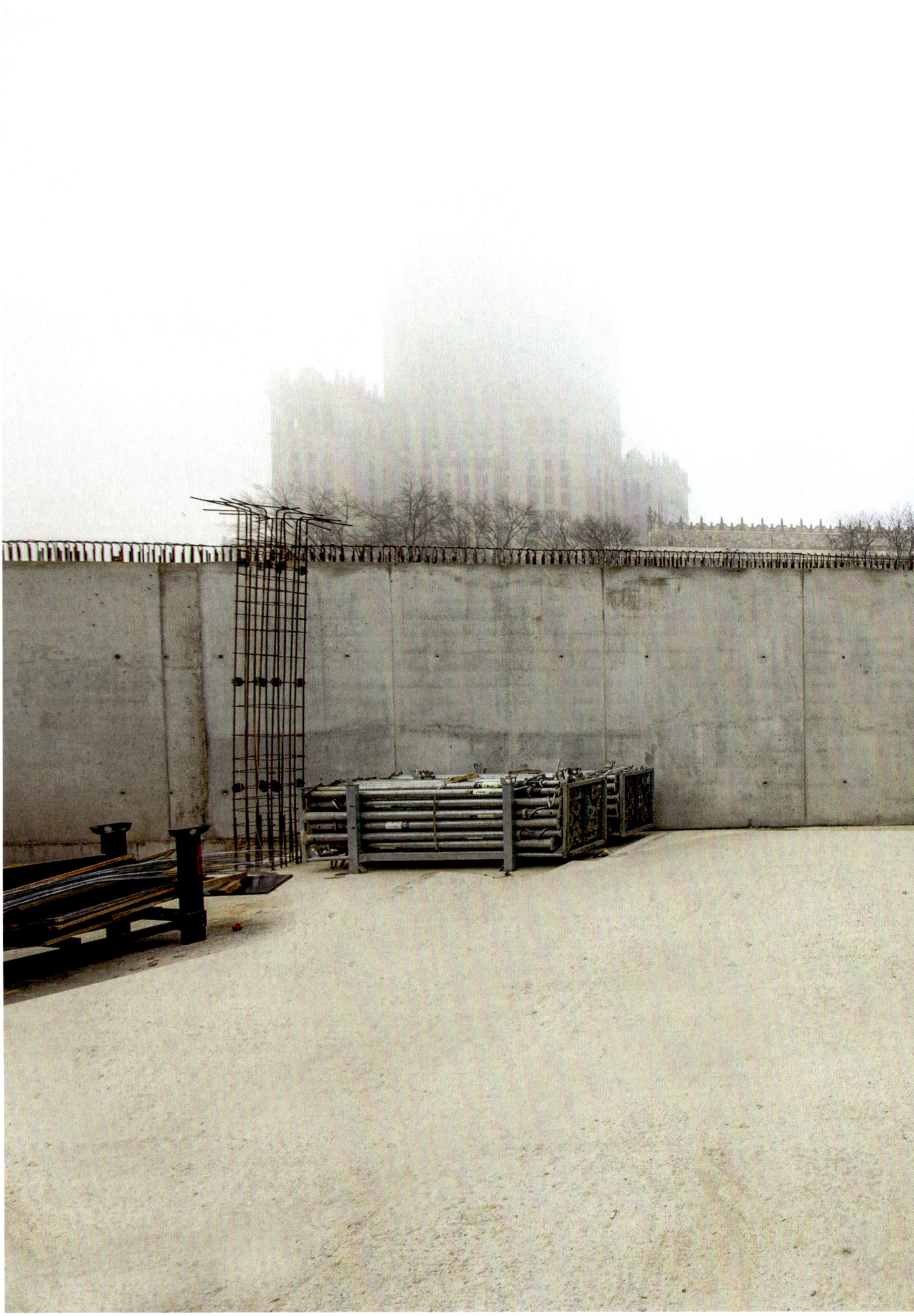

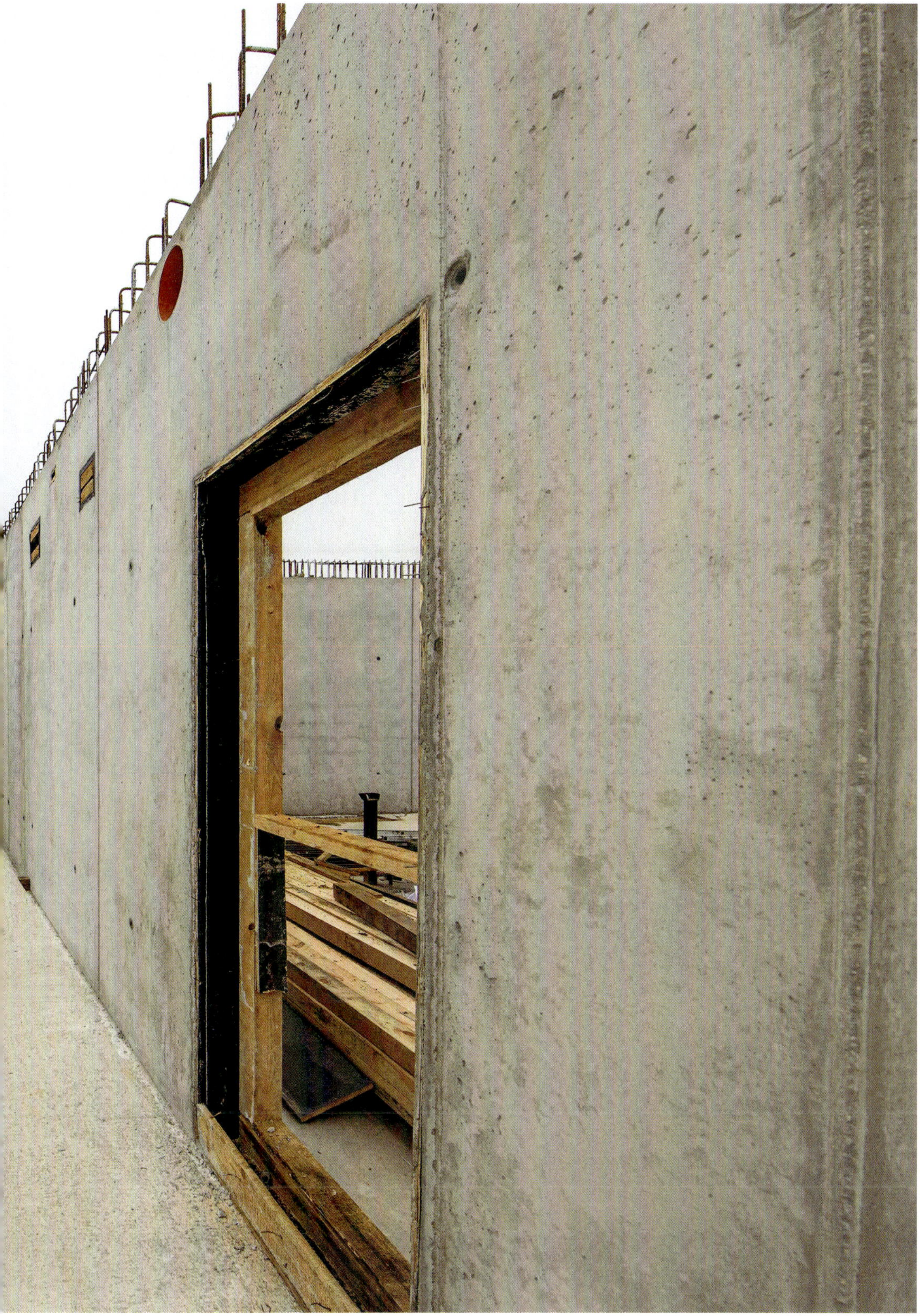

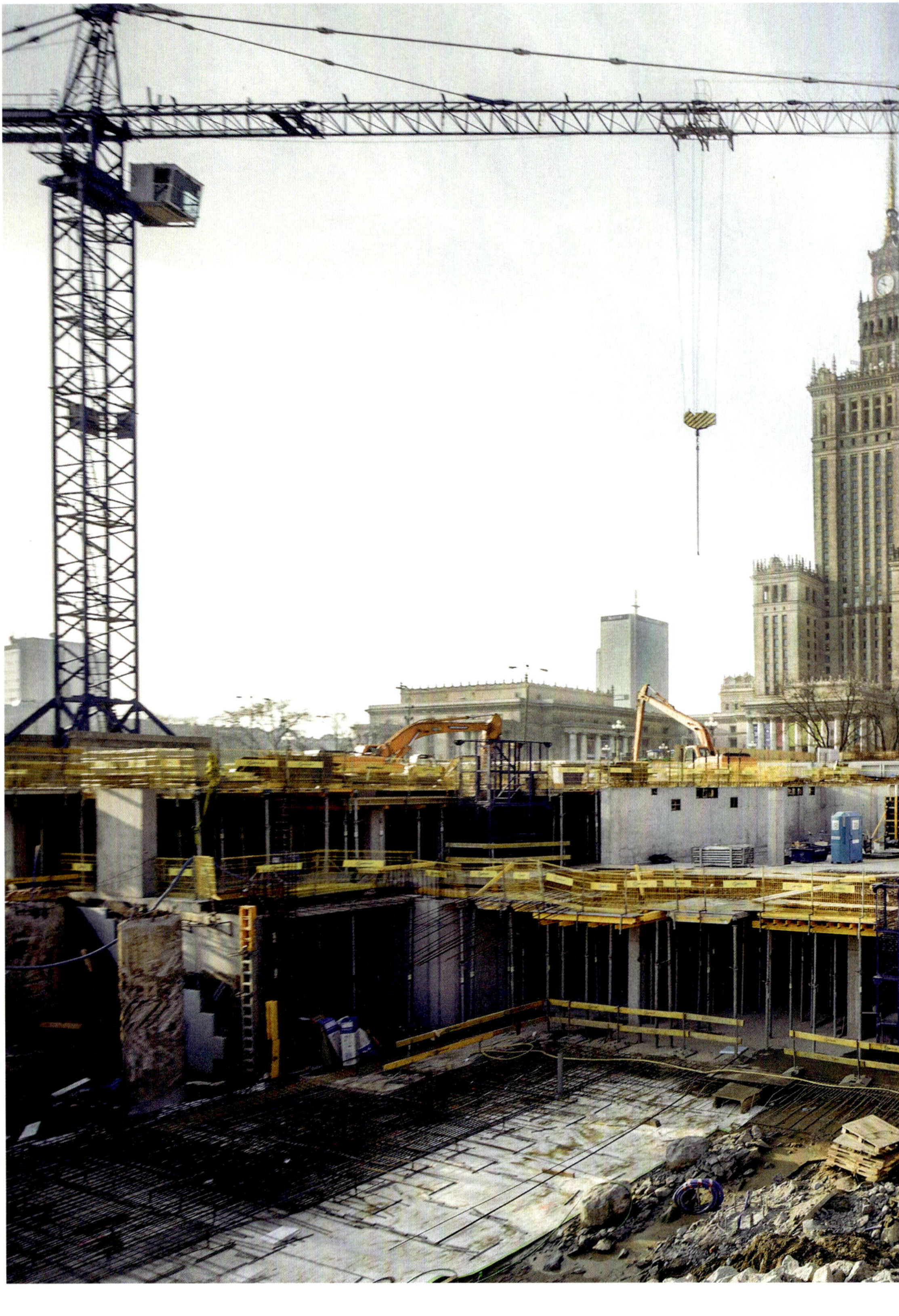

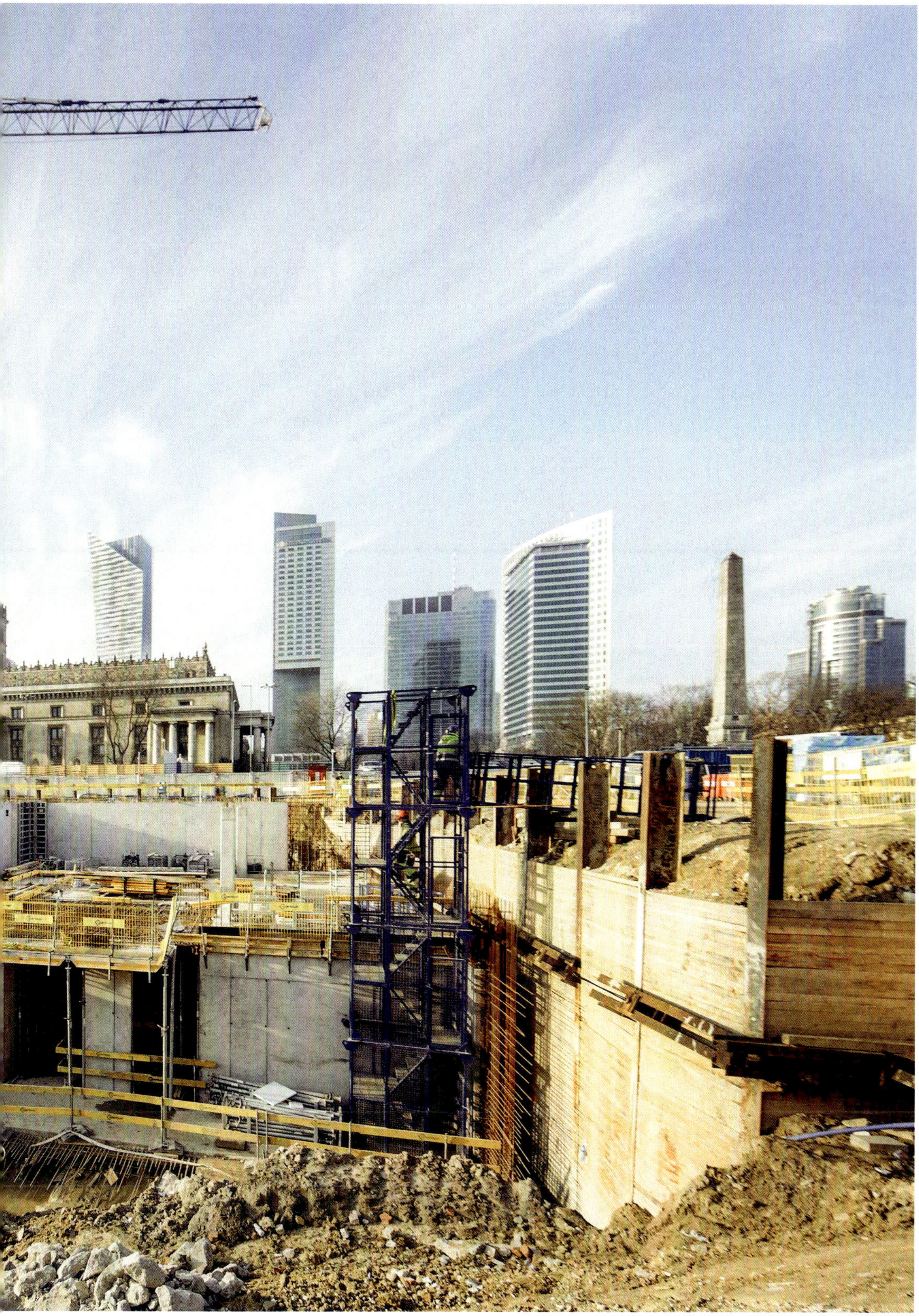

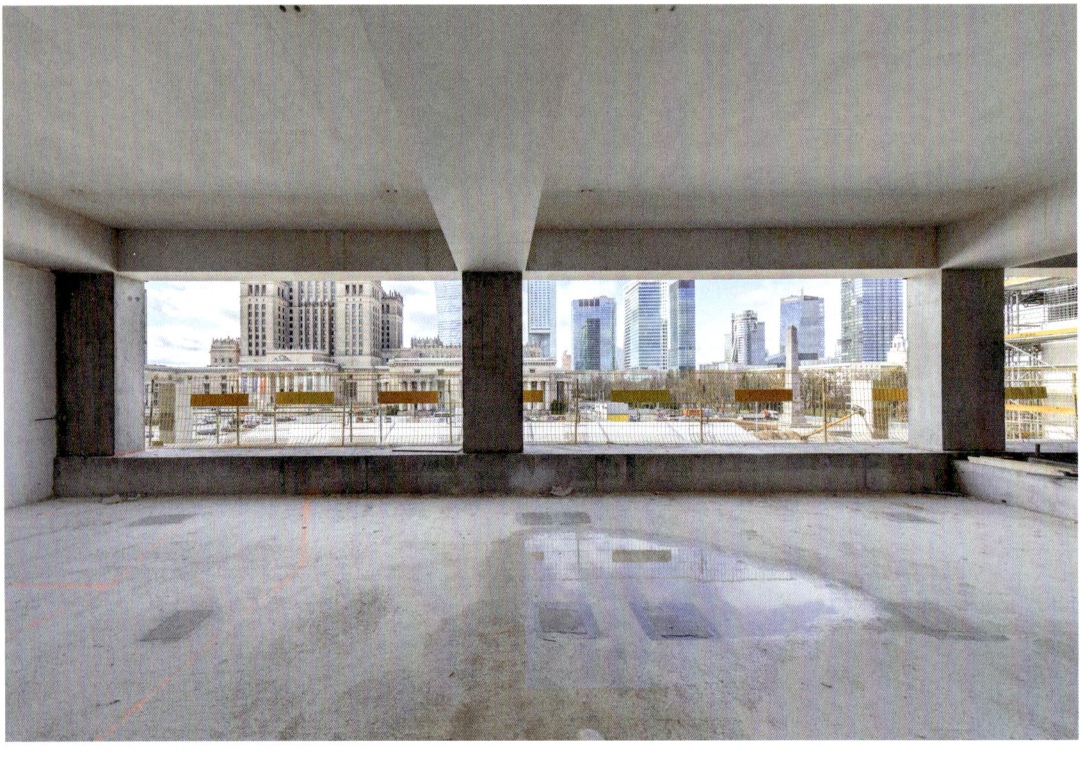

THE MUSEUM AND THE SQUARE 2024

Maja Wirkus is an artist and photographer with a thematic focus on architecture. She is the author and editor of *We Are Millennium Stars* (2024), and the co-author of *CIAM Archipelago. The Letters by Helena Syrkus* (2019). She has contributed to numerous international exhibitions and books, including for C/O Berlin, Haus der Photographie der Deichtorhallen Hamburg, Kunstverein am Rosa Luxemburg in Berlin, and the Museum of Modern Art in Warsaw (*Emilia. Meble, muzeum, modernizm*, 2016). Maja also conducts artistic research with Eric Pries under the name "wirkuspries."

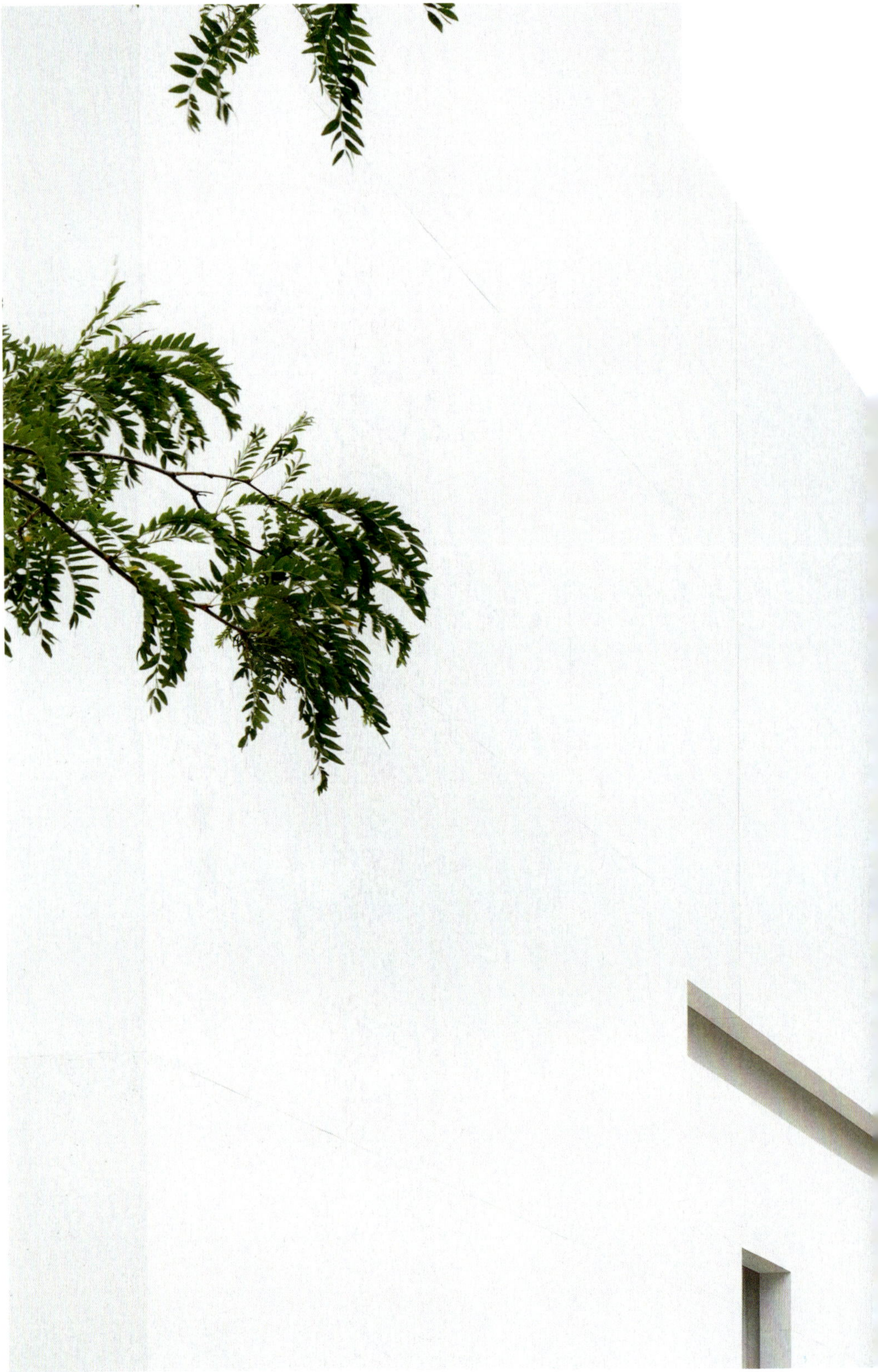

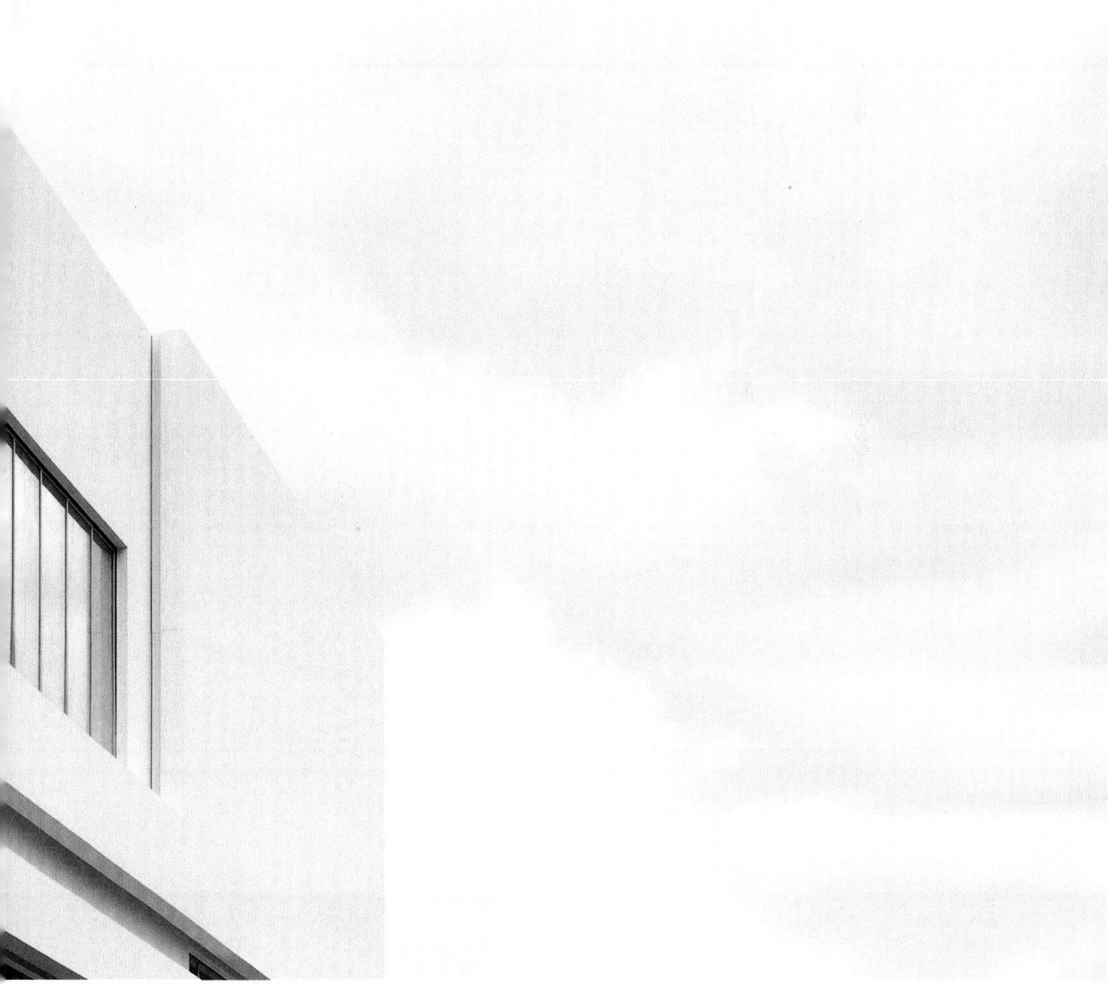

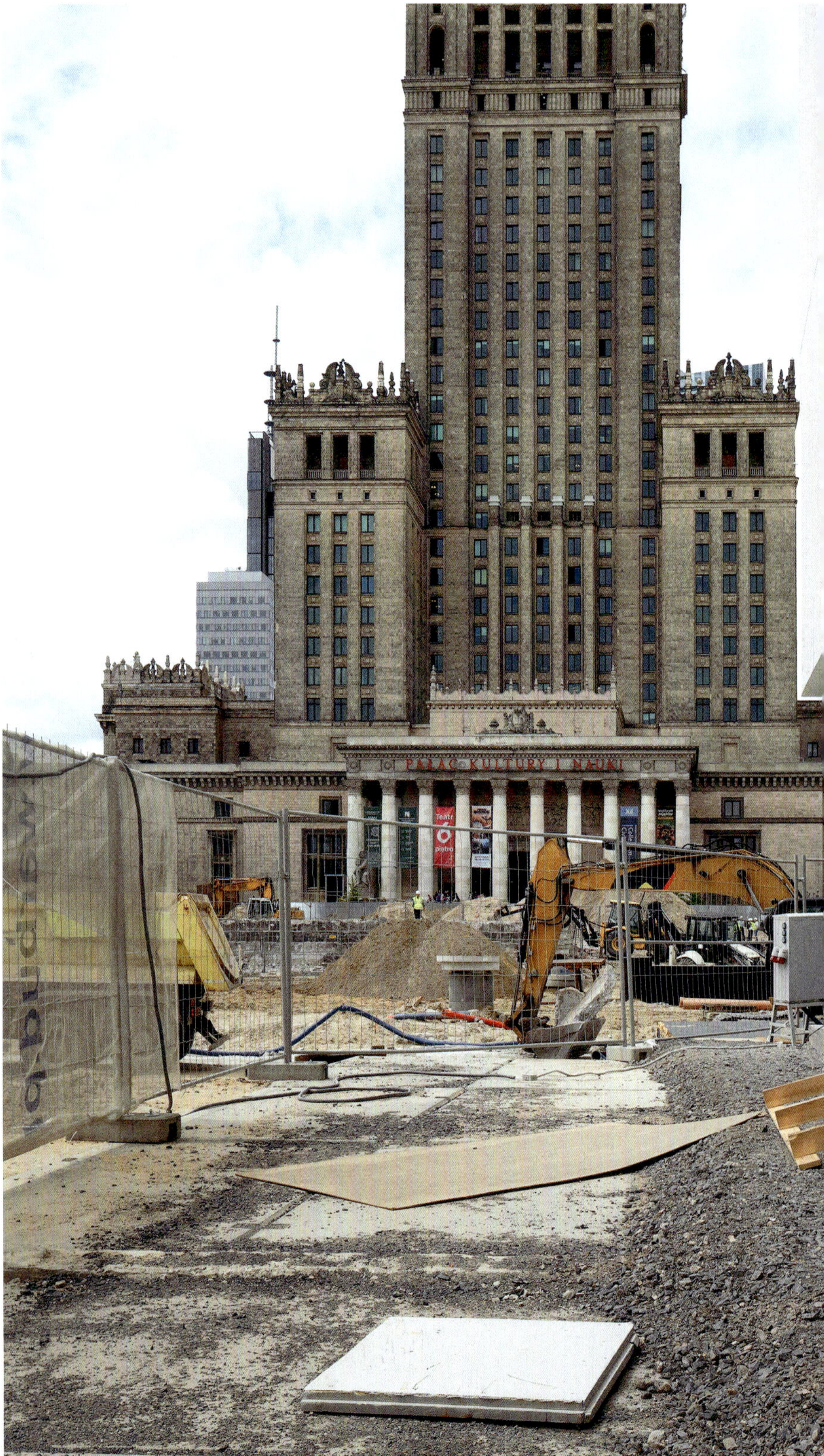
PAŁAC KULTURY I NAUKI

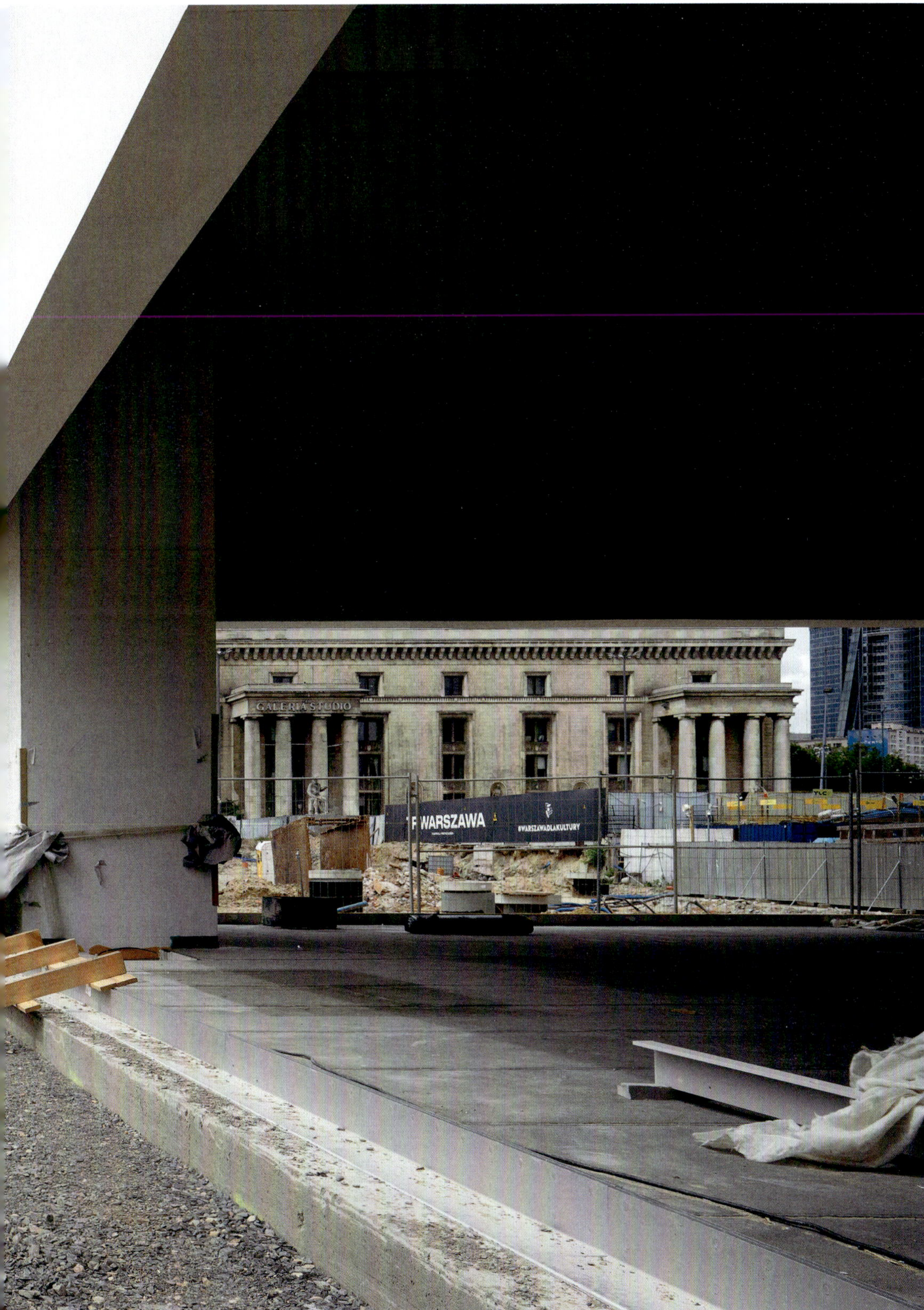
GALERIA STUDIO
WARSZAWA
#WARSZAWADLAKULTURY

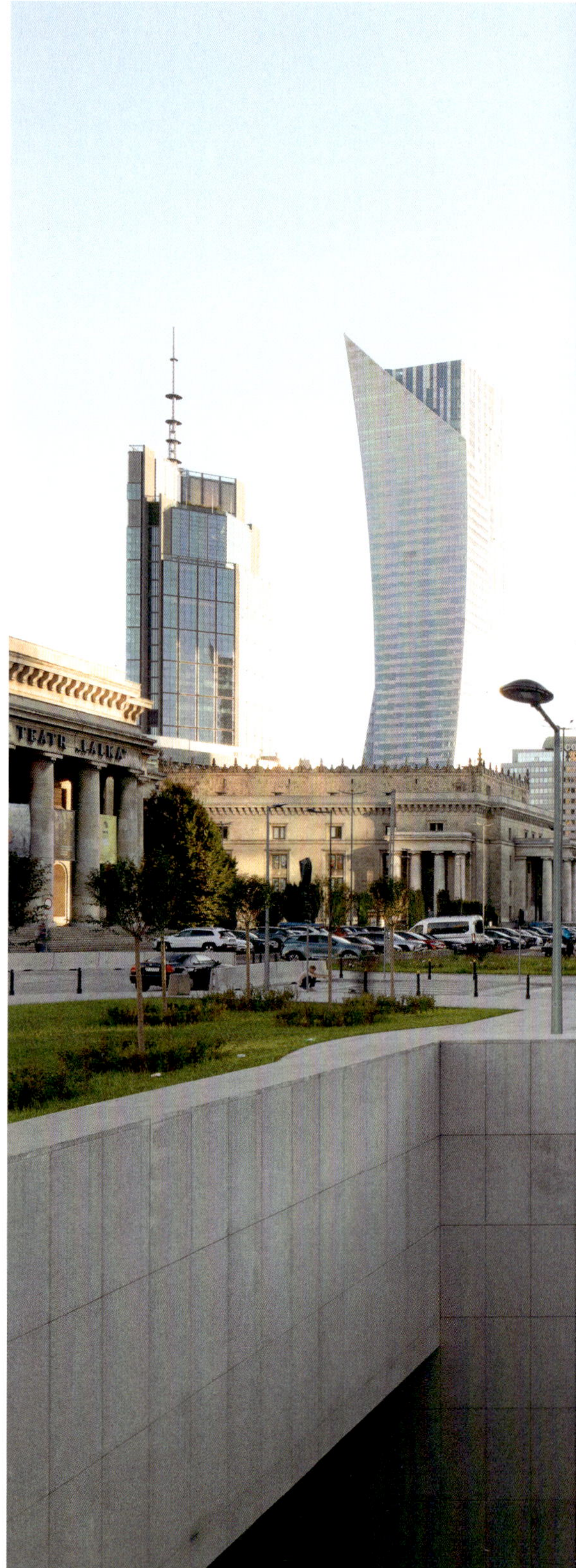
TEATR „LALKA"

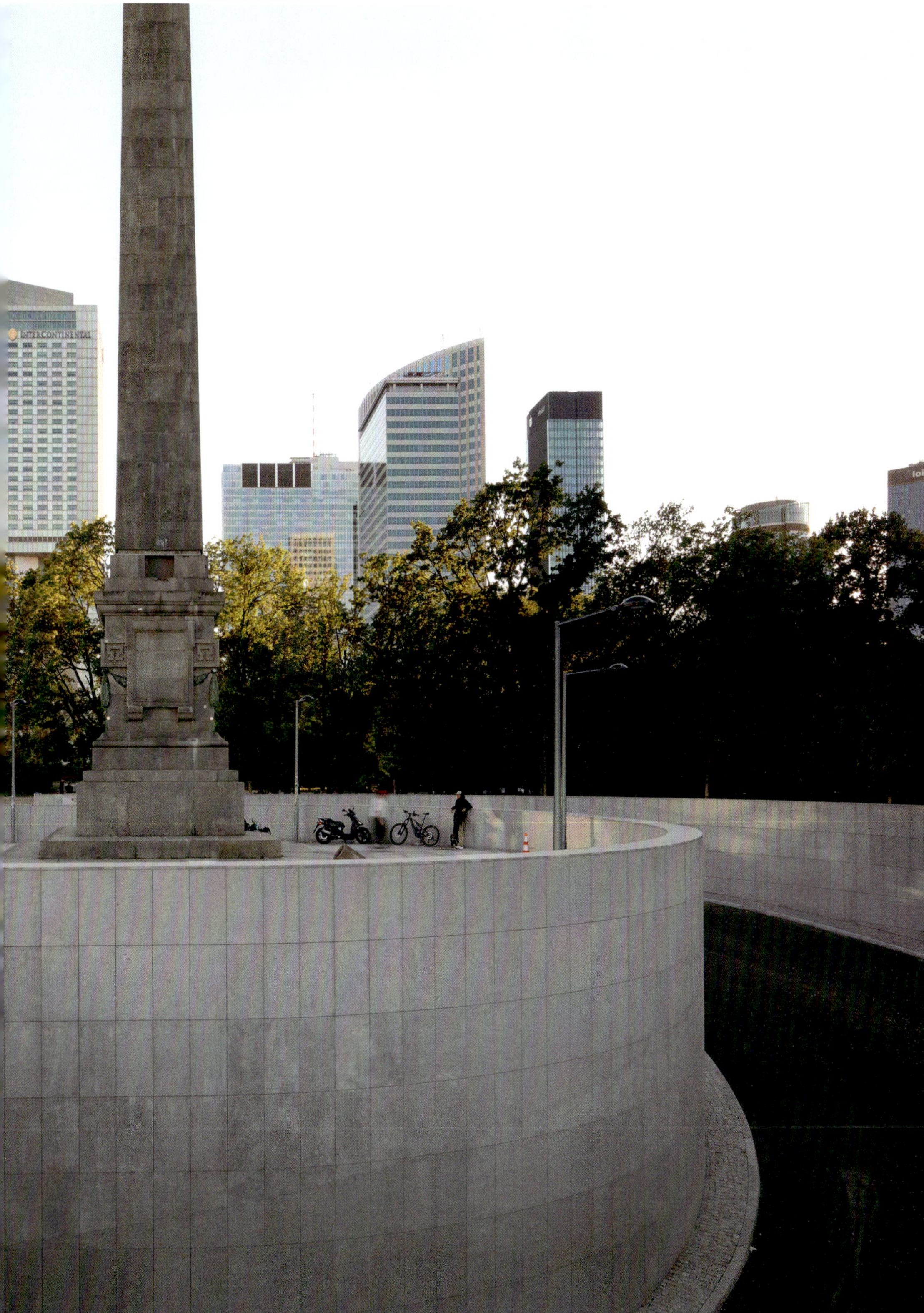
INTERCONTINENTAL

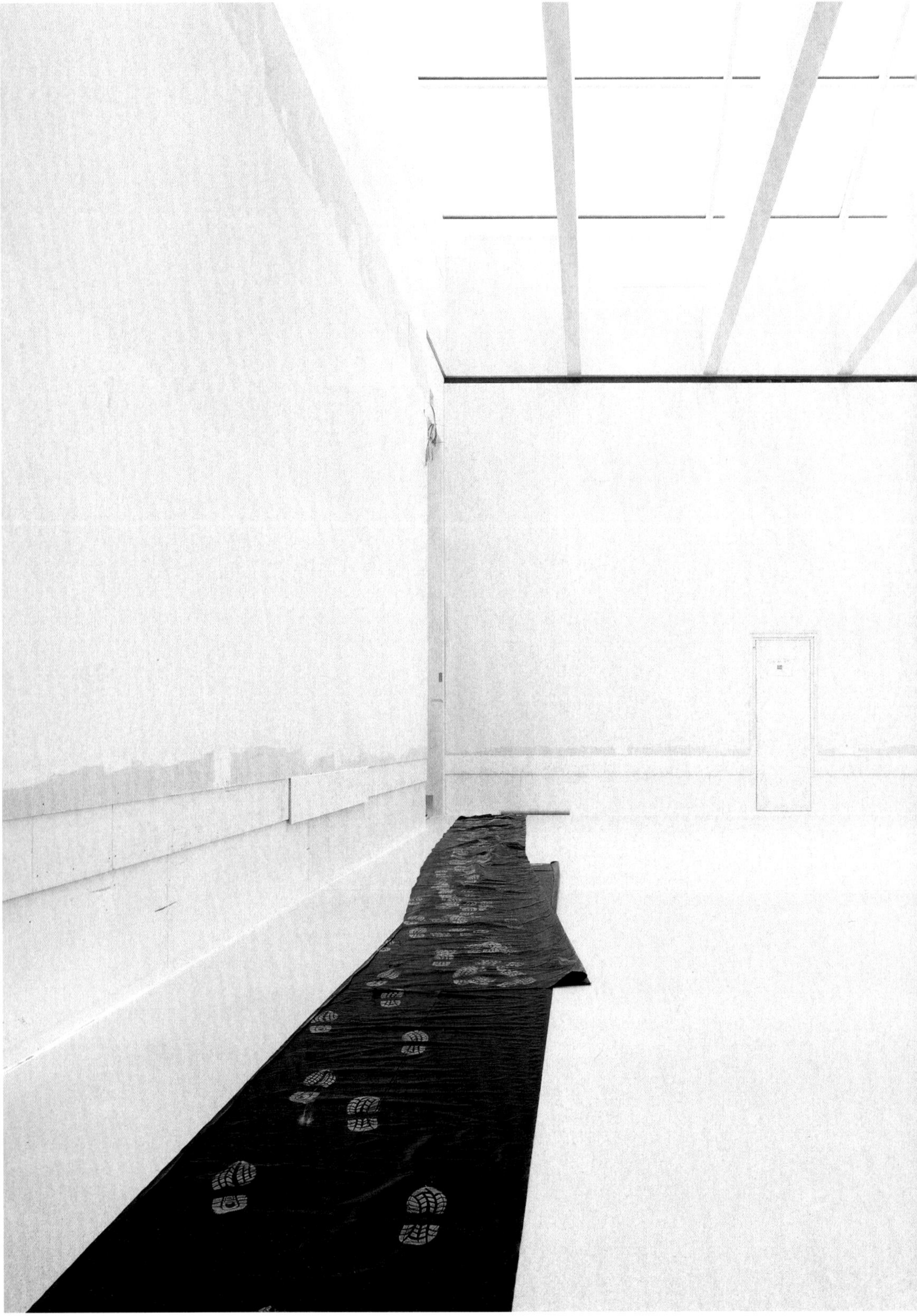

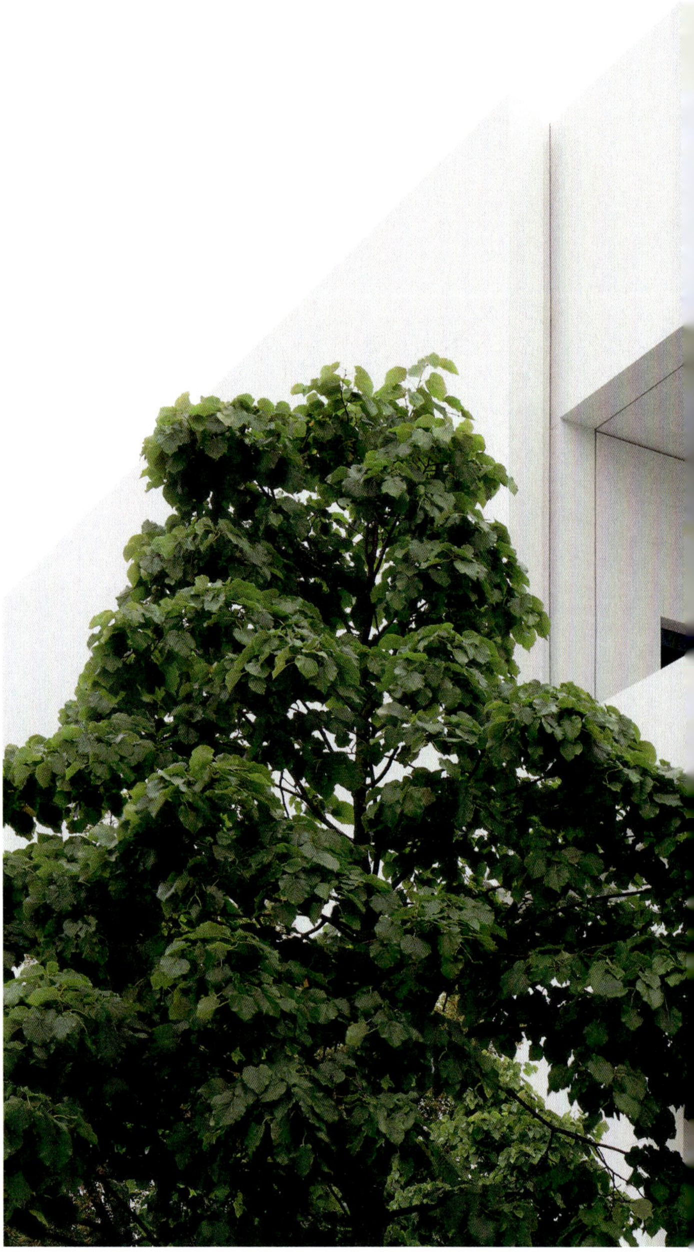

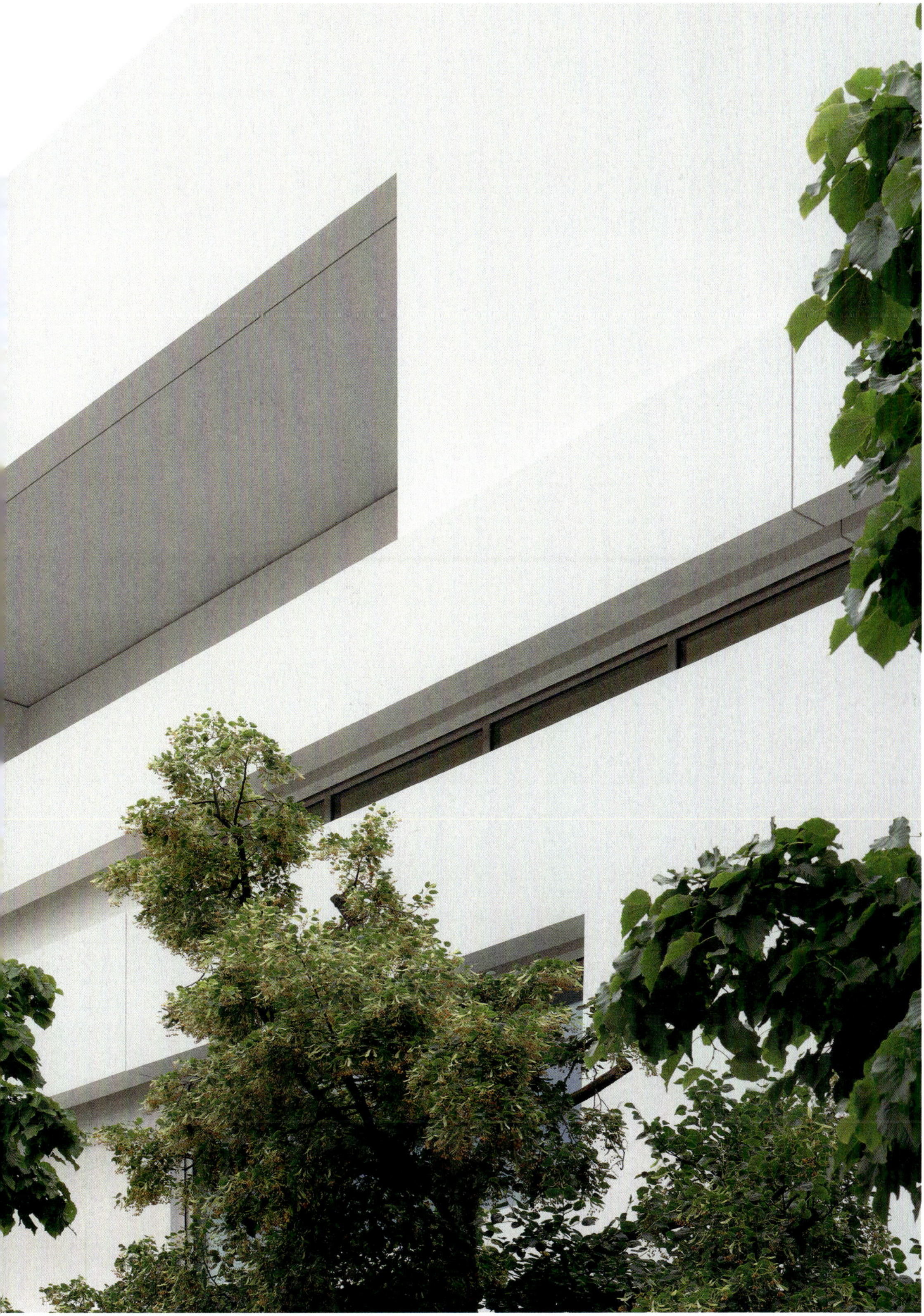

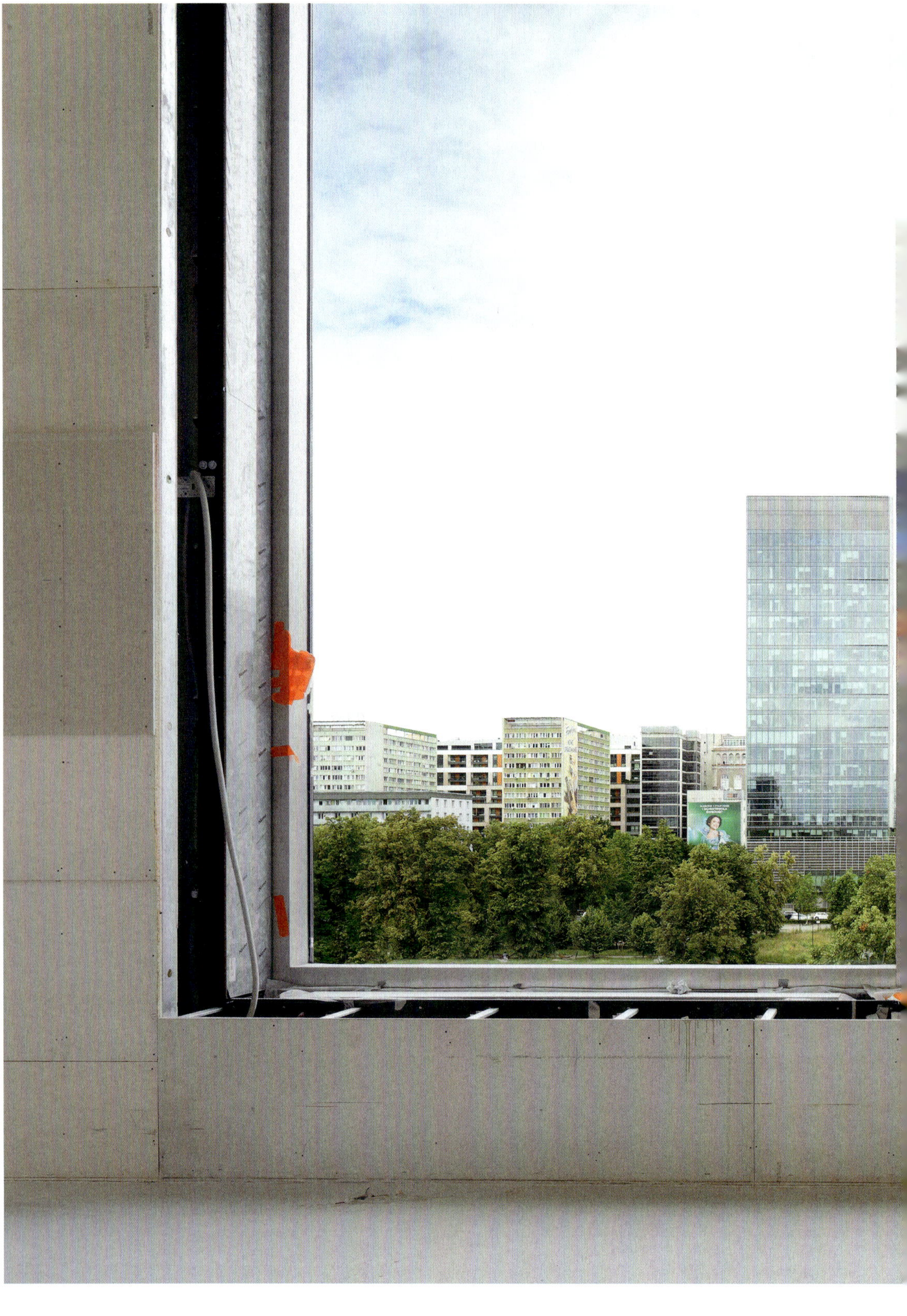

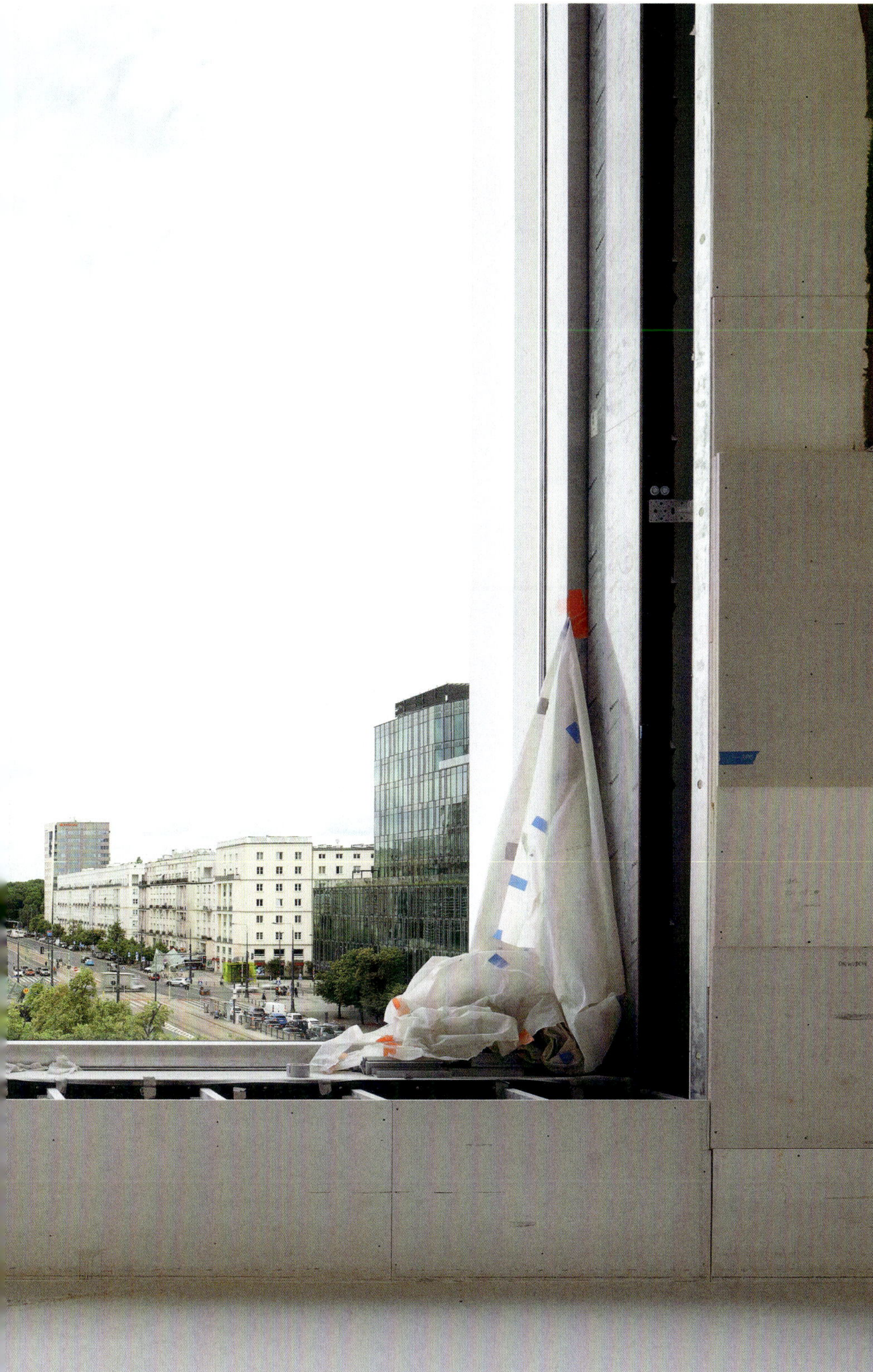

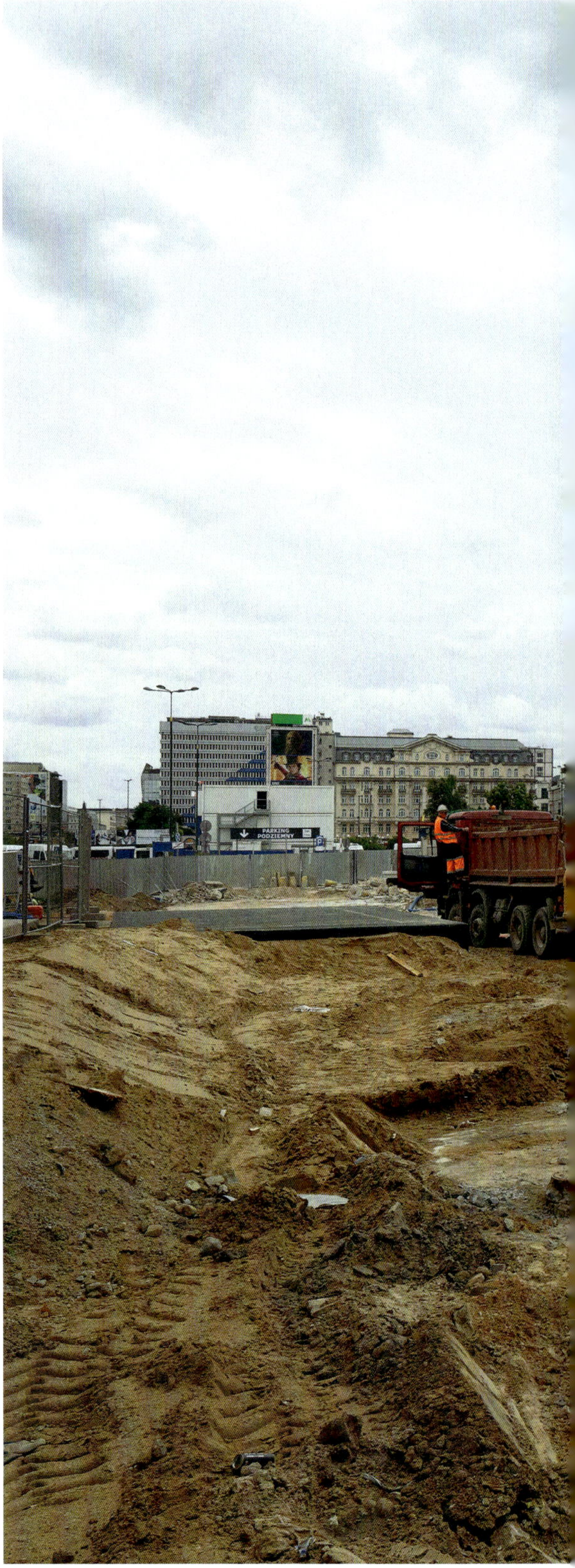
PARKING
PODZIEMNY

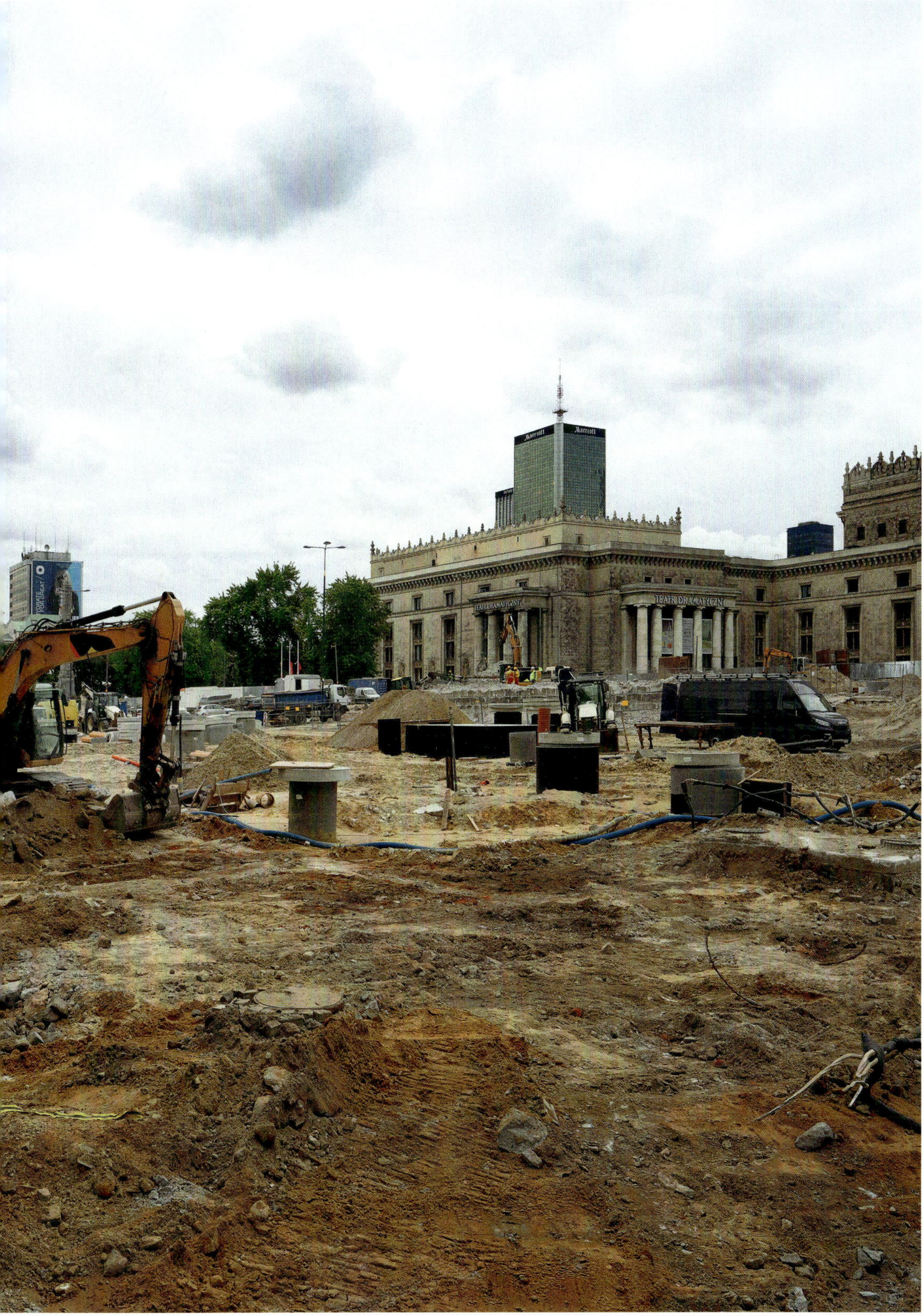
Marriott
TEATR DRAMATYCZNY

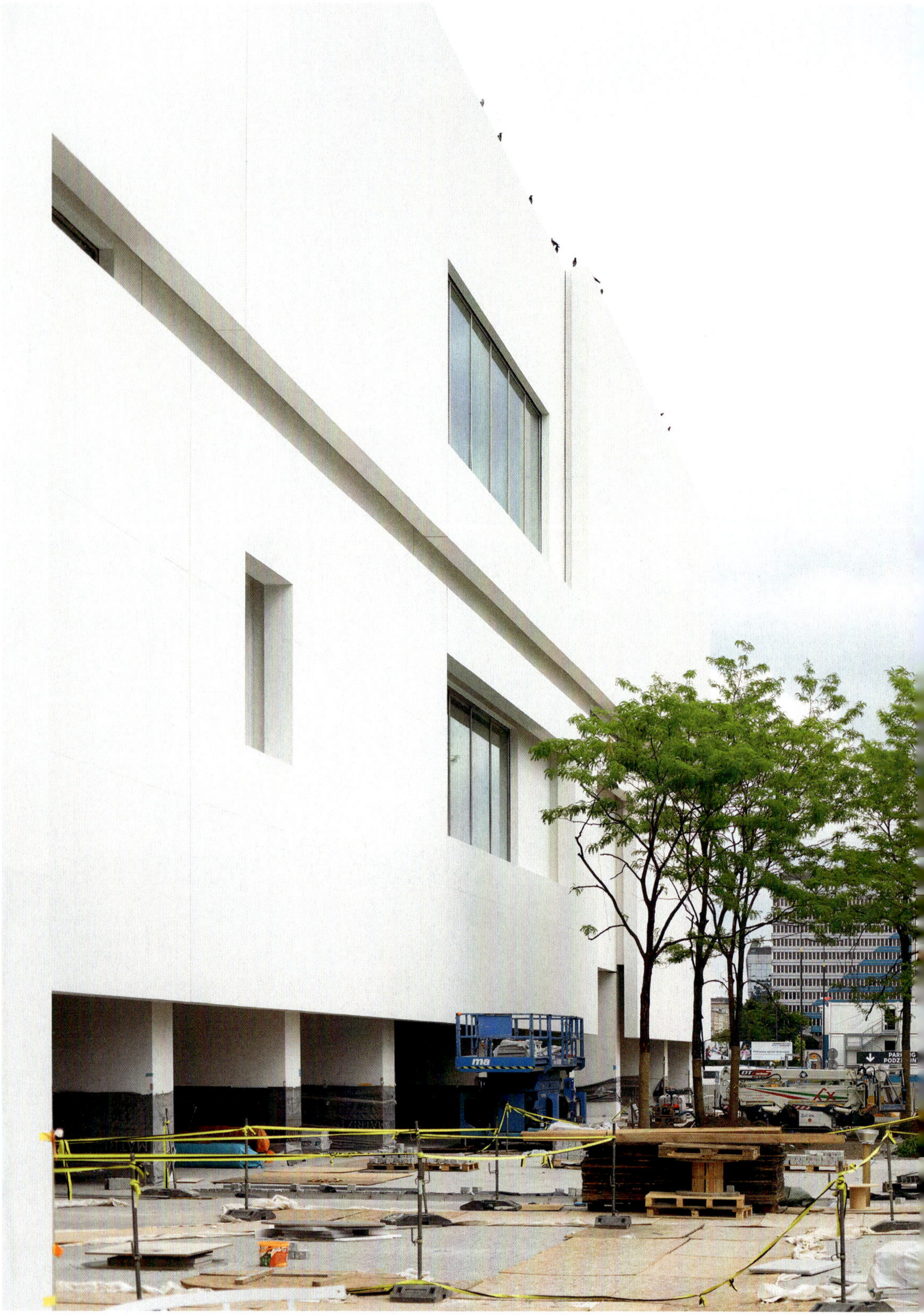

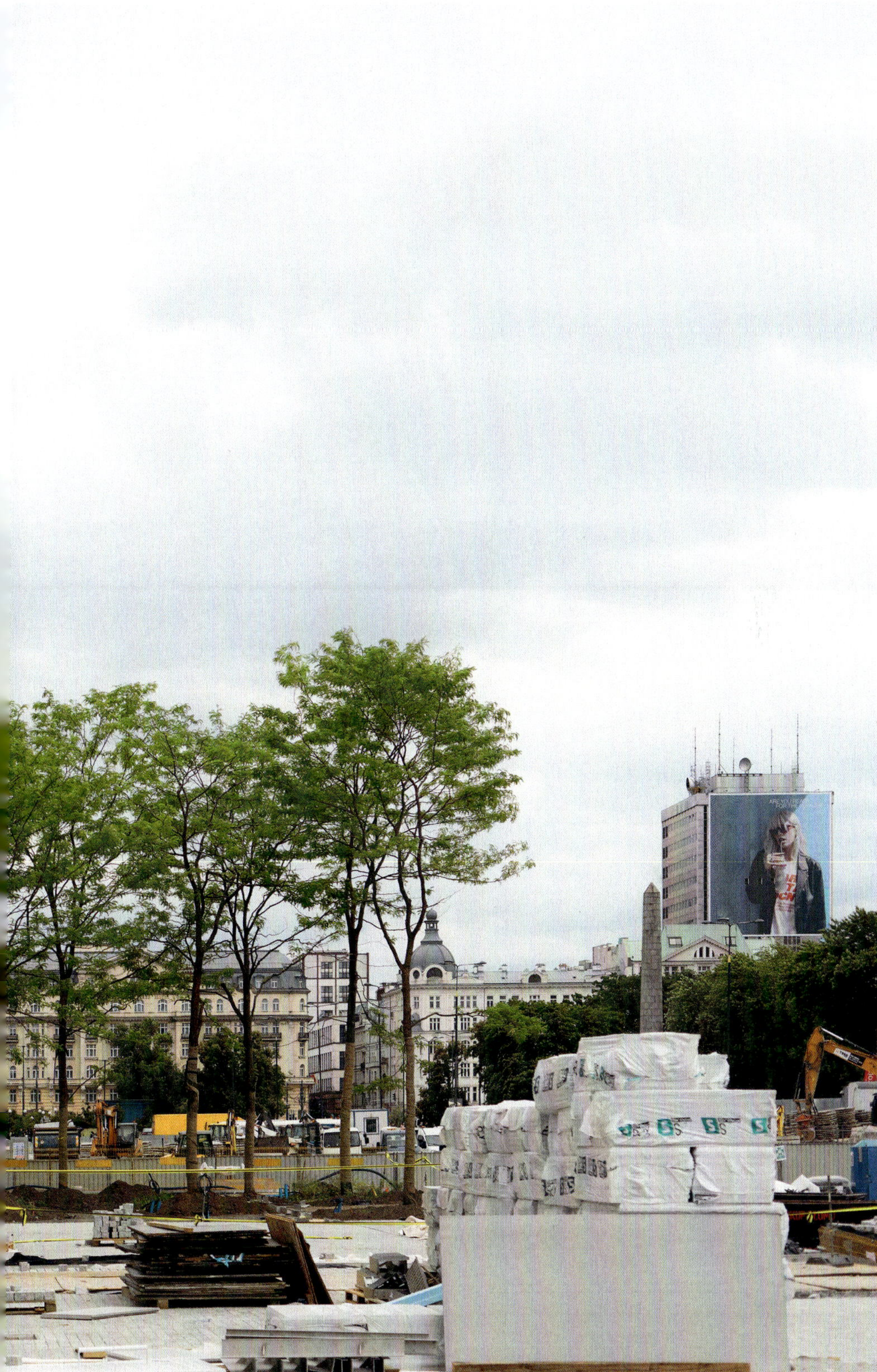

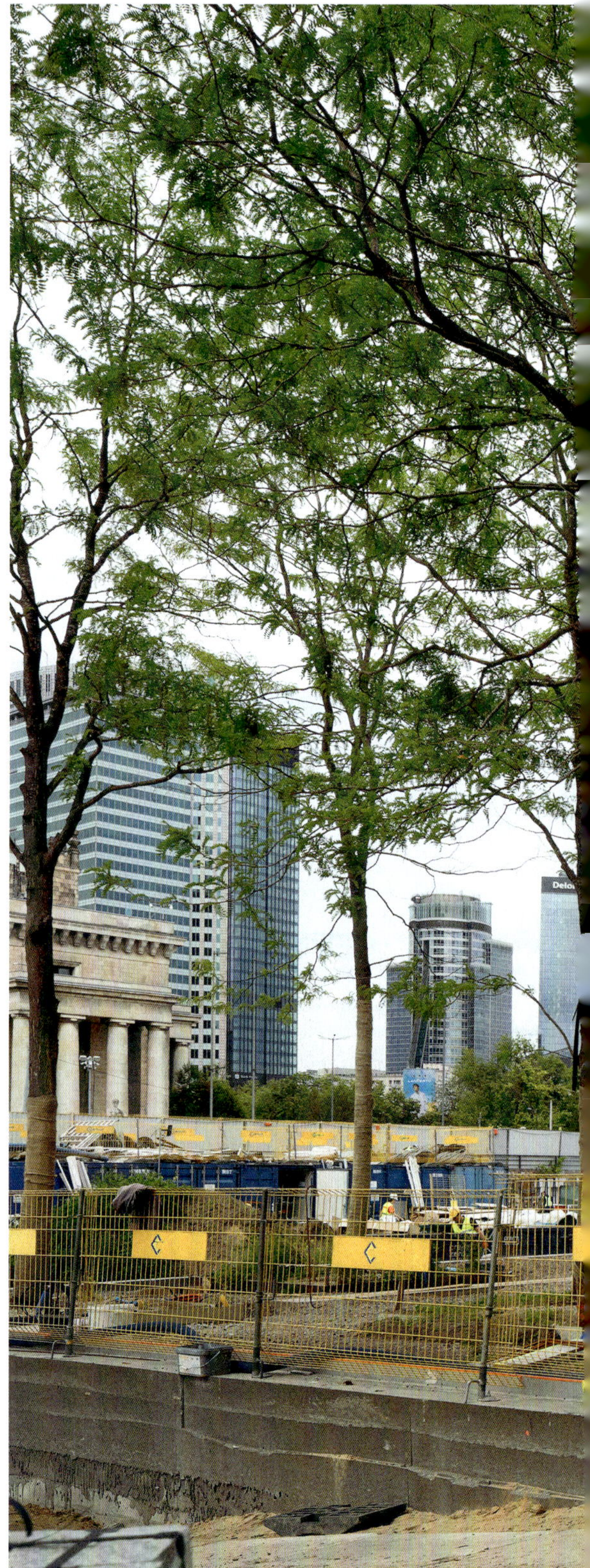

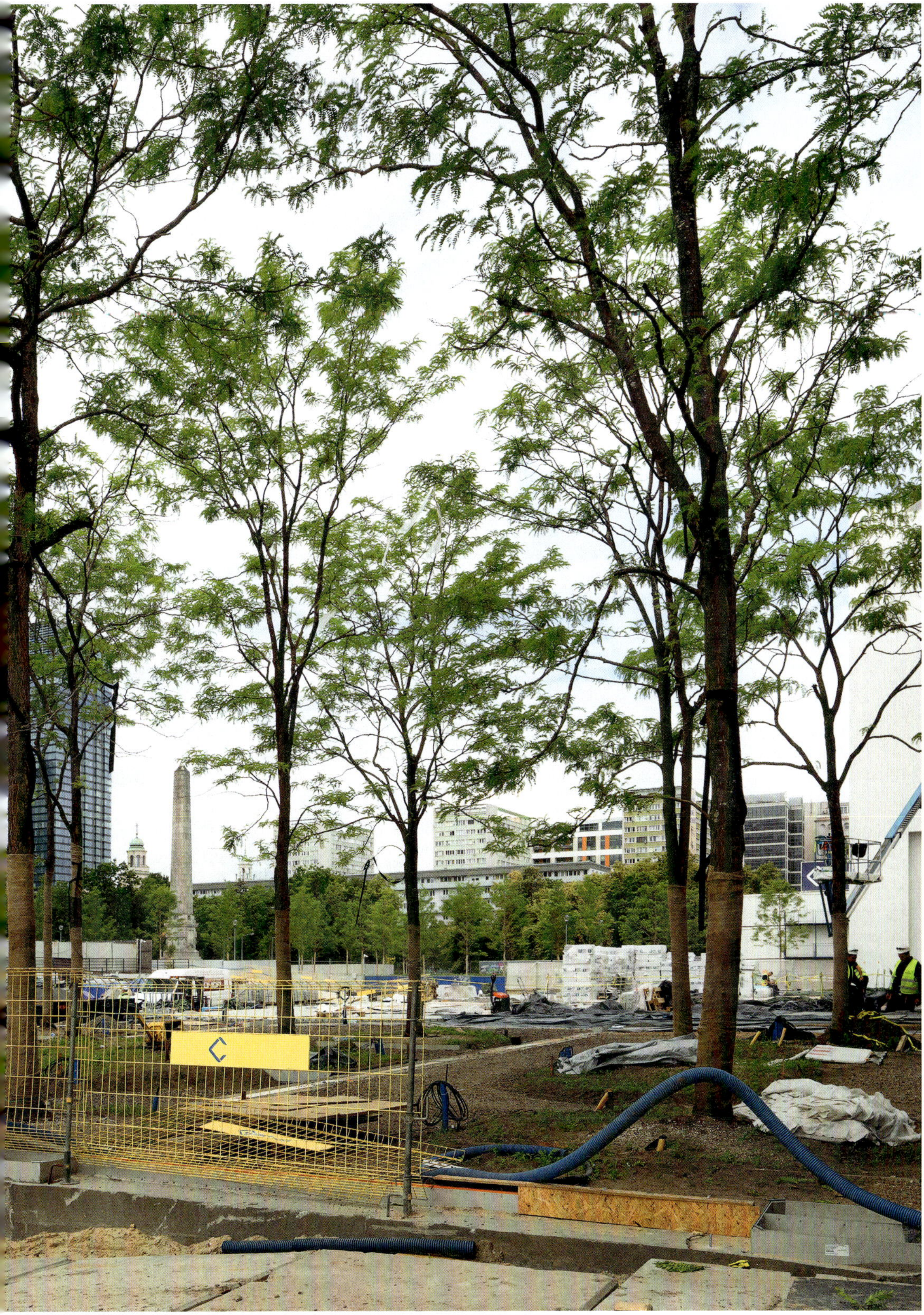

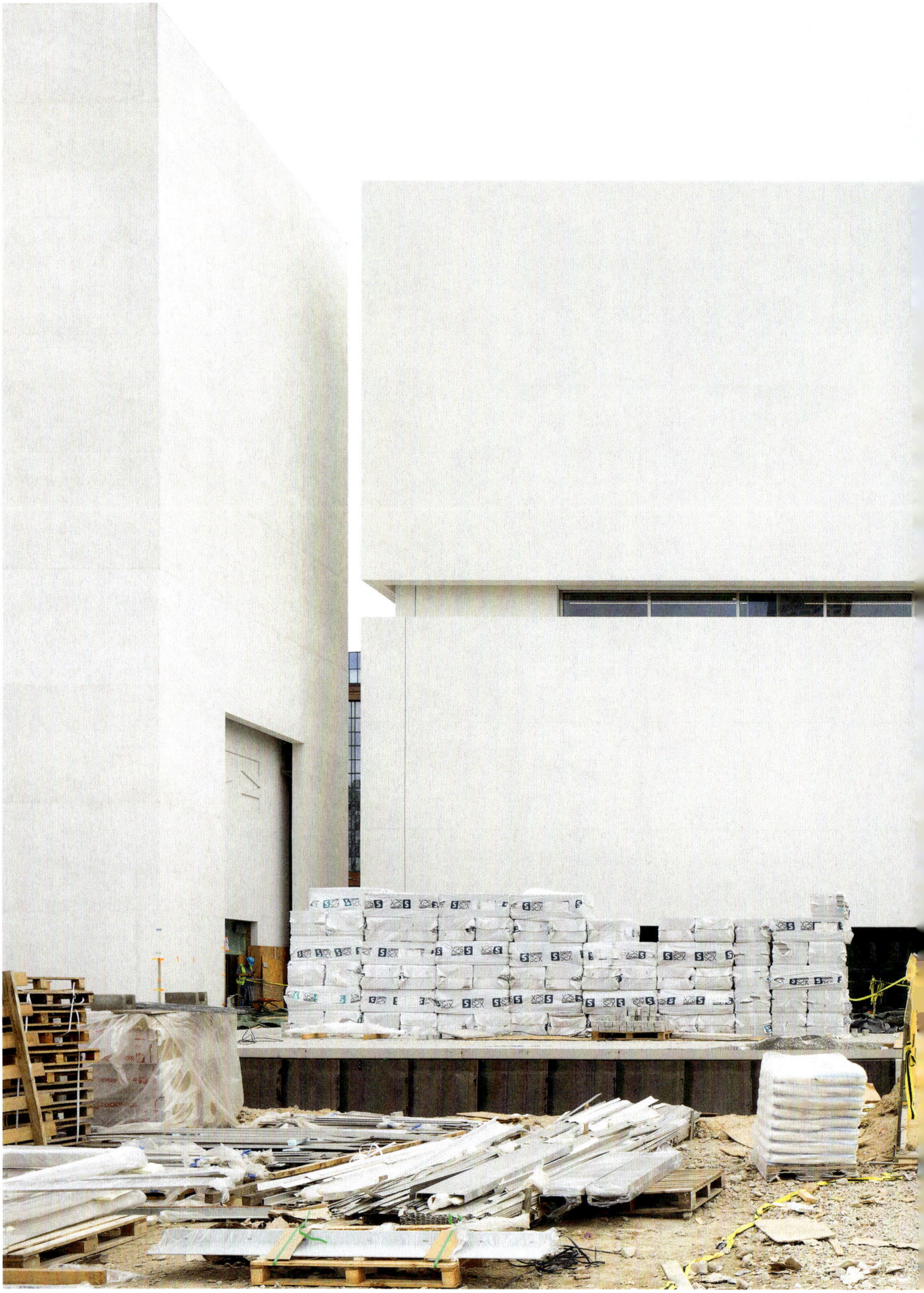

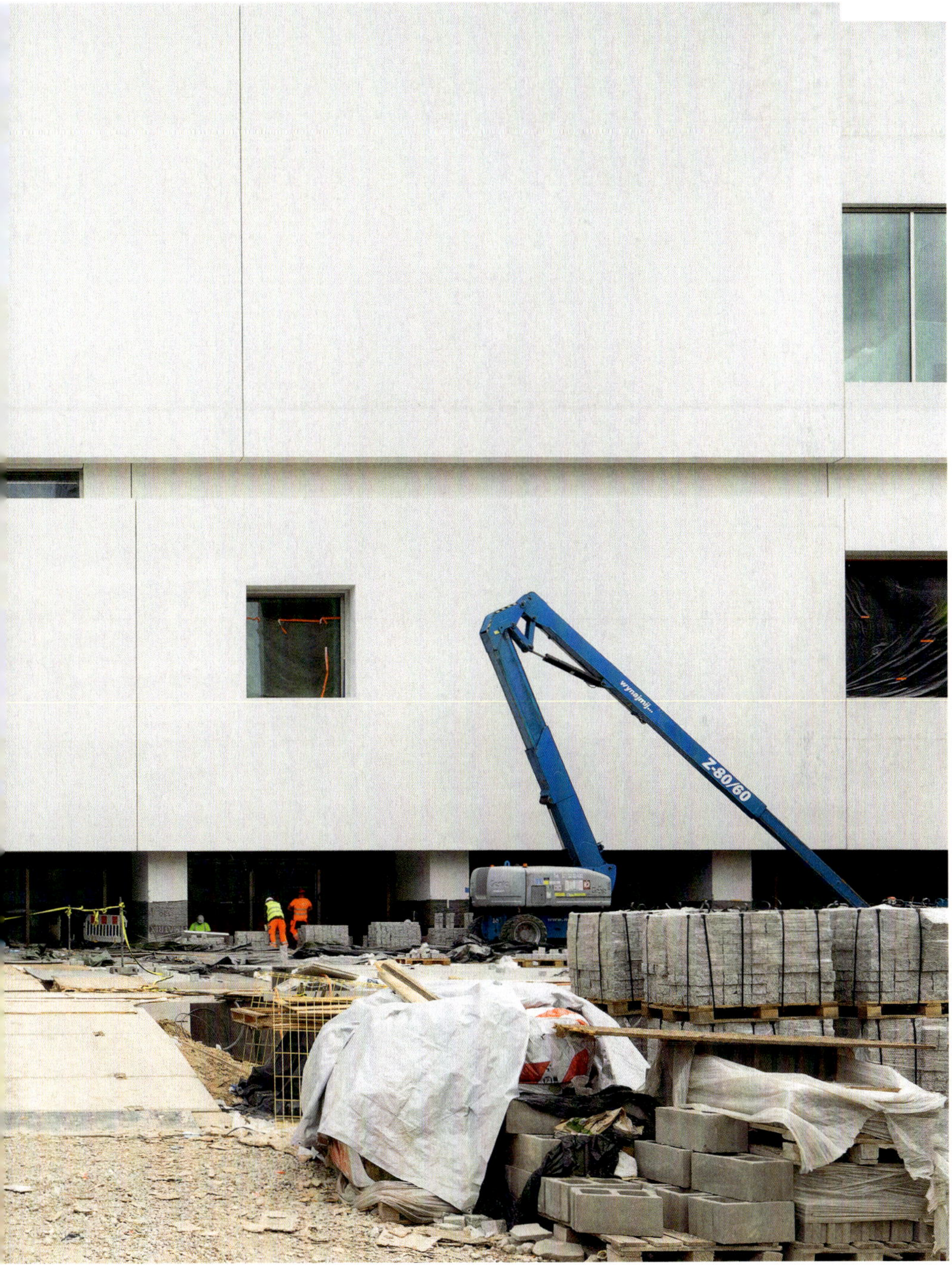
Z-80/60

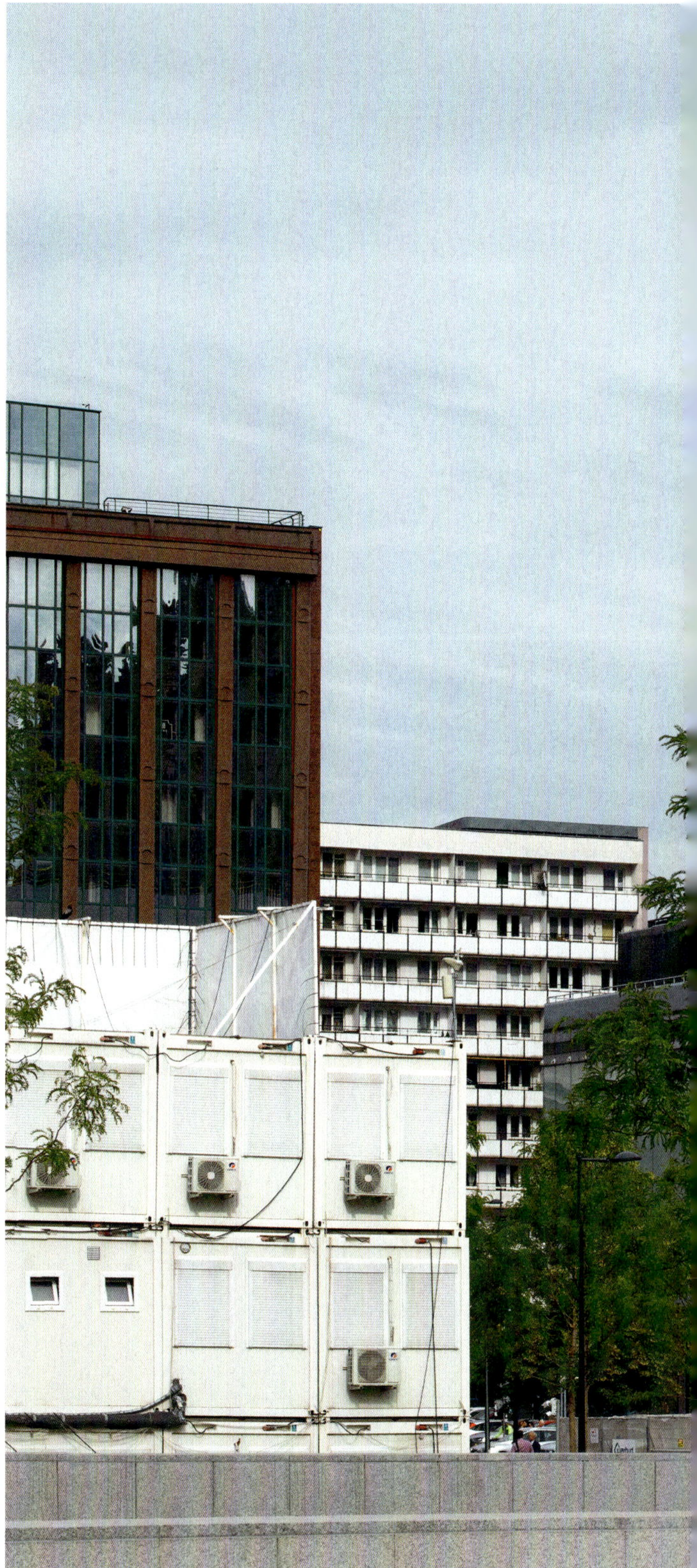

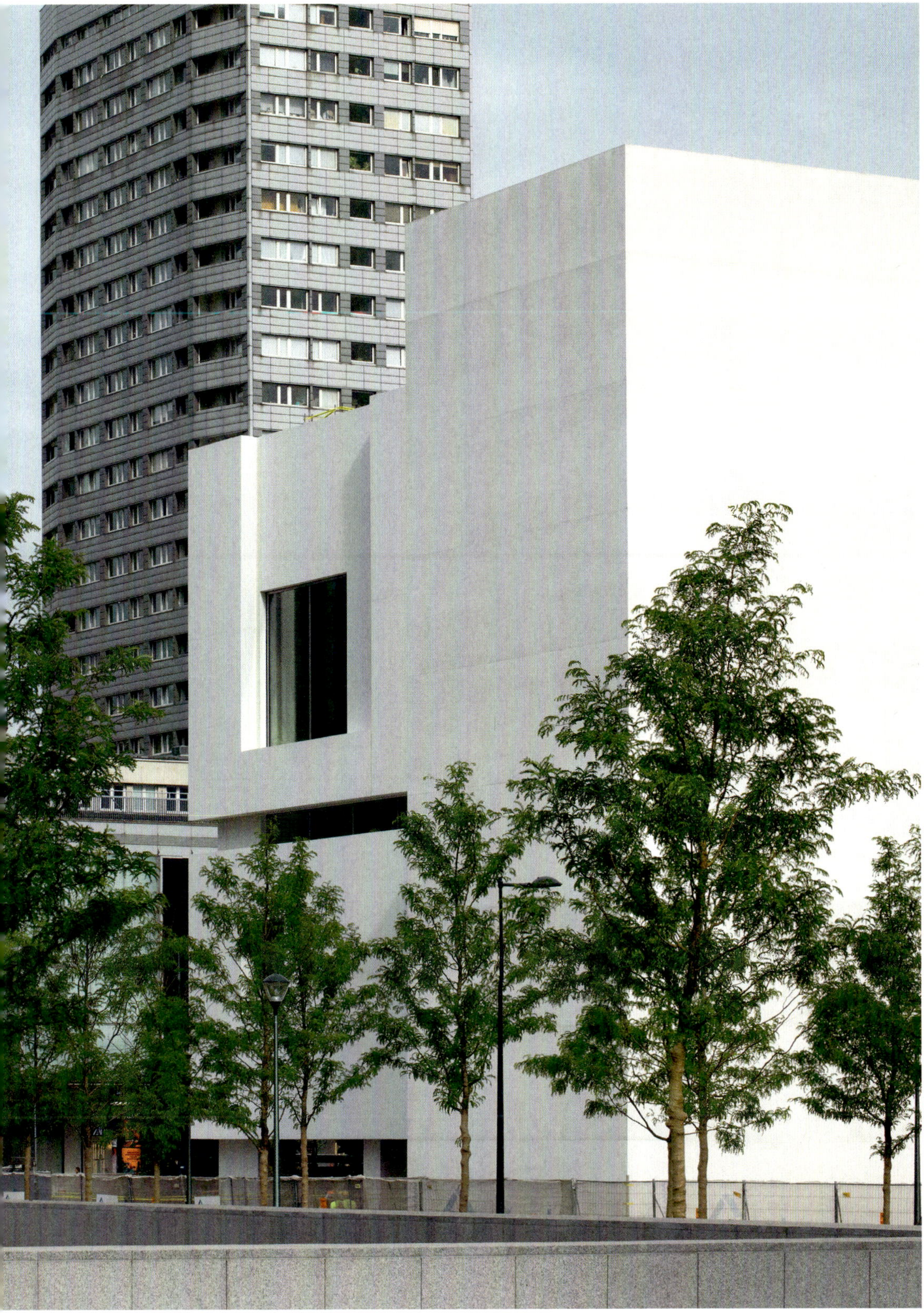

IMAGE CREDITS

- p. 21 photo: Marta Ejsmont
- p. 25 photo: Michał Murawski
- p. 26 courtesy of the artist and the Kulik-KwieKulik Foundation
- p. 28 [FIG. 4] photo: Scott Frances, courtesy of Thomas Phifer and Partners; [FIG. 5] rendering: rysuj.pl, courtesy of the Office of Architecture and Spatial Planning of the Capital City of Warsaw
- pp. 31, 32 courtesy of the artist and the Kulik-KwieKulik Foundation
- p. 36 collection of the Museum of Modern Art in Warsaw
- p. 37 photo: Grażyna Jaworska / Agencja Wyborcza.pl
- p. 42 photo: DESA Unicum, private collection, courtesy the Estate of Alina Szapocznikow / Galerie Loevenbruck, Paris
- p. 45 photo: Ashleigh Stewart
- p. 49 photo: Michał Murawski
- p. 56 photo: Rob Hornstra © Rob Hornstra / The Sochi Project, CC-BY-SA-3.0
- p. 57 Vladimer Kurtishvili private archive © AA Architecture Ambience
- p. 62 [FIG. 14] photo: John Karwoski, courtesy of John Karwoski; [FIG. 15] photo: Uwe Brodrecht, CC-BY-SA-3.0; [FIG. 16] photo: Xavi López, courtesy of photoXL@yahoo.com
- p. 66 photo: Bartek Zalewski, collection of the Museum of Modern Art in Warsaw, purchased with the financial support of the Minister of Culture and National Heritage
- p. 69 photo: Dawid Żuchowicz / Agencja Gazeta
- p. 71 [FIG. 19] photo: Adam Stępień / Agencja Wyborcza.pl; [FIG. 20] photo: Michał Murawski
- p. 72 photo: Kuba Snopek
- p. 78 photo: Bartek Stawiarski
- p. 84–87 © Artur Żmijewski
- p. 88 photo: Henri Cartier-Bresson © Henri Cartier-Bresson / Magnum Photos, courtesy of FORUM Polish Photography Agency
- p. 91 © The Estate of Alina Szapocznikow / Galerie Loevenbruck, Paris. All rights reserved
- p. 94 courtesy of the artist and the Kulik-KwieKulik Foundation
- p. 95 © The Estate of Alina Szapocznikow / Galerie Loevenbruck, Paris. All rights reserved
- p. 97 photo: Sławomir Kamiński / Agencja Wyborcza.pl
- p. 100 [FIG. 5.1] photo: Krzysztof Pijarski; [FIGS. 5.2–5.3] photo: Sławomir Kamiński / Agencja Gazeta
- p. 103 courtesy of National Digital Archives (NAC)
- p. 104 [FIG. 7] photo: Bartek Stawiarski, collection of the Museum of Modern Art in Warsaw; [FIG. 8] © The Estate of Alina Szapocznikow / Galerie Loevenbruck, Paris. All rights reserved
- p. 108 [FIG. 9] photo: Michał Murawski; [FIG. 10] photo: Adrian Grycuk / CC BY-SA 3.0
- p. 113 photo: "Sunflower" SCC team, courtesy of "Sunflower" SCC
- p. 114 photo: Yulia Krivich, courtesy of "Sunflower" SCC
- p. 117 [FIG. 4] courtesy of "Sunflower" SCC; [FIG. 5] photo: Yulia Krivich, courtesy of Yulia Krivich
- p. 118 [FIG. 6] courtesy of Yulia Krivich; [FIG. 7] photo: Yulia Krivich, courtesy of "Sunflower" SCC
- pp. 130–138 courtesy of Zygmunt Borawski
- p. 149 photo: Marta Ejsmont
- pp. 168–175 courtesy of Christian Kerez Zürich AG
- p. 180 courtesy of Thomas Phifer and Partners
- p. 183 photo: Scott Frances, courtesy of Thomas Phifer and Partners
- p. 186 courtesy of Thomas Phifer and Partners
- pp. 210–222 © Marta Ejsmont
- pp. 224–245 © Maja Wirkus

Strategic Partners of the Museum

Audi

INVEST KOMFORT

Patron of the Museum and the Museum's Collection

EY Shape the future with confidence

Partners of the Museum

e·on

TPM SZTUKI NOWOCZESNEJ W WARSZAWIE

Partner of the Education

Fundacja EFC

Legal advisor

DZP more than law

Partners of the Museum's Opening

k takt on

INSTITUT FRANÇAIS Pologne

RAFFLES EUROPEJSKI WARSAW

LUKULLUS cukiernia warszawska

MULLENLOWE GROUP

WAREXPO

ves.

Media partners

tvn WARNER BROS. DISCOVERY

onet

POLSKIE RADIO

TYGODNIK POWSZECHNY

AD

VOGUE POLSKA

zwierciadło

MAGAZYN OPINII Pismo.

KINADS REKLAMA W KINIE

MINT

Michał Murawski
A FORM OF FRIENDSHIP.
THE MUSEUM ON THE SQUARE

MANAGING EDITORS
Maciej Kropiwnicki, Łukasz Mojsak

EDITING AND PROOFREADING
Darren Durham

TRANSLATION
Marcin Wawrzyńczak

DESIGN CONCEPT, LAYOUT AND TYPESETTING
Ludovic Balland Typography Cabinet GmbH, Basel
Ludovic Balland & Annina Schepping

TYPEFACE
Qwerty © Ludovic Balland

LITHOGRAPHY
Krzysztof Krzysztofiak

COVER PHOTOGRAPHS
© Maja Wirkus, 2024

ACKNOWLEDGEMENTS
The author and editors would like to thank the following for the provision of images without fee: Zygmunt Borawski and A-A Collective, Marta Ejsmont, Adrian Grycuk, John Karwoski, Yulia Krivich and the "Sunflower" SCC team, Kulik-KwieKulik Foundation, Xavi López, National Digital Archives (NAC), Witold Pietrusiewicz and the Office of Architecture and Spatial Planning of the Capital City of Warsaw, Kuba Snopek, Ashleigh Stewart, The Estate of Alina Szapocznikow / Galerie Loevenbruck, Paris

PRINTED AND BOUND BY
Argraf Sp. z o.o., Warszawa

DISTRIBUTED BY
The University of Chicago Press
press.uchicago.edu

Available as an e-book edition

PUBLISHED BY
Museum of Modern Art in Warsaw,
Pańska 3, 00-124 Warsaw
sklep.artmuseum.pl

ISBN: 978-83-67598-15-6

CO-PUBLISHER
Adam Mickiewicz Institute

Ministry of Culture and National Heritage Republic of Poland

CULTURE.PL ADAM MICKIEWICZ INSTITUTE

Co-financed by the Minister of Culture and National Heritage of the Republic of Poland

instytucja kultury miasta stołecznego Warszawy